JOHN WINSTON LENNON
Volume 1 1940–1966

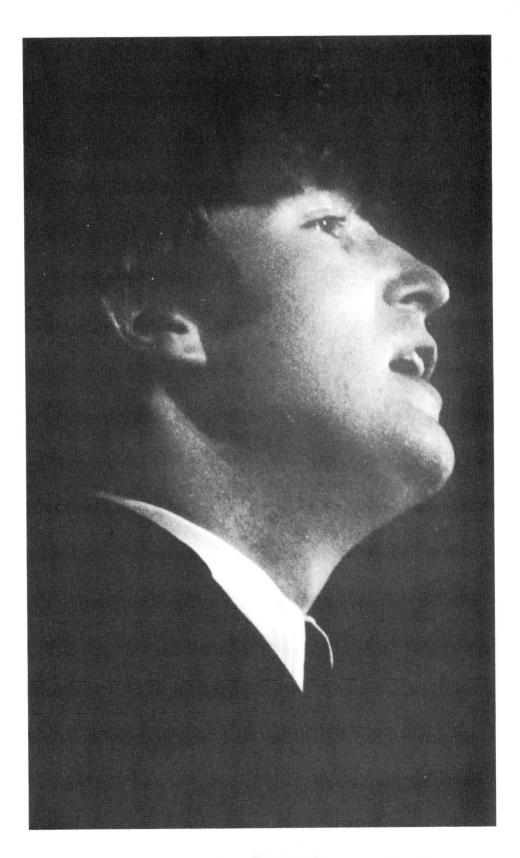

JOHN WINSTON LENNON

VOLUME 1 1940–1966

RAY COLEMAN

SIDGWICK & JACKSON
LONDON

First published in 1984 in Great Britain
by Sidgwick and Jackson Limited
Reprinted August 1984

Copyright © 1984 by Ray Coleman

ISBN 0-283-98942-4

Phototypeset by Falcon Graphic Art Ltd
Wallington, Surrey
Printed in Great Britain by
R.J. Acford, Industrial Estate, Chichester, Sussex
for Sidgwick and Jackson Limited
1 Tavistock Chambers, Bloomsbury Way
London WC1A 2SG

For Julian Lennon

ACKNOWLEDGEMENTS

The author and publishers gratefully acknowledge the permission of Bill Harry, editor and publisher of *Mersey Beat*, for the right to reproduce John Lennon's first published writings; Michael Oldfield, editor of *Melody Maker*, for excerpts of interviews with John Lennon in that publication; and Patrick Humphries, who contributed a large part of the chapter on John's music. The comments by Paul McCartney on John's relationship with Brian Epstein in Chapter 11 are reproduced by kind permission of Capital Radio, London, and interviewer Roger Scott.

The words to the songs 'Help!', 'I'm A Loser', 'In My Life', 'Norwegian Wood (This Bird Has Flown)', and 'You've Got To Hide Your Love Away' are copyright © Northern Songs Ltd, and are reproduced by kind permission of ATV Music, 19 Upper Brook Street, London W1. The words to 'Please Please Me' are copyright © 1962 Dick James Music Ltd, and are reproduced by kind permission.

CONTENTS

LIST OF ILLUSTRATIONS

AUTHOR'S NOTE

When John Lennon's dearest friend, Stuart Sutcliffe, died at the appallingly premature age of twenty-one, John told Stuart's distraught fiancée, Astrid Kirchherr: 'Make your decision. You either die with him or you go on living your life.' John would want *his* survivors to heed that same sentence: he loathed martyrdom, or too much accent on history. He always looked ahead rather than over his shoulder.

Yet since the murder of John Lennon on 8 December 1980, millions of people have felt enriched by looking back on his life. He continues to touch us with the power of his songs that will stand for ever, and with the continuing evidence of his searing honesty.

History will record him as one of the great pacemakers of the twentieth century. Teddy boy, pop star, rebel student, propagandist for peace, poet, artist, songwriter, musician, bandleader, sloganeer, philosopher, wit, loving husband and doting father – Lennon was all these things and more. The founder and power-house of the Beatles, he became a catalyst and dream-weaver for a generation's ideals.

Without him, the Beatles would never have existed, still less have become popular music's finest group; without him, they would have had no cutting edge, conscience or originality. And the 1960s, and its people, would have been very different and much colder.

I knew John Lennon for eighteen years, but no one ever knew the complete person. He slipped through our fingers as a questing, restless spirit. We all snatched at parts of him. 'He was a simple,

xi

complex man,' says his widow, Yoko Ono. So as in any biography, the blemishes as well as the strengths in the man's behaviour and character are reported here. He was brilliant, warm, tender, sensitive and generous. He was also infuriating, tough, aggressive, naive and woundingly abrasive. He bruised many victims, sometimes physically, often verbally. But even to have been tongue-lashed by Lennon was fame of a kind.

I saw him in Liverpool, a young man in a hurry before the Beatles achieved anything; and then in dressing-rooms, recording studios, hotel rooms, cars and planes and trains all over the world; at home during his first marriage to Cynthia, when he was wary of fatherhood and fame; and with Yoko from 1966, indivisible, interdependent. John Lennon's music, a rich legacy, testifies to his enjoyment of the highest of highs and the lowest of lows. He was a butterfly and a bee. But it's an extraordinary fact that all the many women who passed through his life, whether rejected girlfriend or divorced wife, or grieving widow or aunt, still love him madly. The paradox of this achievement is that he remains very much a man's man.

In preparing this book, the first of two volumes on his life and work, John's relatives and friends have been a tremendous source of inspiration, information, observation and illustrative material. The biography is no fanciful tale but an unvarnished account of the man straight from the mouths of his acquaintances. They have portrayed John Lennon in his truest and most human light; their memories will allow readers to form their own ideas of an often misinterpreted artist.

My special grateful thanks to John's indomitable, ever-loving Aunt Mimi for hours of patient conversation and memories; to John's first wife Cynthia for her total, often painful, honesty and for allowing me to reproduce for the first time her insightful, precious letters from John, as well as photographs; to his son Julian, for his interest and recollections; and to Astrid Kirchherr for setting the scene in Hamburg and for the loan of Stuart Sutcliffe's drawings of John, published here for the first time.

I should like to thank Pamela, Miles and Mark for their tolerance and for sustaining me in two years of research.

This book's accuracy is guaranteed by the assistance of Mark Lewisohn. Britain's most knowledgeable, indefatigable researcher on all things Beatle poured enormous energy and enthusiasm into checking facts, picture collation, and compiling the exhaustive chronology of John Lennon's life. Mark's guidance and suggestions have been invaluable since the book's inception and I thank him warmly.

My gratitude is due to many people, particularly in Liverpool, for their generous help: to Helen Anderson for great practical assistance and inspiration; Uncle Charles Lennon for remembering; Michael Isaacson for a memorable, informative night; Tony Barrow; Don Short; Brian Southall at EMI Records; William Pobjoy, John's headmaster at Quarry Bank High School and his housemaster Eric Oldman; Dick and Stephen James; George Martin; George Melly; Victor Spinetti; Rod Davis; Ron King; Helen Shapiro; Johnny Beerling; Billy J. Kramer; Richard Lester; Clive Epstein; Kenny Lynch; Gerry Marsden; Cilla Black; Arthur Howes; Hilary Williams; Liz and Jim Hughes at the Cavern Mecca, Liverpool; Bob Wooler; Bill Harry; Joe Flannery; Michael McCartney; Janet Webb; June Furlong; Ann Mason; Thelma Pickles; Phyllis McKenzie; Derek Taylor and Neil Aspinall.

I thank my agent David Grossman for his constant encouragement and Carol Beerling for transcribing many hours of taped interviews.

Thanks, above all, to John Lennon for treasured memories. To know him was to love him.

Ray Coleman
Shepperton, England
February 1984

CERTIFIED COPY OF AN ENTRY OF BIRTH

GIVEN AT THE GENERAL REGISTER OFFICE, LONDON

Application Number 9257 9

REGISTRATION DISTRICT Liverpool South

1940. BIRTH in the Sub-district of Abercromby in the County Borough of Liverpool

Columns:—	1	2	3	4	5	6	7	8	9	10*
No.	When and where born	Name, if any	Sex	Name and surname of father	Name, surname and maiden surname of mother	Occupation of father	Signature, description and residence of informant	When registered	Signature of registrar	Name entered after registration
463	Ninth October 1940 Liverpool Maternity Hospital	John Winston	Boy	Alfred LENNON	Julia LENNON formerly STANLEY	Seaman (Steward) 9 Newcastle Road Liverpool 15	J. Lennon Father 9 Newcastle Road Liverpool 15	Eleventh November 1940	Edward J.R. ——— Registrar	

CERTIFIED to be a true copy of an entry in the certified copy of a Register of Births in the District above mentioned.
Given at the GENERAL REGISTER OFFICE, LONDON, under the Seal of the said Office, the 20th day of July 19 83

BXA 863403

This certificate is issued in pursuance of the Births and Deaths Registration Act 1953. Section 34 provides that any certified copy of an entry purporting to be sealed or stamped with the seal of the General Register Office shall be received as evidence of the birth or death to which it relates without any further or other proof of the entry, and no certified copy purporting to have been given in the said Office shall be of any force or effect unless it is sealed or stamped as aforesaid.

CAUTION:—Any person who (1) falsifies any of the particulars on this certificate, or (2) uses a falsified certificate as true, knowing it to be false, is liable to prosecution.

*See note overleaf

Form A502M Dd 8264441 100M 3/82 Mcr (3056)

NB

PROLOGUE

Aunt Mimi, who brought him up, never smacked him; but she long ago lost count of their arguments. They were usually about his studies or homework or the trouble he was getting into because of his terrible discipline at grammar school. Two or three days a week, at about ten o'clock, the phone would ring in her house, Mendips, 251 Menlove Avenue, Woolton, Liverpool.

'Oh Lord,' she'd say under her breath, knowing it was another call from the secretary at Quarry Bank High School. 'What's he done *now*?' John would have been disruptive, or involved in mocking teachers. He was often caned.

'And yet, you know,' says Mimi, 'the main reason he was such a worry to me while he was growing up was because I knew he had *something. He* knew he had it too. But he didn't know where exactly to put this talent he had, or where it might lead him.'

Day after day, Mimi would berate him. The reports coming from school told of his indolence, his troublemaking and his potential expulsion unless he changed. And every time she scolded him, Lennon would say something like: 'I know what I want to do, and it's not coming from the teachers. It's in *here*.' And he would bang his chest.

'That's all right, dear,' said Mimi, 'but don't neglect your work.' She knew he was right, but she was worried that he would end his schooldays with no qualifications. She was right about that too.

But young Lennon, even from the age of ten, confronted authority. He was simply not interested in orthodox schooling. 'I'm not having people bending over my shoulder, rubbing my work out and telling me it's no good,' he would tell his aunt. But in

Mimi Smith he met a dead end. She offered more resistance than any schoolteacher. She loved and cared for John Lennon with a passion and determination that he was not to understand until much later in his life. But she wasn't having her nephew playing a dangerous game with his future.

'The school reports are bad, John. I won't have it. How are you going to get yourself a job if you don't do well at school?'

'But the teachers are so boring, Mimi.' He was good at English, art and French, awful at arithmetic, and made little effort at anything.

'Go to your room. Go on. Go, John. Do some homework.'

John stood for as long as he dared by the door of the morning-room at Mendips, a semi-detached house in a respectable suburb. Mimi kept it immaculately clean and well furnished. 'You wait,' he said. 'One of these days, I'm going to be famous and then you'll be sorry you were like this to me.'

'All right then, John. Until that day when you are, get upstairs. Elvis Presley may be a very nice man but I don't want him for breakfast, dinner, and supper.'

Eight years later and after scores of similar scenes with Mimi, John Lennon went back to Mendips, a successful Beatle, his face, his music, and his personality celebrated throughout the world. She cooked him his favourite: egg and chips and tea.

'He reminded me,' says Mimi, 'of what he'd said at that doorway when he was about sixteen.'

'Remember I said I'd be famous?' he said.

'Well,' said Mimi, thrilled but totally unimpressed. 'What always worried me, John, was that you wouldn't be so much famous as *notorious*. You were certainly *that* as a child. Think of the worries I had. If the Beatles hadn't come along, you could have ended up on the scrap heap without any school qualifications, and you'd soon have got through the bit of money I had. . . .'

'Oh Mimi, if the Beatles hadn't happened I'd always have been able to write or paint or draw.'

She reminded him of her favourite phrase, when she would banish him to the front porch with the £17 guitar she had reluctantly bought him from Hessy's store in Liverpool. He had nagged her when he was sixteen to 'let me get the music bug out of my system'.

'The guitar's all right as a hobby, John, but you'll never make a living from it.'

John replied, 'Well, I can always be an illustrator.'

The castigation, so typical of Mimi in its opinionated certainty, reverberated around the world as the Beatles story gained speed and the legend of Lennon's tough but caring aunt grew stronger.

'He was a worry to educate at school, and he kept telling me he was bored at college. I'd have to lay down the law: "Get on that eight-thirty bus until your time as a student is up, John. *Then* you can mess about with the guitar." '

When he became a pop star and laughed at his aunt's reprimands, John said to her: 'Actually, Mimi, you were quite right. I'd never have made it as a single performer as a guitarist. I was never good enough. But, y'know, I always guessed something would happen. And I met Paul and we met George and – well, it turned out great, didn't it, Mimi?'

October 1950. Ten-year-old John outside Mendips, Menlove Avenue, Woolton, the middle-class home where his Aunt Mimi brought him up

1

THE REBEL

'Oh God, Buddy Holly's dead'

She loved him but the smell of scallops in his hair and on his body drove her crazy. Liverpool scallops were slices of potato surrounded by a greasy, thick batter, dipped into fat and deep-fried. John Lennon was addicted to them. Most lunchtimes, as a student at Liverpool College of Art, he would cross the road to the chip shop in Falkner Street and pile himself up with a bag of chips and a bag of scallops. He would take them back to one of the classrooms, perhaps play the guitar while eating, and enthral a few students. The gentleness of his playing contrasted vividly with his hell-raising personality. To many students this reprobate seventeen-year-old was absolutely magnetic.

But he stank. 'It permeated from his head, through his clothes, and his entire body reeked of greasy scallops,' recalls Helen Anderson, one of the students who adored the 'lovable swine' who dressed like a teddy boy. She would nag him to wash the grease out of his hair and get rid of the DA ('duck's arse') style at the back. 'Get lost,' Lennon would snap. The greased-back hair, DA at the rear, sideburns, drape jackets, crepe-soled shoes, tatty checked shirt, and drainpipe trousers, all based on Elvis Presley whom he regarded as the king, were central to Lennon's personality. For they made him stand out from the rest of the students. Nothing was more important to him than individuality.

Helen Anderson had a unique, direct line to John Lennon's thoughts: he would confide in her about his love affairs. She was a patient listener and admirer of his wit, and since there was never any suggestion that they would become lovers she became a platonic friend and confidante.

1

She possessed a major attraction for John Lennon. At sixteen, she had actually *met* a pop star of the day, Lonnie Donegan, whom she had painted in oils for the astronomical fee of fifty guineas. There had been stories in the newspapers about her artistic talent. 'Hey, are you that bird who painted Lonnie Donegan?' John asked her on her first day at art school. He was impressed.

As John's undisciplined, hilarious behaviour made more of an impact on her, Helen would go home and tell her mother every day about John's crazy antics that had broken up the class. She demonstrated how John crept up behind people and suddenly boomed one of his favourite songs into their ear. It was Screaming Jay Hawkins' hit, 'I Put A Spell On You'. Helen and John's special friendship was sealed when he regularly gave her his trousers to narrow the legs into drainpipe style. 'Take these in for me, would you, Heloon,' he would say. 'They're too bloody wide.' (Heloon was his nickname for her because she always laughed uproariously at his outrageous behaviour.) Dutifully, she would take John's black trousers home and return them next morning tapered. The 'drainies' were worn *underneath* his 'regulation shape' trousers until he reached the bus stop on his way to college, where he slipped them off. That way, his Aunt Mimi would not see over breakfast that he was a latent 'ted'. He had to find many similar methods of fending off her wrath about his untidy appearance.

Those who were at art college with John Lennon are unanimous: he was destined either to be a great public figure, a triumphant star with unique gifts, or he would be a layabout, a burden on society who achieved nothing. There would be no halfway for this extraordinary teenager who roared through Liverpool, making an impact on everybody who was willing to be touched by him.

'Even at sixteen I knew he was destined to some sort of grandeur and greatness,' says Helen Anderson. 'In his first six months at college, his paintings were very wild and aggressive. Every one he did incorporated the interior of a night club and they were very strongly drawn, very dark, and there was always a blonde girl sitting at the bar looking like Brigitte Bardot. There were always musicians in John's early drawings, a band on a bandstand, dim lights, something sleazy. I always liked them. But very few people noticed his work in his early days at college.'

To the teachers Lennon was a pest, a danger. His work, erratically presented, was the last thing they worried about. It was his behaviour as a catalyst for trouble in every classroom that they outlawed in unison. Eventually, Lennon and the masters became polarized, just as they had done at his previous school, Quarry Bank High School, Woolton. The more they bored him with their orthodox, predictable, unyielding methods of education which he abhorred, the more he would seek his own route. 'The masters were not interested in him,' says Helen Anderson. 'He was a nuisance to the entire college, distracting everybody else who wanted to learn.'

Lennon didn't care. He had his gang, camp followers like the laconically funny Geoff Mohammed, who was a perfect foil for John's pungent humour. There was Tony Carricker, who joined in the crowd who laughed almost non-stop at John's ribaldry. And there was even June Furlong, the twenty-seven-year-old nude model who was the subject of the life class in which they would all have to draw her body. Even she became convulsed with laughter on many days when she was supposed to be a serious art subject. Lennon discovered early in his teen years what was to be one of his most endearing characteristics when he was in deep trouble; he could always make people laugh with his very distinctive, cruel, exploitative sense of humour.

In the very warm life class of room 71 at the college, fifteen students were set their weekly task of drawing June. Some would doze off when the teacher left the room. Suddenly Lennon would give out a little giggle. Nobody would take much notice. Two or three minutes later, his giggle would be louder. That would disturb people, especially those trying to concentrate on drawing. A real laugh followed, and a few minutes later his loud, hyena-like cackle totally broke up the class. By then everyone was hysterical at John's calculated disruption. To top it off, Lennon then jumped out from behind his easel, ran into the middle of the room where June was sitting, naked, rocking with laughter and trying to stop her body from shaking for the benefit of the students who wanted to continue to draw it. Finally, for his *pièce de résistance*, Lennon brought laughter to the entire life class by leaping around the room where silence and decorum was the rule.

During another life class session, the whole class produced proper drawings of the nude which were soberly dissected by the teacher, Teddy Griffiths. When John came to hand in his effort, he had perversely drawn nothing of June. He produced a drawing of the only item on June's body – her wristwatch. Students were aghast at his nerve – and originality.

While John's eccentric behaviour, non-conformist dress and swearing in front of the teachers were enough to make him prominent, a less rational, disturbing side to his character emerged soon after he joined the art college. He quickly developed a bizarre obsession for cripples, spastics, any human deformities, and people on crutches. He had a particular fascination for warts. It was a subject that was to manifest itself throughout John Lennon's years of fame. It took root, firmly and with a gaggle of students embarrassed at their own sick sense of humour in laughing at him, here at art college.

Deformities cropped up in his drawings all the time. So did his dry wit, the quality that dominated his personality. For a seventeen-year-old he had a subtle sense of humour way ahead of his time. There was always life and movement in his drawings, to redeem that streak of cruelty. Every person he portrayed had a physical affliction, usually a wart sticking out of the side of the head. Asked why, John would shrug it off, with the implication that if you had to ask, you weren't on his wavelength, so there was no point in discussing it.

By 1958, in his eighteenth year, with all the guns blazing at the art college which bestowed upon him lots of freedom in dress, and demeanour, but which was unsuccessfully grappling on all fronts with his wildness, John Lennon could not be missed. He was desperately short-sighted, which somehow added to his mystique among the girls. He wore teddy boy clothes and his black horn-rimmed spectacles, worn only under the greatest pressure, for he had an ego, were held together at the joints by Elastoplast. He rarely had any money, and borrowed it permanently from his gang. He scrounged ciggies all the time, somehow managing to get through between ten and twenty Woodbines a day. He drank too many pints, usually black velvets, in Ye Cracke, the students' pub in Rice Street near the college, and since he could not take much beer without feeling its effects, he frequently behaved either obnoxiously or violently. He kept losing his artist's materials and would constantly ask his Aunt Mimi, with whom he lived, for more money on the pretext of needing a new pen or other equipment.

He was a startlingly talented, non-conforming artist, but so lazy that even his close college friend, the serious intellectual Stuart Sutcliffe, could not drag John's attributes into line and get him properly on course. Music, rock 'n' roll, Elvis Presley, Chuck Berry, Little Richard – it was all too much of a pull for Lennon, who would stalk the college with a guitar strapped to his back, ready for the lunchtime sessions over scallops and chips in Arthur Ballard's classroom with two other kids from the more academic

John's familiar hunched frame was captured by fellow student Ann Mason
when he sat for more than two hours for this painting in March 1958

Liverpool Institute next door. Their names were Paul McCartney and George Harrison.

On 4 February 1959 John walked solemnly into the classroom, visibly shaken. It was not often that students saw John Lennon vulnerable, broken, unhappy. 'Oh God, Buddy Holly's dead,' he muttered. Holly, a vital pioneer of early rock 'n' roll, a singer of plaintive love songs wedded to jerky, haunting melodies, was one of John's idols. He had died in a plane crash in America. Unlike many of the students John did not cry over the news, but went silent for the day and took some time to snap out of the shock. Lennon always buried his feelings deeply.

It was the third great emotional death to mark John's life, and he was still only eighteen. Seven months before Buddy Holly's death John's mother, Julia Lennon, had died instantly at the age of forty-four after being knocked down by a car when leaving the home of John's Aunt Mimi, with whom John was living. The death of Uncle George, Mimi's husband, who doted on John and had bathed him, protected him and been a warm and loving father-figure during his childhood, had rocked John at the age of eleven. And now, just as John was getting inspiration from Buddy Holly, and totally absorbing the wonderful, embryonic sounds of American rock 'n' roll music, it was like another death in the family.

For the teenager who had come from a broken home, despite all his natural inner orthodoxy, respect, and sentimentality, there seemed only one way to get through his early life after eighteen years punctuated by physical fights and emotional scars. That was to erect a cocoon of belligerence, aggression, sick or vicious wit, and castigation. The real John Lennon, from his birth until his death, was a vastly misunderstood man. His drawings and his spoken word may have injured or hurt, and he was capable of wounding with pertinent jibes that shot straight through the heart of the victim. But he always aimed his arrows at people he could not respect, and beneath that abrasive exterior beat a heart of pure gold. Eventually, it was to come out in his music as he mushroomed into one of popular music's most beloved, searingly honest artists who, more than anyone else in his field, wore his heart, as well as his art, on his sleeve. In 1959 the personality of John Lennon was changing quickly, but the world had not heard of him. A few were privileged to see the man shaped by his own grit as he rampaged through first Quarry Bank High School and then made an indelible mark on Liverpool College of Art before becoming an emblem for youth: artist, poet, and philosopher. The family, students, and friends who saw John Lennon as a schoolboy and teenager testify to one undeniable fact that marked him then as it marked his entire life: you could loathe him or like him. But you could never feel neutral about him. And you certainly could not ignore him.

Cynthia Powell knew that she had fallen helplessly in love with John Lennon when, one day in the art college lecture hall, she noticed one of her closest friends, Helen Anderson, apparently stroking John's hair. Helen was sitting immediately behind John; Cynthia, a few seats away, began trembling with jealousy at the sight of another girl touching him.

To this day Cynthia believes that Helen and John were romantically linked, at the very least. Helen denies it. She was part of a coterie of Lennon college friends who formed his essential audience. Helen says she was not fondling John. Instead she was trying to straighten out his DA hairstyle which she hated. But the fact that Helen cared enough to make her presence known to John, and the banter between them, was enough to arouse Cynthia's envy.

A year older than John, and a serious, formal art student, Cynthia Powell seemed theoretically, to other students, the unlikeliest choice for a loud-mouthed, troublemaking teddy boy who was roaring through art college in the days when words like beatnik and bohemian evoked images of dangerous living. She lived her life, particularly at college, 'by the book', as a conscientious, ambitious student. But Cynthia had four key attractions that were to attract John. Firstly, she had the potential in his eyes to look like Brigitte Bardot, his strongest fancy. Many of his previous girlfriends had to bow to his demand: 'Grow your hair long, like Brigitte.' He would do drawings for them of how they were expected to look. One student, Joni Crosby, looked even more like Bardot, and Lennon drooled over her in the canteen. During tea break he said to Helen Anderson, day after day: 'Bloody hell – she's fantastic – just like Brigitte Bardot.' Secondly, Cynthia came from snooty Hoylake, 'over the water' on the Wirral, and 'spoke posh, talked proper', which he believed made her unattainable to a lad from Woolton. Thirdly, she was plainly besotted over him and would do anything to please him, even dye her brown hair blonde and grow it long. Fourthly, and crucially, she was serene. As an eighteen-year-old art student Cynthia had a composure that marked her out from the others in college. Lennon, the college performer who strove to make an impression by cackling in class, smoking when it was against the rules, and bucking the system at every twist and turn, was chemically attracted to Cynthia because she was supercool and different. *Vive la différence* was a characteristic that was to *drive* Lennon all his life. The orthodox and the predictable usually bored him, although he always clung strongly to traditional values in human relationships and family life.

Cynthia and John had two other important things in common. Cynthia was fatherless, her commercial traveller father having died when she was seventeen, so, like John, she knew the burdens of being a teenager with one parent; and Cynthia was, like John, hopelessly short-sighted and wore spectacles. But in his earliest days at college, he played her attractiveness to him very cool and hung around with other girl students on a platonic basis.

In the tradition of the busking art student, John and two college girls, Helen Anderson and Ann Sherwood, spent afternoons drifting across the ferry from Pier Head to Seacombe. This route was chosen because it was the cheapest boat; when they arrived they would walk the three miles down the promenade or along the sands to New Brighton, with John playing the role of entertainer. 'Be funny, John!' 'Sing us a song, John!' they would ask him. And John, his guitar slung across his black jacket, would love being the clown, the star of the show, for Helen and Ann. The girls had dutifully done the work Arthur Ballard had set them, and the afternoons were free for them. John told them he could not be bothered to do his work, so needed no persuading to have a musical day at the seaside.

Musically, his repertoire was funny but thin. 'He only strummed his guitar. It was obvious he wasn't much of a player then,' says Helen Anderson. His songs included Buddy Holly and Little Richard with a little Elvis Presley thrown in. He'd ad lib with everyday phrases and extemporize on the songs which he was to be heard jokingly playing around with in classes: he'd wander around looking over people's shoulders at their work, mumbling 'Sugar In The Morning, Sugar In The Evening, Sugar At Suppertime', 'When You're Smiling', and the one everyone laughed at:

I like New York in June, how about you?
I like a Lennon tune, how about you?
Holding Rabbis in the movie show, when all the
Lights are low, may not be new, but I like it,
How about you?

Says Helen Anderson: 'He definitely had a thing about Jews and loved taking the mickey out of them. The slightest chance to work them into a song and make it funny, he'd take it. But it wasn't nearly so cruel as his thing about cripples and afflicted people.'

In 1958, as John Lennon swept through art college, world events that were changing a post-war Britain from uncertainty into prosperity were making an enormous impact on young people. Khrushchev became Russia's premier, marking the start of a cold war; the first transatlantic commercial jet service began; and an aeroplane crashed on take-off in Munich, Germany, killing twenty-three passengers including eight Manchester United footballers. There were terrible race riots in London's Notting Hill, the first serious riots of their kind; General de Gaulle was forming his first French government; and magical, influential pop music names like Elvis Presley ('Jailhouse Rock'), Jerry Lee Lewis ('Great Balls of Fire'), the Everly Brothers ('All I Have To Do Is Dream'), The Coasters ('Yakety Yak'), and the Teddy Bears ('To Know Him Is To Love Him') were forging a vital new impact for popular music fans who listened to it in bed under their blankets on the barely audible, but adventurously hip, Radio Luxembourg.

The following year the M1 became Britain's first motorway, to presage a new era of speed and travel; the giant E.M.I. Records discontinued the use of 78 r.p.m. records in favour of 45 r.p.m. singles; and history was made by ten thousand members of the Campaign for Nuclear Disarmament marching from Aldermaston to London, the biggest demonstration of its kind until then. Musically, there was lots for Lennon and his friends to drool over, including Buddy Holly's 'It Doesn't Matter Any More', and Elvis Presley's 'I Got Stung'. Against all the good sounds that were grasped by Lennon, he developed an instinctive hatred for what he regarded as the bland, antiseptic music of new British stars like Cliff Richard, Adam Faith, and Craig Douglas.

The Lennon of these years, torn inside by a fractured family life, did not suffer fools. He was a young man in a hurry. But he did not know his destination. What he did recognize, immediately he felt it, was love. He had had torrid relationships with girls before he met Cynthia Powell. But with her, something else gelled to make her his automatic and serious partner. With the arrogance that characterized him he accepted that she was, in the words of Helen Anderson, nutty about him and prepared to be used as a doormat, to please John's every whim and lend him her art materials. But no, to John that wasn't all: many girls were ready to be servile towards him, to laugh at his weakest jokes and physically titillate him in his quest to learn everything about sex during an era when it was taboo among teenagers. Cynthia offered much, much more than those attractions to which he had become accustomed. From Cynthia came also intelligence and the great, unspoken heatwave that was to make them inseparable for about eight years: love, understanding, care, and devotion. John returned it, for, with the death of his mother and the desertion of his father, the need for an anchor to his life was much more real than might have been apparent to the students who saw him as a court jester. All he needed was love, music, an escape route from the humdrum, routine, wage-earning future that many of his contemporaries seemed to regard as inevitable. To John Lennon, even at seventeen, nothing was inevitable. Deep down inside, he saw himself as special. His method of saying so was to project a rough and tough exterior, because he had no platform or power to do anything about it. Yet physically, mentally, and because her tranquillity offered a useful antidote to his excesses, Cynthia was his perfect partner.

Reflecting on those years, Cynthia is in love not merely with John – whom she will love to distraction until the day she dies – but with the sweet, innocent, yet passionate romance of the college years together. 'He had a strange fascination for many of the girls, like Helen Anderson and Thelma Pickles,' says Cynthia. 'He wasn't the sort of chap you'd swoon over. What concerned me, and drew me to him at first, was that he was so lazy about his work. He didn't give a damn and I got worried, being a conscientious type, that he would get into trouble and get kicked out of college. Everyone knew that he was in art college on sufferance. No teachers wanted him there, except Arthur Ballard, who was a similarly artistic type and saw some potential in John. I cared more about his future and his work than he did. I saw in John so much talent, as an artist, but if he got chucked out of college, which was likely, where would he go? I was a lot older than him, mentally.'

The story of their first encounters sounds like fiction but is fact. Cynthia, in her second year at art college, was among a dozen students who had chosen to attend lettering class twice a week. Everyone there felt positive about the subject, except John Winston Lennon. He quickly became the talk of the class because he had been shoved there through a series of rejections by teachers who had grown tired of his disruptiveness in other classes. Lennon was not a candidate for the lettering class, either; his natural style was to draw cartoons of whatever his teachers had ordered.

Cynthia remembers that the two lettering class days, on which

One of the earliest photographs of John and his future wife Cynthia together, before she dyed her hair blonde at his request. This was taken in October 1958 in the alleyway alongside John's regular college pub, Ye Cracke in Rice Street. Seated in the front, from left to right, are students June Harry, Pat Jordon, Jim Reynolds and Hazel Dorothy

In this college photograph taken in September 1958 by Thelma Pickles, one of his girlfriends, John's greased-back hairstyle shows his affinity with Elvis Presley. The students in the picture, taken near Liverpool College of Art, are (from the left on the back row), John Lennon, Carol Balfour, John Wild, Jeff Cane, Gill Taylor, Peter Williams; (seated, from left) Marcia Coleman, Ann Preece, Violet Upton, Helen Anderson, Diane Molyneux; (front from left) Ann Curtis, Sheila Jones

she would study John, became her 'fix'. For the rest of the week they were separated during studying hours and she would roam the corridors of the college hoping for a glimpse of the boy who was the unruly focal point of the students but had become her obsession. It was all too much for a conventional girl from Hoylake who already had a steady boyfriend who was saving for their future in a building society.

To be hooked on Lennon was also slightly dangerous because of his notoriety. 'On lettering days he always arrived late, anything up to half an hour,' says Cynthia. 'He looked a mess. He had scruffy black trousers, quiffed hair with a slight DA at the back, and it was an attempt to look like a teddy boy. But often, even though he was late, he'd have a screwed-up drawing under his arm to present to the teacher. And it would get him off the hook, in a way. Arthur Ballard would hold it up to the class and say: "Now look, this is the kind of original idea and inspiration we're looking for." ' The fact that it was unrelated to lettering didn't matter. Lennon had quickly found a way to buck the system.

'After I'd first experienced John in lettering,' says Cynthia, 'I couldn't get him out of my mind.' On lettering days she would arrive in the classroom earlier than anyone else to sit near where he had been sitting in the previous lesson. What finally drove them together was a playful test, among all the students one morning, of each other's eyesight. 'We had identical short-sightedness, and when we started talking about what we couldn't see – like when the bus was coming – we were away,' says Cynthia. Major romances have been built on stranger events, but for Cynthia Powell the moment of that discovery was magical. She blessed her disability, for her passion for the wild one was now all-consuming.

Still, she thought that she, with her short, permed brown hair, tweedy skirt, twinset and Hoylake image, was too proper for Lennon. Cynthia could not see her attractiveness to him adding up to much. She loaned him materials during lettering, she had similarly bad eyesight, and he was always a fraction more polite to her than he was to the other students. But that was all. Her teenage crush seemed to offer no way out.

But fate smiled on her. As the college's vacation loomed for the summer of 1958, one of the students thought it would be fun to have a lunchtime end-of-term party. They got permission to use the smallest room in the college and one of them brought a record player. That year's hits were the Everly Brothers' 'All I Have To Do Is Dream', Conway Twitty's 'It's Only Make Believe' and 'Tom Dooley' by the Kingston Trio. Cynthia's eyes rarely left

Lennon at that party, but she had teenage blushes of embarrassment at herself, too. When John walked over and asked her to dance, slowly, to the song 'To Know Him Is To Love Him' by the Teddy Bears, she nearly collapsed with excitement. 'I think John was slightly embarrassed too, which was unusual for him,' she says. 'Perhaps he knew what was happening to us. It was painful and beautiful.' The other students looked on amazed at the unlikely combination.

As the party began to break up, John asked Cynthia if she was involved with another man. He said he'd like to meet her, out of college.

'I'm awfully sorry,' Cynthia said. 'I'm engaged to this fellow in Hoylake.'

John's retort to this was: 'I didn't ask you to marry me, did I?'

Cynthia, flustered, thought she had let him slip through her fingers, for the Lennon reply seemed cutting and final. But he wasn't as dismissive as she feared. He said to Cynthia and her best friend, Phyllis McKenzie: 'Let's go and have a drink.'

Cynthia and Phyllis had never before been to the college boozer, Ye Cracke. Here, black velvets were drunk and Woodbines smoked most lunchtimes, by hard-up Lennon, surrounded by his cronies. To Cynthia and Phyllis, adjourning from college to anything other than the train and bus home wasn't done; but suddenly Cynthia understood what college life was supposed to be like. Lennon was, however, still far away in the crowd of men and made no attempt to chat her up in the bar, so she began to leave. She thought the dance with John, and the drink, probably marked the start and end of their relationship.

As she neared the door, Lennon's voice boomed out above the pub chat: 'Didn't you know Miss Powell was a nun, then?' It was a typically Lennonesque dig at her propriety. She spun round, their eyes met, and she walked over to his side. He persuaded her to stay. Both had had a few too many drinks and little to eat during the day when so much had happened. As the drinking session continued, it was obvious that John Lennon and Cynthia Powell were going to be together.

That night, they left the pub and spent all night together at the rented bedsitter in Gambier Terrace, a convenient two-minute walk from college, of John's best college friend, the serious-minded Stuart Sutcliffe, to whom Lennon turned when he tired of the audience of students who simply wanted him to act funny. Increasingly, John and Stuart became best friends. There was never any discussion about what they had in common: it was intuitive. Sutcliffe and Lennon bounced off each other because they had the same speed of thought, restlessness, and a natural talent. In Stuart's case, though, it was a talent he marshalled and nursed.

Three months older than John, Stuart was a model student, a star pupil, and he wanted to become a famous painter. His drawings of skulls and skeletons, particularly, were outstanding and appealed to Lennon's interest in the macabre. A year ahead of John in college, Stuart was concentrating on painting and sculpture and worked long, arduous hours. 'He was very spotty with horn-rimmed glasses and, just like John's, they were taped up at the edges,' recalls Cynthia. 'As a student, he was precisely the opposite of John, because he was working himself to death, totally dedicated. He wasn't eating properly and didn't have much to do with girls. His work was all-important to him.'

As Stuart and John became more friendly, Sutcliffe became more of a leveller to Lennon. 'John needed Stuart really badly,' says Cynthia. 'He was going down the wrong road with these two characters, Tony Carricker and Geoff Mohammed, and he probably realized it because John wasn't stupid. It was Stuart who persuaded John to concentrate more on his art and less on messing about,' says Cynthia. 'When John saw Stuart's work, he was inspired by it. He started painting a lot more seriously himself, slapping great canvases around. Before, he had been working too tightly on little cartoons and on smaller areas. Suddenly, Stuart drew him into the painting rooms often and John at last had a mate to help show him the way. After college, Stuart would stay on and say to John: "Don't worry about it. Just slap it on, a bit here, a bit there," whereas John had always been very wary and careful and detailed. Stuart was great fun in art and their minds were right for each other. John obviously looked up to him, and he was bringing John out as an artist.'

But it was too late to hold John back from what was becoming his major interest: music.

Strong though Stuart was in trying to pull John towards serious work, Lennon had by now reached the point of no return. If a lesson or a day went by without his causing mirth in the classroom, he would have been diagnosed ill by those who were expecting him to perform.

'He was the biggest mickey-taker I've met,' says Helen Anderson. 'He picked on all kinds of characters in school, whatever their backgrounds, and tried to find some way of laughing at them. There was one, awfully nice well brought-up fellow with frizzy red hair, whom John persisted in annoying by calling him Snodgrass and making everyone laugh. John wouldn't let go of something once it stuck with him: "Snoddy" this and "Snoddy" that, to the annoyance of this very straight student. Another poor student named Derek had the habit of picking his nose in front of everybody and didn't realize he was doing it. We'd be in the middle of a lesson, with everybody silent, and suddenly John would scream out at the top of his voice: "Dirty picky nosey, Derek!" Of course it broke up the class. We all fell about laughing.

'He used to make horrible jokes against the singer Alma Cogan, impersonating her singing "Sugar In The Morning, Sugar In The Evening, Sugar At Suppertime". He'd pull crazy expressions on his face to try to imitate her expressions. We all had hysterics. He was a real comedian.'

Curiously, when the Beatles became famous, John was to become friendly with Alma Cogan and visit her home.

'We could always tell when he was about to come out with a gem of a joke or a phrase,' says Helen Anderson. 'His nostrils and cheeks would swell up. He was such a wit, he made an impression on everybody in the whole college. But contrary to what Cynthia believed, I loved him and adored him but never fancied him.' He was a natural comic, but in a style that wasn't expected. When students asked his name, when he first arrived at art college, he would say: 'Simply Simple Pimple. John Wimple Lennon.' He would preen a little when he gave his real middle name of Winston – not because he felt nationalistic about having been named after Britain's great wartime prime minister, Winston Churchill, but because it sounded posh and was different and unexpected.

Stories of his outlandish college behaviour abound. One panto day, the annual event for which the students dressed up and went around the city shaking collection boxes for charities, seven students got together to dress up. John roped in Paul McCartney and George Harrison from the Liverpool Institute next door, together with Ann Priest, Rod Murray, Helen Anderson, and Mona Harris. At John's instigation, he and Paul and George were to dress up as vicars. They found yellow sweatshirts which they wore upside-down with their legs inside the sleeves, and dog collars with black tailcoats. The Lennon plan was to 'raid' every café in every department store in Liverpool. They marched in shaking their tins and everybody would turn round to look. Within a few minutes John would stand up on a table and shout:

'My lords, ladies and gentlemen. On my right, in the red corner. . .' and Paul would jump up. 'And on my left, in the blue corner. . .' and George would come out. The two would start fighting on restaurant tables, in every chain store, to attract attention. And they were ceremonially thrown out of every place they entered – but not before raising a few pounds by the sheer noise and audacity of their stunt.

Later that day the students went to the city's Adelphi Hotel, where John persuaded the staff to lend him a bucket and a mop. A crowd of several hundred gathered outside the hotel to watch Lennon, still dressed as a vicar, singing loudly and mopping the zebra crossing. He was the star turn; the others were giving him moral support, loudly and successfully, and shaking their tins.

The light, undisciplined attraction of college life greatly appealed to John. After the formality of his previous school, where he had trouble fighting the system and had been an academic disaster, art college at least seemed to give him the chance to behave as a young adult. There was the array of pretty girls, many of whom looked on him as a card as well as a tearaway; there was encouragement from Arthur Ballard, who, even though he didn't care for John's refractory style, knew the boy had something and did his utmost to encourage him; there was the security of the gang of Geoff Mohammed and Tony Carricker and Jeff Cane. There was, eventually, Cynthia with whom he had a fast-moving love affair.

'Before me,' says Cynthia, 'there was another girl he mentioned to me named Beth whom he was pretty serious about. But her parents couldn't stand John. He kept saying to me: "Don't worry, they've banned me from seeing her anyway, they think I'm a ruffian. They won't have me round." ' Lennon had met her when he was fifteen and a pupil of Quarry Bank High School. The fact that he talked openly about her infuriated Cynthia during their early romance, and reached breaking-point when, one night, he did not arrive for their nightly meeting. 'He quickly admitted he'd been to see Beth, to see if it was finished between them, and it was definitely all over and we were together.'

Unknown to Cynthia there were other girls in John's life before their romance blossomed, and during their love match John would vanish from the college on some afternoons and go off with them. One of his gang would support him by spinning a story about where John had gone. Lennon frequently found himself arm in arm with a casual girlfriend walking back to college, and suddenly thrown into a panic at the sight of Cynthia. He would flee round the corner in case she saw him. Outwardly sharp-tongued and tough though he was, even at that age Lennon did not want to hurt Cynthia, whom he quickly christened Cyn. She was on a pedestal, classier than any of the other girls with whom he had quickie affairs, and the last thing that could be risked was Cynthia discovering his unfaithfulness. Cynthia, to this day, is blissfully unaware that there was any other heavy romance for John in his college days . . . which is exactly what John wanted her to believe.

With Stuart fast emerging as his bosom mate, and trying in vain to pull him solidly into art as a career; Cynthia having a powerful love affair with him and meeting him whenever she could; and the teachers throwing up their hands in dismay at the eighteen-year-old who wouldn't listen, John Lennon in 1958 was a complex, talented young man. His restless mood was partly summed up by the way he moved around. 'He gave off this feeling that he was already battling through life, even at eighteen,' says Cynthia. 'Whenever he was going anywhere or doing anything, he walked like lightning, as if he was being shot from an arrow. It was a kind of panic. He would look round as if someone was chasing him. He staggered, quickly, as though he believed that if he moved quickly, people might miss him.

'Those of us who loved him for his lunacy and his cutting remarks realized that inside John was a lot more than he was showing. It was trying to get out and hadn't found the right way. The teachers couldn't care less because they just judged his appearance and his track record, which wasn't very good. And they feared him because they didn't understand him. Stuart was intelligent enough to see something special in John. I did, and so did just a few of the girls at college. But the people who realized he was destined to be either a giant or a bum were few and far between in those days. Most people thought he was a dangerous, loud-mouthed, troublemaking layabout. He really needed his friends. . . .'

The key to understanding the psyche of the errant teenager who arrived at Liverpool College of Art lies in his wounded childhood. Years later, he was to recapture the pain of those years with songs that spine-chillingly re-enacted the tensions of his early agonies. But the real pressure of nursing John Winston Lennon through his first twenty-two years of problems, while all the time believing that he had a special talent and ought eventually to 'go places', fell to one woman, Mary Elizabeth Smith, John's Aunt Mimi.

John's father, Alfred Lennon, was away from Liverpool at the time of his son's birth. He worked as a ship's steward, and his adventurous, romantic work, coupled with his carefree attitude to life which took him on passenger liners to otherwise unattainable places like New York, is what attracted John's mother to him. The son of a freight clerk, Alfred Lennon – Freddy to his friends – was born at 57 Copperfield Street, Toxteth Park, on 14 December 1912. He was one of five brothers and had one sister.

John's mother, Julia – known in her family as Juliet – was born on 12 March 1914, the youngest of five daughters of George Ernest Stanley, and Annie (née Millward). Julia was a cinema usherette before she married Freddy on 3 December 1938.

Named John after his paternal grandfather, he had a decidedly Irish heritage. Lennon is the anglicized version of O'Leannain, a clan strong in the Galway, Fermanagh and Cork areas of southern Ireland. John's grandfather went to Liverpool from Ireland, as many did in the mid-nineteenth century, to seek better prospects of work in an England that was becoming industrialized faster than their own country. Born in Dublin in the 1850s, grandfather John Lennon – nicknamed Jack – was an occasional singer who spent some years singing in a group in America. At the age of nine, in 1921, Freddy Lennon became an orphan when his father died of a diseased liver. Freddy went to the Bluecoats orphanage in Liverpool.

Julia and Mimi's father was an official with the Glasgow and Liverpool Salvage Company, and often travelled on salvage work, retrieving submarines from the bottom of the Atlantic. His father had been a musician. Julia's mother, Annie, was the daughter of a solicitor's clerk; in the jobless Liverpool of the 1930s, a family like this was, for Julia and Mimi, something to be treasured, to be proud of, to mark out your values and aspirations. Compared with thousands of Merseyside people, they came from a privileged background.

Auburn-haired, slim and vivacious, Julia was attracted to Freddy by one major characteristic their personalities had in common: they were both fun-loving and carefree. A year after their marriage at Mount Pleasant Register Office, Freddy was on the high seas as a head waiter, eventually berthing at New York. 'Freddy was a ship's steward on troop ships carrying soldiers between Liverpool and Southampton and France,' says Charles Lennon, his brother and John's uncle. 'They also went over to Canada to bring troops back.' He returned home for the Christmas of that year but was soon off again, and was jailed when one

Aunt Mimi, whom John grew to love and respect. This picture, taken in
March 1971, shows her with a cat John brought home as a stray

boat on which he sailed reached North Africa and he was accused of stealing a bottle of vodka. Erratically, he would write home to Julia from his ships saying he was doing well, singing songs like 'Begin The Beguine' during crew concerts; but his absence, during these dark war years, was placing an impossible strain on their marriage. In one letter, he wrote to Julia saying his date of return was uncertain and he suggested she should get out and enjoy herself and not sit around and mope.

Julia did just that, for she saw the marital storm clouds looming. By 1942 she considered Freddy to have left her for good, and she moved in with a new man, a hotel waiter called John Dykins. He was later to be nicknamed Twitchy by John because he had a pronounced facial tic. Julia wrote to Freddy asking for a divorce, and later asked for one when they met, but Freddy always refused. They were never divorced.

Julia had three illegitimate children outside her marriage, and John Dykins was the father of two who were John's half-sisters: Julia Dykins, born in Liverpool between January and March 1947 and Jacqueline Dykins, born in Liverpool between October and December 1949. Another child was fathered by a Norwegian ship's captain. John met his two half-sisters on his occasional visits to Twitchy's house.

Charles Lennon says, 'Fred worshipped Julia and told me he'd never give her the satisfaction of a divorce. He was broken-hearted when their marriage collapsed. He would have done anything to have her back but kept saying their future was ruined when she met Dykins. When Fred and Julia were together, they were very keen on music: he would sing and she would play the ukelele. I can hear him now, serenading her with those Italian love songs in Newcastle Road.' The reason for their final parting is contentious. Some people say Fred genuinely hoped for a reunion when he returned from sea but half expected her to leave him. Charles Lennon maintains that Julia had got together with her new regular man, Twitchy, by the time Freddy returned, and there was no chance of a reunion. Freddy Lennon died in Brighton, England, in 1976.

From his first days on earth, Mimi treasured her nephew, and her husband, John's Uncle George, 'thought John had been put here entirely for his pleasure', says Mimi. With no children of their own and Julia isolated by the frequent absence of Freddy, Mimi made John a welcome fit for a king at her house in Woolton, where Uncle George ran a dairy farm around the corner from their home. Mimi could offer a stable home and was much better placed to raise a child than her sister who, on her separation from Freddy, was no longer entitled to payments each week from the shipping line for which he worked. Julia continued to live with her parents in Wavertree, a short bus ride from Mimi. Increasingly John was left in the care of Mimi, who needed no encouragement to have him for days and weeks at a time. Her husband George, too, entertained him by occasionally taking him early in the morning to see his cows being milked. John's pre-school years were idyllic.

By the time Julia had moved in with Twitchy, and John was five, Freddy Lennon suddenly reappeared in an attempt to patch up his marriage and reclaim his son. One day he arrived at Mimi's house and, against her better judgement, persuaded her and John to let him take his son to Blackpool for the day. Walking John on the Blackpool sands, his father asked John what he wanted to be when he grew up. John answered: 'Prime minister, or on the stage.'

Freddy had a vague plan to take him to New Zealand and start a new life there, but it was a plan that went horribly wrong. When Freddy did not return to Mimi with John after several days, Julia found out where he was and arrived, unannounced, in Blackpool. She said bluntly that she wanted John back; she had set up a new home with a new man, and, she insisted, could offer John a better childhood than Freddy. The uncertainty of his father's life at sea was no substitute for what Mimi and she could offer.

The scene that followed in that Blackpool flat was traumatic for a five-year-old. By then he had got used to a comfortable family pattern: he lived with Mimi, who insisted on caring for him as Julia was involved with Twitchy, but every day Julia would visit her son at Menlove Avenue. Gradually, he started to understand and come to terms with the situation, developing a rapport with his exuberant mother as well as a deep mutual affection for Mimi. 'Mimi' and 'Mummy' ran well together as the two women in his life; Uncle George was there as a benevolent, kindly man, an anchor and something of a substitute father.

One day, John said to his aunt: 'Why can't I call you Mummy?'

She answered: 'Well you couldn't very well have *two* Mummies, could you?'

Now, with his real parents arguing before his eyes over who was to have him, young John Winston Lennon was emotionally wracked. He had always hoped for the return of his father from seafaring, and 'Pater', as he called him, had given him a good time in Blackpool, romping in the sands every day. But his mother had been more constant than his father in his young life. Here, now, was a hideous tug-of-war.

It was Freddy who put John in the most hopeless situation. 'You have to decide if you want to stay with me or with Mummy.'

A tearful John replied: 'I'll stay with you.'

Julia intervened: 'Now John, are you sure about that? Do you want to go to another country with him, or will you stay here with me?'

'With Daddy,' sobbed John, tears pouring down his cheeks.

Freddy was triumphant and said to his wife: 'That's enough, Julia, you've had your answer. Leave him alone.' Freddy had already unsuccessfully tried to woo Julia back from the happiness she was enjoying with her new man.

Despite all her inner torment, and with the tears welling up inside her, Julia decided it was all over. She turned round and walked out of the door of her flat. She had lost her son.

When the door closed, the finality of his mother's departure and the uncertainty of a future with his father were too much for John. He ran after his mother, crying uncontrollably, and eventually found her in the street. 'Mummy, Mummy, don't go, don't go.'

They hugged each other in the Blackpool street, and Julia delivered him back to Liverpool, safe into the loving arms of her sister Mimi, who was to care for him with conscientiousness, strictness – and passion. Julia was so excited at having her son back that she forgot to get a train ticket at Blackpool and was apprehended by police when she arrived back at Lime Street Station. She explained her predicament and returned the next day with the money. Mimi's life, and much of Uncle George's, now centred totally on the little lad who had survived so much and who, soon after she had sent him at the age of five to Dovedale Road Primary School, had been described to her by the headmaster, Mr Evans, as 'sharp as a needle'.

Even at this age, John's character was shaping quickly. Part of his resilience, reaction against authority, aggression, and fierce independence may be traced to that anguished parting of his parents in Blackpool, when they threw an impossible decision into his young face. A second facet of his character was formed by the warm sanctuary of Mimi's home life. She brought him up with a rod of iron and a heart of gold, which he was never to forget.

2
CHILDHOOD

'I was either a genius or a madman'

Even as a toddler John was defiant, determined, and a leader. When he played cowboys and Indians, in the garden of Mimi's home, she recalls: 'He had to be in charge. Always. The other boys had to be the cowboys and he *had* to be the Indian. And when he said they were dead, they were dead. "Pretend properly," he would tell them.'

Nostalgia hardly suits Aunt Mimi, a tall, bold woman with a striking, no-nonsense, uncompromising personality, but she will make an exception and enjoy reminiscing on her favourite topic: John Lennon. She sits in the bungalow at Sandbanks, Dorset, which John bought for her in 1965. That year it became obvious that she could not survive, with sanity, the gathering hordes of fans rounding on John and Mimi's beloved home in Liverpool. 'The fans were not only sleeping in the driveway all night, without me knowing. They were phoning me from all over the world. . . America, Australia, everywhere. We kept changing the phone number but the fans found the new number every time. The Post Office said they'd run out of new numbers for me.'

John said one day: 'You're going from here, where do you want to live?' Mimi was visiting him at his Beatle home in Weybridge, Surrey.

'Bournemouth would be nice,' said Mimi.

'Let's go,' said John.

He set off with her in his chauffeured Rolls-Royce, headed south, and made her choose the pretty bungalow overlooking Poole Harbour where, within months, the passing holiday launches would carry finger-pointing passengers on pleasure trips. And on the megaphone the guides would shout: 'Over there on the right, is where John Lennon's Aunt Mimi lives.'

Mimi, who went there seeking solitude and anonymity, groaned. 'Why can't they leave me alone?' In 1983, after an illness, Mimi moved back north to within a few miles of her former home: she wanted company and went to stay with her sister Anne.

In 1965, when he moved Mimi from north to south, John Lennon was considered to be generally at his most acid-tongued, and had a reputation as the 'hard man' of the Beatles. Yet Mimi had ample evidence that, underneath, he was unchanged. He disagreed with her on a major point of sentimentality; he wanted her to keep Mendips, even though she was leaving it.

'Mimi, I grew up there. Let's keep it,' he said, as they drove south.

'John, if I leave there, it has to be sold. Have you ever been back to an empty house? A gloom comes over it. Sell it.'

'Well,' said John, 'spend six months up in Mendips and six down here in Bournemouth. I don't want anyone else owning that house where I grew up.'

Mimi was adamant. She wanted a total break. Not for the first time, she won her point with John. He was never easily persuaded about anything, but Mimi was at least his equal at digging in. He loved and respected her for that, and even his 1965 status as a wealthy Beatle would not change either Mimi or him. Mendips was sold, initially to doctors. Today a sign outside the neat house reads: 'Official Notice, Private. No Admission, Merseyside County Council.'

The house is still on Liverpool's tourist route. At dead of night, cars bearing people on pilgrimages from all over the world pull up outside, and dreamy passengers of all ages sit and stare. This, they reflect, is where John and the Beatles were born. If the walls of that house could only talk. . . .

Mimi remembers everything. From his birth, she was utterly enraptured by everything about the baby who would become world-famous. Because he was due to be born at the end of September, doctors planned a Caesarean operation on Julia Lennon. 'She was overdue and I was phoning the hospital every five minutes,' says Mimi. 'The same question they got tired of hearing: "Has Mrs Lennon had her baby yet?"'

' "No, not yet."'

'The Caesarean became unnecessary. At six-thirty on 9 October I phoned and they said: "Mrs Lennon has just had a boy."'

'Well, we were five girls as sister in my family, and I nearly went off my nut. I said, "Mother, mother, a boy, a boy!" The air raids used to start at that time, dusk, so I ran to the maternity hospital to see her.'

That night, Hitler's Luftwaffe pounded Liverpool in one of its fiercest raids on a major city and port. 'I was dodging in doorways between running as fast as my legs would carry me,' says Mimi. 'I was literally terrified. Transport had stopped because the bombs began always at dusk. There was shrapnel falling and gunfire and when there was a little lull I ran into the hospital ward and there was this beautiful little baby. But they had this rough blanket around him and I said immediately: "Take this blanket off his face, it's too rough." Just as I lifted him up, the warning sirens went off again and visitors were told we could either go down into the cellars or go home but we couldn't stay. John, like the other babies, was put underneath the bed for safety. I ran every step of the way home.

'When I got home, I said: "Mother, he's beautiful."'

'My father said: "Oh hell, they always say that. He'd *have* to be better than any other."'

'I said: "He *is* better than all the others. You know, the others are all wrinkled and he isn't." ' '

Within a week, Julia and baby John had left hospital and went to live at 9 Newcastle Road, Wavertree. He was a model child but there were early signs of determination: in his high chair with his feeding table in front of it, he would prefer to try to spoon feed himself rather than be fed. At ten months he was toddling, unsteadily, but trying hard.

When Julia and Mimi decided that John would be brought up by his aunt, Uncle George entered the picture very firmly. A gentle soul, George Smith came from three generations of farmers. 'They started in a very small way,' says Mimi. 'The great-grandfather had only one cow, and the next a bigger business, until George carried on as a big breeder, and the milk was supplied mostly to hospitals.'

At four and a half John was taught to read and write by George, who sat him on his knee and worked the lad through the *Liverpool Echo* every night. 'Syllable by syllable, George would work at him till he got it right. John couldn't spell at that age, of course, but he could get down what he wanted. My husband went through all the headlines in the newspaper with John every night.'

The habit may have accounted for John's avid newspaper-reading habit throughout his life. During the Beatles years, he told me he got many ideas for song lyrics from reading newspapers. He was always quick to identify the idiosyncrasies of each newspaper, and was almost obsessively interested in the news of the day. It was a rare earthquake indeed that escaped his attention.

There were no toys in John's early life – the nearest was a plastic duck which swam in the bath with him. Books were his passion, particularly the *Just William* series by Richmal Crompton, which mirrored his own personality as a naughty but humorous boy. *Alice in Wonderland* was another favourite: he would re-read it until he could recite passages by memory. 'He never showed the slightest interest in games or toys,' says Mimi. 'I had twenty volumes of the world's best short stories and we had a love of books in common. John used to go back and read them over and over again, particularly Balzac. I thought there was a lot of Balzac in his song writing later on. Anyway, he'd read most of the classics by the time he was ten. He had such imagination and built up the stories himself when he and I talked them over.'

John had no illnesses when he was a child – just chicken pox (which he called chicken pots) when he was eight. 'He was never really ill for one day in his life, except for the occasional cold,' says Mimi. She ran her house, and disciplined him, the way she had been brought up: 'No picturedromes. He never gave me any trouble when he was young, and he never asked for much. I don't believe in people giving children money to go to the cinema just to get rid of them. He had three interests: painting and drawing in bed, if he was down with a cold; having his friends of the same age round; and reading.'

In his bedroom haven above the porch, the studious little Lennon was quiet for hours, aided by an extension speaker from the lounge radio, with long electrical wires stretching down the stairs from his room. With his pencils and crayons and drawing books, he would be totally happy apart from the occasional shouts like: 'Change the programme on the wireless, Mimi.'

Two special favourites were *Dick Barton, Special Agent*, the thriller serial that came on every night at 6.45 p.m., and *The Goon Show*. Says Mimi: 'When Dick Barton was in trouble, his face used to go deathly white. He couldn't sit down for worry. While it was on, George and I had to be absolutely silent. And with the Goons, he imitated their accents all the time. "I'm the Famous Eccles," John would say, and he would drive me crazy with non-stop mimicry of the various accents. He loved that play on words.'

Late at night, Mimi would get her instructions from above when her nephew was ready to go to sleep. She had tried to instil in him the value of money. 'We weren't short but we weren't rich and I couldn't bear waste, particularly of electricity. This little voice would shout down on so many nights, "Turn landing light out, Mimi." '

On his children's post office set, he would write letters to his Uncle George, saying: 'Dear Gerge, will you wash me tonight, not Mimi?' Young John didn't take long to work out the benefits of living with his doting aunt and uncle: Mimi would forever be the staunch disciplinarian and he was destined to spend his entire life persuading her that he wasn't all that bad; George was easily won over, and, especially when he was in trouble with Mimi, the kind uncle would bail him out with an encouraging word, a pat on the head.

'I had no time to go playing ducks in the bath with him,' says Mimi, 'but George would do anything John wanted when he was little. They adored each other. George would see him to bed with a smile, most nights.'

Bedtimes were happy, with George usually having to recite a nursery rhyme to John, traditional favourites like: 'Let Him Go, Let Him Tarry' or 'Wee Willie Winkie'. Mimi, ever practical, would be more concerned with scrubbing his knees.

Mimi would berate her husband, in the kindest fashion: 'George, you're ruining him. We can't have two fools in the house. One's enough.' No matter what he wanted, John could get it out of her husband. Whenever John was being rebuked or pulled into line by Mimi, George would give him the nod and a wink to go upstairs and look under his pillow. George, anticipating trouble, had put a sweet or a biscuit there for his surrogate son.

When John reached the age of five and it was time for primary school, Mimi applied her usual diligence to the task of choosing 'not just anywhere, but the best possible'. After inspecting various state schools in the area she settled on Dovedale Primary, just down the road from Penny Lane. To get there, some three miles from Mendips, John would be taken by bus past the Salvation Army hostel in Strawberry Field, down to Penny Lane.

From his first visits to the school, John was considered bright. On his informal look around Dovedale, the school secretary asked the five-year-old to run an errand, to take a letter to a nearby classroom for her while she and Mimi talked. 'She remarked even then on his confidence and said: "What a smart little boy," ' says Mimi.

At the first parents' meeting to discuss their children's progress,

September 1947. Aged seven, a pupil of Dovedale Primary School, Allerton

A childhood Christmas sketch by John and a note on a telegraph form to Mimi's husband, George. The postcard is from his Aunt Elizabeth in Scotland

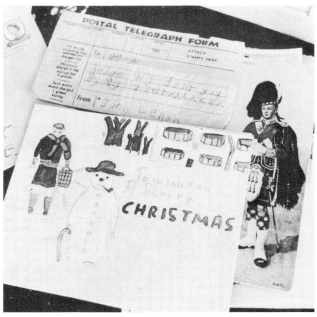

May 1948. John, aged seven, outside the front porch of Mendips. Aunt Mimi would banish him there when his guitar playing became too much for her

the headmaster, Mr Bolt, told Mimi: 'There's no need to worry about him. He's as sharp as a needle. But he won't do anything he doesn't want to.'

In his first school, Lennon's individuality rose quickly. Doug Freeman, now a farmer in the Lake District, went to Dovedale with John. 'To me, he was always stuck out as somebody different, even from the age of five or six. Whatever he did, he was going to be unusual. If there was anything out of the ordinary going on in the school it was centred on him. You definitely noticed him, even at that age. He was on a totally different wavelength from the others, and although he was sometimes causing trouble and disagreements, as kids do, no teachers could ever work out properly what it was about him that was different. It stuck out a mile. The teachers could never tie him down to anything. He was always the centre of attention; he was different from anyone else in the school.'

Sliding in the snow or ice in the school playground slopes and playing marbles was a favourite hobby among all the boys, but Lennon would not join in the communal games: he was off on his own, leading a pack. 'Always on the borders of getting into trouble, but never quite going over the edge,' recalls Doug Freeman. 'We were all a little bit frightened of him, too, and it stuck out to parents then that he was different. The mothers had their eyes on him as if to say: "Keep away from that one." ' Rather like the notices he puts up around some of the fields near his farm, Freeman makes this analogy: 'Chemically treated – beware.' John, he avers, had to be treated similarly – with great caution.

Art quickly became John's special subject at Dovedale. He was getting on well in all subjects, though with a notable weakness in mathematics, but in art he excelled. In an exhibition in the school hall, when he was ten, John's drawing startled several pupils. He drew a picture of what several boys recognized as Jesus Christ, in itself an adventurous move. Twenty years later, John Lennon's bearded facial appearance, when he was not wearing the 'granny spectacles' which were to become his trademark for a time, exactly resembled that drawing of Jesus which he had done at Dovedale Primary School. 'It was certainly strange. The similarity of the drawing, and the John with very long hair we later saw, was uncanny,' says Doug Freeman.

Comedian Jimmy Tarbuck, who went to Dovedale with John, recalls: 'Even at the age of eight he stood out, and had his gang of admirers. He wasn't easily missed at school – he wasn't the sort of kid to stand in corners, studiously reading his books. Oh no, he had a load of energy even then. If there was a playground fight, he'd be involved in it. He could be quite aggressive and when I saw him out of the classroom he'd be making his opinions known, though he always talked very slowly.' Tarbuck remembers going on a school camping trip with John to the Isle of Man. 'It wasn't so much what he did that was special, but the way he spoke,' he reflects. 'You could register, even as a kid, that here was an oddball. Now I can see that he was a genius all along.' Tarbuck did not go to grammar school with John, but caught up with him when the Beatles emerged and the comedian was one of the regulars at Liverpool's Cavern. 'He was a bit of a teddy boy then, very sarcastic, but also very funny.' In later years, the two went round London together on club crawls into the early hours. 'By then I was a comic, but John made *me* laugh. He would put down people with one crushing sentence. Some artists don't suffer fools gladly. John never suffered them at all.'

As an embryonic Beatle Lennon said, looking back on his troubled childhood: 'I had a feeling I was either a genius or a madman. Now I know I wasn't a madman, so I must have been a genius.'

John was fourteen when Uncle George died from a haemorrhage. When he came home from holiday in Durness, Scotland, with Aunt Elizabeth to be told by Mimi of George's sudden death, John went red-faced and ran to his room. After the separation of his parents, this was the second bitter blow to his young life. In the recurring arguments with Mimi about his lack of discipline, lovely Uncle George had been his mate. They had gone for walks together. He adored the man's gentleness. Mimi, heartbroken by the death of her husband who had not suffered a day's illness, put a brave face on but was quiet for days. Coincidentally, John was now seeing more of his mother. With the new man in her life, Twitchy, Julia lived a short bus ride away at 1 Blomfield Road, Spring Wood, Allerton. Apart from her maternal attraction, John found in her a total contrast with the authoritarian Mimi. Julia was effervescent, smiling, full of *joie de vivre*. And she enjoyed practical jokes. Most importantly to John, she tended to look down on authority.

Three years before Uncle George's death, John had sailed effortlessly through the 11-plus examination. He arrived home from Dovedale one afternoon and casually told Mimi: 'I've got it – I'm through.' His primary school days, though showing early signs of his individuality, had not caused Mimi any disturbance, so she was hardly surprised.

Uncle George had prepared for the great day, anyway. 'It's

outside, what you were promised if you passed the exam,' he said. John immediately went out for a ride across the golf course opposite Mendips, on his new emerald green Raleigh Lenton bicycle. He used to show it proudly to the other boys who went to the garden fetes in the grounds of the Salvation Army hostel at Strawberry Field in Woolton: Mimi took John to these often.

John was glad to be leaving Dovedale; even at eleven he felt he was outgrowing it, with its uniform of a black blazer, with a dove as the badge, and grey shorts. He had made his little stabs against school rules by often not wearing the blazer when he should have done, or by arriving at school assembly with his tie askew and top shirt button undone. Only a few boys were similarly careless in their dress. 'It was also a school where sport was encouraged, and John was totally uninterested in it,' says Michael Isaacson, today the boss of a highly successful London advertising agency. He had the totally unique experience of being a year older than John Lennon, and seeing him arrive at all three schools: Dovedale Road Primary, Quarry Bank High, and Liverpool College of Art.

'He didn't do particularly well, academically, at Dovedale. Certainly nobody talked of his prowess at any subject although there were often drawings by him on display, just as there were by other boys. I do remember him at Dovedale as not making a lot of effort. But he had obvious talent, because getting through the 11-plus in those days wasn't an easy task. Only the minority passed. He was a bright, alert boy and you could see from his face that he was no fool. If he'd decided to be an academic, I imagine he'd have made a very good one.'

Even at primary school, John and a few others found a way of bucking the system and making a profit: he would take his dinner money, payable for school lunches, and not hand it in to the teacher. Instead of eating school lunch, he and three or four others would go down to Penny Lane on some days and buy sweets and their own 'lunch' – custard tarts. But he was shrewd enough not to get found out.

Quarry Bank High School was a different matter. When he went there, in September 1952, the sharp-eyed Lennon quickly realized he was going to be up against much sterner authority, more strictness, and rules. It was a state grammar school with pretentions to being a public school; the masters wore caps and gowns and the headmaster, E.R. Taylor, a tall, rangy-looking man and a devout Methodist, used the cane.

Lennon got the measure of the school very quickly and decided there was only one route for him: to confront it. He had done well

John with his mother, Julia, in the garden of her sister's house (John's Aunt Anne) in Rock Ferry on the Wirral, July 1949

in any fights at Dovedale, but here at Quarry Bank there were bigger boys. Combined with the aura of academic and disciplined heaviness about the school, it was intimidating, but on entering this formidable school John had a major asset: his two friends from Dovedale had also passed the 11-plus. While one of them, Ivan Vaughan, had gone to the more prestigious city school, the Liverpool Institute, another from the 'gang of three', Pete Shotton, was joining John at Quarry Bank. Mimi was pleased to see that John was not going to a city school but was continuing his education at a suburban grammar school. She would be able to keep an eye on him more easily if he didn't have long bus journeys. She scarcely knew what awaited her.

Quarry Bank High School's motto was *Ex Hoc Metallo Virtutem* (From This Rough Metal We Forge Virtue). In his black blazer, with red and gold stag's head badge, John cycled there each day, up the long Harthill Road and passing the old sandstone quarries on one of which the school was said to be built. Like most schools, it divided its pupils into houses. These were named according to the district in which the boy lived. It followed that boys from the middle-class homes would be together and boys from the rougher areas would be together. In pecking order of poshness and toughness, Childwall was the number one house, Allerton number two, and Woolton (John's house) was number three. The 'harder' houses were Wavertree and Aigburth. John, in a middle-class house, was thus expected to behave, like most of the others, with reasonable decorum and discipline.

But he didn't. 'From day one, he roared through the school,' says Michael Isaacson. 'He set out to be a noise, aided and abetted by Pete Shotton who had the face of an angel but was exactly the opposite.' John was, however, the leader in any partnership, and Shotton became his lieutenant in the hundreds of misdeeds that became legendary in a school that was to deliver brilliant students to universities.

John soon decided that he had no respect for most of the teachers, and academically he plummeted. A bright boy from Dovedale when he arrived, he failed to concentrate in lessons, did not do much homework, and dropped to the B stream by the third year. By the final term of the fourth year he was twentieth in the bottom class of the C stream. His school reports told Mimi more than she needed to know: 'Certainly on the road to failure. . .hopeless. . .rather a clown in class. . .wasting other pupils' time.' Mimi, worried by one report, took him to have his eyes tested. John read a figure 5 as an 8. Mimi's eyes watered with sadness as she realized that her young boy needed glasses. 'But he had said he wouldn't wear National Health glasses, so I had to buy him thick black-rimmed ones – even then on condition that when he grew up he could have contact lenses,' says Mimi. John hated wearing the spectacles, and the fact that he couldn't see the blackboards properly without them may have contributed to his general despair about learning much at Quarry Bank.

Skiving, swearing, and smoking became the three key activities in John's life at Quarry Bank. Every morning and night, Mimi would try to instil in him that it was his future at stake, as he dressed in the smart blazer that Mimi had had made specially at Uncle George's tailor in Woolton village. ('It lasted longer that way – and it looked nicer than the school outfitter's,' she says.) By the time he reached school, invariably late for assembly, John's uniform was liberally arranged around his body so that he looked as if he'd just tumbled out of bed in it.

Since the Quarry Bank badge was a stag, Lennon must have taken this to mean he could cavort around the place like a field. 'His uniform', says Michael Isaacson, 'looked as if it had survived World War One. He rarely wore a tie until he was admonished for looking dishevelled.'

Lennon was particularly harsh on student teachers. 'He and Shotton could virtually send a new teacher who was standing in or studying at Quarry Bank for three weeks, to a mental home. They'd take no notice of anything he said, and do no work, and the teacher's only route would be to send them to the headmaster,' says Isaacson.

Lennon was caned literally scores of times but the stick made no difference. He would receive it for rudeness to teachers, refusing or ignoring their instructions to do work to a set pattern, missing assembly, scoring a direct hit with a peashooter during a lesson, being late in class, looking slovenly, swearing, or causing a disruption in the school. The punishments mounted through a simple fact of schoolmasters' expediency; once a boy became notorious, like John, he was picked on, whether he was causing trouble or not. Caning had no effect: he got so used to it that he emerged from the headmaster's study with a smile afterwards. His view was: if *that* was the worst that could happen to you for leading such a liberal school life, it was worth suffering a raw hand. Pete Shotton, who often followed Lennon into the caning session, saw John coming out with a smirk on his face, smiled back, and was admonished even more strongly for not treating the matter seriously.

In nearby Calderstones Park, Quarry Bank schoolboys did cross-country runs. Michael Isaacson was captain of athletics, and head of the Woolton house which included Lennon. 'John and his bunch were the constant bane of my life. He would do anything to make the cross-country runs a total and utter mess. In sport Lennon was a total drop-out. Not only did I not want him in any run, because my job was to get Woolton house as high as possible; I didn't want him anywhere *near* the run, because he'd do his best to screw up any effort we were making. Half of the lads were running their hearts out, the bulk of them did it because that's what they had to do, and half a dozen boys were so tubby that running was an effort. And of course, it was those fatties whom Lennon and Shotton would verbally torture if they were anywhere near. They'd stand there looking as if a dust cart had been dropped over them, smoking and swearing, mocking the fatties, and – if I'd let them – tripping them up as they ran. I saw they were dangerous to have around during any athletics and told them to get out of my way, very early on after a few experiences like that in Calderstones Park. Lennon and Shotton were as thick as thieves and they went out looking for trouble.'

Stealing became a habit too. In Woolton and Allerton sweet shops he would ask shopkeepers for a quarter of sweets from a jar that was behind the counter and difficult to reach. The time needed to reach down the jar enabled Lennon to whip a bar of chocolate from the counter, unseen.

'Every situation I remember John in,' says Michael Isaacson, 'he led. The guys who were frightened of him, which was quite a lot, kept out of his way. He had a sharp tongue and didn't mind a fight. But those who adored him just followed.'

While the school curriculum was boring him increasingly, so that he plunged down in position in each form, John continued the flicker of interest in art which he'd shown at Dovedale. He hung around the art room, recognized Michael Isaacson as the older boy from Dovedale, and admired Isaacson's prowess which was to win him the title of Young Cartoonist of the Year, at the age of nineteen, in a national contest in the *New Statesman* newspaper.

'I was never a mate of John Lennon's but we always got on OK. He knew I wasn't a pushover and he never tried anything on me,' says Isaacson. 'Despite having no real encouragement, I got a feeling he was good at art, early on at Quarry Bank. So he'd come in and have a chat when I was in the art room drawing cartoons, which were my forte. I had a sense of humour rather like his. My drawings were satirical.

'Despite his troublemaking, I quite liked him and he was very, very funny. I was having plenty of my own trouble with the school, which was very anti-Jewish, so we had this much in common at Quarry Bank; my attitude was to outrun them all and to be the top athlete and captain of athletics, to prove a point; John's attitude towards the school was "To hell with the whole lot of them." I'd say I was constructive, he was destructive. We had lots of laughs about this and the worse he got, the more I enjoyed it – as long as he didn't interfere with my hopes to win the athletics cup for Woolton house. I knew there was no way I could get him to jump three inches or run three yards. So he was happy to be told forcefully to clear off at games time.' Sport simply bored his restless mind. Even dear Uncle George's attempts to teach him to bowl met a dead end.

The more he dug a trench for himself, the more aggressive he became. The more appalling his school results, the more he would incur the unflagging persistence of Mimi. She was particularly upset about this in John as she was conscientious beyond reproach. Long before the phrase 'latchkey children' was invented, Mimi believed firmly that her duty was to be in the house whenever John arrived home from school. 'Wherever I was in the village, by early afternoon I'd watch the clock and make sure I was back home by about three to prepare his meal. He never came home to an empty house.'

But the decline in his school work coincided with his increased visits to see his mother, particularly at weekends. Julia could play the banjo a little and tried to teach him a few chords; even at the age of four, he had received from her a £4 guitar. Her playing was limited, but the fact that she chuncked along and smiled was good enough for John. He was getting closer to his mother, and her casual approach to life, combined with a prankish sense of humour, was marvellous for a boy living with an aunt who was loving and caring but strict.

At Mendips, there were three cats in John's life. Tich, the marmalade-coloured half-Persian, died when John was at college. Tim, the half-Persian, was a stray found in the snowy street by John and became a specially pitied favourite. Sam was another cat he loved. And there was Sally, the mongrel dog who died when John was at art college. John often walked the dog around Woolton. As a young boy, John doted on the cats. Every day, he would cycle to Mr Smith the fishmonger in Woolton village to buy pieces of hake for his pets. Later, as a Beatle on tour, he would phone Mimi to ask how the cats were getting on without him.

'Nothing but the finest', was Mimi's motto for John during his growing years.

The solid middle-class values which Mimi Smith instilled into John were to earn her his love and respect when he grew up. As a Beatle, he would often phone her during his travels and say: 'Remember the old days, Mimi, when you told me off?'

And she would reply, 'There was always a reason, John. You had no job to go to. I was worried.'

John would laugh, secure in the knowledge that all was well in music.

'He only became obstreperous between the ages of fourteen and seventeen,' says Mimi. 'When he moved from Dovedale to Quarry Bank, the school reports became worrying to me. He'd bring them in, and throw them through the window before I could get to them. I knew something was wrong. "You've got a brain, be thankful and use it," I kept saying. He'd just look at me, even then, and in that tired way say: "Oh. . .Mimi." And then when he looked at me I couldn't go on any more. He'd give me a "squeaker" of a kiss on the side of my face and I'd say: "Don't soft soap me now," but he knew how to get round me.' Mimi, a great collector of books herself, remembers he could not get enough books to read; an encyclopaedia absorbed him at the age of twelve, particularly a section on magic.

Mimi's chief memory of the child is that he was not one to waste a minute. 'He was always looking for something to do or read, a very active child. And he loved to talk, about growing up and why I was so strong on discipline, and he listened.' He seemed interested especially in why she made a point of always being in the house when he came home from school around four o'clock.

'Because it's my duty John, to be here,' Mimi answered.

John said, 'But you've no need to.'

'Ah,' said Mimi, 'but when you're older, you'll understand.' And he did, she says. 'He grew to appreciate that, and often mentioned that he never returned from Quarry Bank to an empty house.'

For all his general studiousness and interest in words, he was careless and casual about his possessions and constantly needed money to replace things. He always asked for it at the same time – just before the bus left. That way he knew Mimi had no time to argue. But Mimi confirms that he was not mean; from early childhood he would buy her a bar of chocolate on her birthday, and his card to her would carry his own piece of poetry.

The first signs of John's enjoyment of being on stage came when he was about twelve. During an argument with her over discipline, he would pull funny faces and act out a part, recalls Mimi. 'He'd say, in a funny voice, "You know my name, doooon't you? Aim John *Winston* Lennon." ' Mimi's reaction was 'Save that for the music hall.' But she had a quiet laugh at John's talent.

St Peter's, the Woolton village church, had been the place of worship for Mimi's family for generations. John was sent to Sunday School there from the age of eight, and sang in the choir. He was conscientious about ensuring that he had enough money from Mimi to give to the church collection each Sunday. And throughout his years of living with her, John said he was a believer. 'Somebody's listening up there,' he would say.

He was about eight or nine when he walked into Mimi's kitchen and informed her: 'I've just seen God.'

'Well,' said Mimi, 'what was he doing?'

'Oh, just sitting by the fire,' John replied.

'Oh,' Aunt Mimi said, nodding thoughtfully, 'I expect he was feeling a bit chilly.'

At that age, she recalls, he was 'really good looking with fair hair and beautiful brown eyes, but he was nobody's fool'. He was resolute in whatever he decided decided to do – such as sitting in puddles whenever he was wearing new trousers. 'He was a bohemian, even as a boy. He'd never work at anything he wasn't interested in.

John marked the start of the Beatles years with his Aunt Mimi by inviting Brian Epstein to Mendips. Mimi was impressed with the 'charming, gentle man' who said that he had enormous hopes for the future of the group. He also assured her that John's talent was so special that, whatever the success level of the Beatles, her nephew would 'always do well'.

Brian stayed overnight at Mendips twice, talking of his grand plans to get a recording contract. 'It was his dream,' says Mimi. 'I said, "It's all very well for you, Mr Epstein, you have got your career. But these boys haven't. What happens if you can't get them on the road to a career? What happens then?"'

'Epstein would allow no such dark thoughts. "Don't worry, Mrs Smith. They are so talented. . . ." ' He sent Mimi a pot plant after each visit to thank her for tea. Such politeness went down well with her.

But when John came home in 1962 with a demonstration of their début single, 'Love Me Do', Mimi saw no reason to lose her scepticism. 'If you think you're going to make your fortune with that,' she said sharply, 'you've got another think coming.' She was proved right: it reached only seventeen in the bestseller lists. Next, John and Brian appeared with the demonstration of 'Please Please Me'. She was upstairs when they put it on. 'That's more like it,' she shouted down. 'That should do well.' She remembers clearly John's accurate prediction.

'Mimi,' he said, 'that is going to be number *one*.'

Mimi remembers John's Quarry Men friends visiting her home during their schooldays: 'When Paul first came to Mendips he had a buckle on his shoe. John had never seen anything like it. Then George Harrison came along, with his pink shirt and winklepicker shoes.' Mimi's disapproving stare spoke volumes. 'Mimi,' said John, 'can I have some clothes like Paul and George have – you know, shoes and shirts. . .?'

'Certainly not,' said Mimi, ending the conversation.

When he eventually had to move to London, Mimi missed him terribly. 'But I never said as much when he came to visit me. I was determined that there would be no clinging vine stuff.' The tough guy image which the public saw as a Beatle cut no ice with her: she remembered the little boy whom she had sent for a holiday to Scotland every year to his Aunt Elizabeth, nicknamed Mater by the family. When he had left the house with his Uncle George, he would always return to kiss Mimi and say, 'Don't be lonely or sad while I'm away. Read a good book.'

During early Beatlemania, Mimi kept a low profile. 'I didn't think it was any of my business to be seen and give interviews,' she says. And later, on a visit to Mendips, John said how grateful he was that she never pushed herself.

The old sparring between them resumed one night at the height of the Beatles' fame. She was in their dressing-room at Glasgow. As the time neared for John to go on stage, he ushered her out, saying, 'You'll have to go Mimi, I've got to get changed.'

She rasped, 'Have you any idea how many times I've seen you naked in twenty-four years?'

He laughed. The reaction was typical of the woman who remained completely unintimidated by his fame, money, or egotism.

Mendips, during the Beatles years, was under siege from fans. 'I'd go out and tell them it was no use waiting, but they knew his movements and insisted he was going to turn up,' says Mimi.

June 1964. Aunt Mimi, smiling in Sydney, Australia, has her first experience of Beatlemania

Some had hitch-hiked for hundreds of miles for a glimpse of John Lennon's childhood home, and stood taking pictures. Mimi, worried about some of them and their lack of cash, invited them in for tea and sandwiches. 'They'd beg me to give them John's cup. I'd tell them he'd used them all. They'd absolutely shriek with delight!'

If she went upstairs while playing 'open house' to the fans, she had to lock the kitchen door. 'Otherwise there wouldn't be a piece of crockery left in the kitchen by the time I came down.' She worried about the kids who stood outside in the pouring rain. She asked them in to dry out their clothes. 'Because I didn't have any girls' clothes in the house, I'd have to give them an old pullover of John's. They'd swoon on the spot.'

John's room above the porch was appallingly untidy. He left his clothes all over the place. Sometimes the girls would ask to see his room. She usually refused, but once, 'just to teach John a lesson', she took them up to see the mess he'd left. Instead of being horrified, they made a grab for things.

That same year, 1964, the Beatles played thirty-two concerts in nineteen days throughout Australia and New Zealand, before 200,000 fans. John phoned Mimi two weeks before departure saying: 'You're coming on holiday with me. Get your jabs.'

The whirlwind struck her when she was whisked for the best trip of her life: 'one long party,' she recalls. On the flight through the Far East, John made sure particular attention was paid to her. 'I kept saying: "No special treatment, John."' When they arrived in Wellington, New Zealand, Mimi made sure an exhausted John said hello, amid the pandemonium, to two second cousins he had never met. Mimi's mother's sister's children, John and Ann, did get to meet the hero in the family. 'He was quite interested in his family's history and finding out that they emigrated to become farmers,' says Mimi.

Memories of John's witticisms will never leave Mimi Smith. When American magazines asked her to write her memoirs, John said: 'Tell them! Take the money, Mimi! Tell them I was a juvenile delinquent who used to knock down old women!'

She recalls a press conference at which he was asked how, if he had never been any good at arithmetic, he managed to count his money. 'I just weigh it,' he answered.

And she sees him forever in her mind's eye, sitting in the lounge at Mendips writing poetry and lyrics. 'He never had a pencil out of his hand. He'd write something down, then screw up the bit of paper and throw it away and start again. And he'd say: "You ought to pick these up, Mimi, because I'm going to be famous one day and they'll be worth something." '

And she recalls, with heavy irony, a conversation with John at the start of the Beatles frenzy. 'I told him off about his accent. I said: "What's all this Scouse accent about, John? You weren't brought up as a little Scouser. You know how to speak properly." '

John just looked at her and rubbed his fingers together. 'It's about money,' he replied. 'The fans *expect* me to talk like that.'

3
SCHOOLDAYS

'Just let it roll'

For the first five years of John's education at Quarry Bank the headmaster was E.R. Taylor, whose memory of John is of 'an under-achiever who made no really positive contribution to the life of the school, either in sport or in attempting to improve academic standards'. Says the ex-head: 'He did not share in what we set out to do. When I joined the school in 1947, I took over from an ageing headmaster who had been ill, and most of the staff, like me, had returned from the war. There was a major job to do, in establishing *esprit de corps*, and building up the school's standards. While there was never any question of expulsion for John Lennon, I think he despised what we were trying to do in our traditional manner.' He was not a 'grievous troublemaker', but the school punishment records showed him to have been caned for offences which now seem minor, such as, in the military jargon that lingered from the teachers' army days, 'going AWOL' (absent without leave), a euphemism for playing truant; he also gambled on the sports field during a house cricket match – a travesty in a school that took sport seriously.

'Liverpool,' in the immortal words of the playwright Alun Owen, who wrote *A Hard Day's Night*, 'scars its children for life.' One of the endearing characteristics of the Liverpudlian is to bounce back, never to take a verbal knock or a swipe without retorting with something at least as sharp. At Quarry Bank, part of the penal system entailed the distribution of marks whereby two bad marks resulted in an hour's detention. One teacher devised a way of alternating the marks system with one that had more effect.

'Do you want a bad mark or a very dirty look?' he would ask.

44

Lennon would lead the chorus saying: 'A dirty look.'

The master's leer would break up the class into laughter; and Lennon mocked the dirty look, for he always enjoyed mimicking. That kind of rapport, treating the pupils more as people than as inferiors, always pleased John, who spoke regularly about how he hated being 'talked down' to.

Rod Davis, who became a firm friend of John and the banjoist in Lennon's first musical group, found himself poles apart from John in attitudes towards school. 'I never saw any point in getting punished for anything, so I toed the line. I was probably a goody goody.' He became head boy, a fact that provoked Lennon's incredulity at a fellow skiffle musician managing to be so ortho- dox.

William Ernest Pobjoy was an energetic thirty-five-year-old when he became headmaster of Quarry Bank, taking over from the portentous, authoritarian E.R. Taylor. Mr Pobjoy's first year at the school was Lennon's fifth and final year, so that by the time he took up office the mould of John's irreverence and the trouble- making Lennon–Shotton axis was difficult to break. 'I went in there as a disciplinarian,' says Pobjoy. 'I was determined to stand no nonsense.' But he faced a major thorn in John Lennon. 'I inherited an extremely disruptive boy, the legend of the school. He was presented to me as my most urgent problem, he and his friend Shotton,' recalls Mr Pobjoy, a palpably kind but firm man who tried hard to get to grips with John Lennon as a person rather than confront the problem with force.

'He didn't come my way until I'd been there a month. All the teachers tried again with him at the beginning of a new school year. Eventually he was brought to me as headmaster as a last resort. On that first and one occasion I gave three strokes of the cane, which was the ordinary thing to do in those days.' Shortly afterwards, Pobjoy abolished corporal punishment at Quarry Bank and it has never been reinstated. 'Caning never stops misbehaving. I quickly realized that. And with or without the cane, John didn't stop misbehaving.

'Missing detention and all the other things John did might be regarded now as ordinary schoolboy pranks, but there was another side to it all. He did take advantage of anybody who was weak. He was extremely cruel.' There were incidents between John and some teachers which horrified them all in the staff room. Lennon was often brutally tough on teachers who did not know how to handle him. He raised his fists and flatly refused to obey instructions.

'When I did cane him on that one occasion,' says Pobjoy, 'apart from the usual "This is going to hurt me more than it hurts you", I reasoned with him. But it did not make a lot of difference with John. He was set in his ways by the time I arrived, and changing his attitude in favour of his school work was an uphill task.

'I saw his guardian, Mrs Smith, frequently. She saw him as not her problem but the school's. I recall her saying: "The school should do something about it." Well, with John's early history and parental background it's not easy in difficult family circumstances to get a boy to behave well – or even to work well.'

Mr Pobjoy's worst moment came when he was at an afternoon football match at Goodison Park, home of Everton football club. A tannoyed message called him to the telephone and a distressed deputy headmaster told him of yet another Lennon problem. 'I said: "Oh suspend him." John was suspended for a few days and I saw his aunt again, but he survived right through from that day in February until July, coming to the natural end of his five-year course at the school.

'I recall talking to him about his ability and saying he could achieve a great deal if he set his mind to it. But he was only a failure at school because he attached little importance to academic work. He failed each of his O-levels by a single grade, and could clearly have passed if he'd wanted to. It simply didn't matter to him. He was particularly fond of an English master, Philip Burnett, who was rather advanced in his approach, his ideas, and his own way of life. John was very interested in poetry and wrote it.

'Among the Quarry Bank staff, John was seen as a wayward talent. John had been a thorn in everyone's side at school. As headmaster, I had the difficulty of beginning with him by dealing out a punishment, and that wasn't the best way to being an acquaintance. But he accepted his punishment as the natural consequence of something he had chosen to do.

'He resented any kind of constraint or discipline. He had no intention, even at Dovedale junior school, of being organized by others. He set out to cock a snook at authority and discipline from early childhood.'

Eric Oldman, John's housemaster and chemistry teacher, says: 'He was awkward but there was something *in* him. It wasn't sheer wickedness, but more spirit. He took up my time more than the others because he wouldn't conform so well. On football afternoons, he would slope off and we wouldn't be able to find him. He seemed determined not to conform to the rules.

'But he had a wit and a humour and ability. In chemistry and mathematics, which I taught a little, there was simple lack of any wish to get on. I remember writing, as his senior housemaster when he left Quarry Bank for art college: "Might make nothing of his life or something, if he brings out something *in his own way* to make a success of it." '

Gloom struck when the O-level results came. Mimi was distraught. 'What *was* I going to do? He'd been good enough at English and history, and when he began he picked up French quickly. I couldn't believe the results.'

John's artistic talent had been quite a talking point at Quarry Bank. But, an original even at that age, his drawings did not follow convention and he did not respond to the art teacher's instructions about what he should draw. A regular method of disrupting the class would be for John to pass from desk to desk an exercise book in which he drew bizarre, outlandish caricatures of the teachers. The book was called the *Daily Howl*. Boys stifled their laughter during class as it was passed round, surreptitiously, under desks.

When the end of term neared, Mr Pobjoy discussed John's prospects with him. This was before his disastrous results in his O-level examinations, but the headmaster, with the knowledge that Lennon was a troublemaker, decided to try to plan his future. Pobjoy also had a long discussion with Mimi, whom he had come to regard, if not fear, as what he calls a 'determined, informed and concerned guardian'.

The conversation with her was as electric as ever. 'Well, Mrs Smith, what are your thoughts about John's future? What do you think should be considered?'

'Well,' rasped Mimi, 'what are *you* going to do? You've had him for five years. You should have his future all ready.'

Mr Pobjoy said his standards in English, literature and poetry, were well above average, but in art he seemed to have a particular talent which should be encouraged. If he tried to get him admitted into art college, would Mimi finance his first year there, after which he would qualify for a grant?

'Yes,' said Mimi. 'Any port in a storm.'

'It wasn't very unusual in those days to get into art college without any G.C.E. passes,' says Pobjoy. 'He produced a portfolio of samples of his work and I had to say that he was suitable, without doing too much violence to my conscience. I did believe that he had talent and should be encouraged as a lively intelligent boy. The question was: Would he behave any better at college? He didn't, of course.'

His talent for line drawing, his attention to detail, and, above all, his grotesque sense of humour were obvious in all these drawings. The targets, the teachers, were sitting ducks for his blistering satire when he was fifteen. Lennon had little respect for any of them. And as subjects for his drawings they were appropriately bizarre in their daily behaviour. One master sewed a golf ball into the hem of his gown: he was literally a cracking shot. His walks around the school corridors and classrooms were punctuated by his taking aim and hitting troublesome boys on the backs of their heads with the golf ball. Another teacher was the talk of the school because he stank all day, every day, and the boys would openly put two fingers to their nose whenever he came near them. Yet another had a fifteen-foot-long pole which he held throughout lessons and which he swept through the air when a boy wasn't listening. He had perfect aim so that the pole smacked the offending boy across the back of his neck.

So John did not need to use much of his fertile imagination to satirize the schoolteachers. But the pungency of his wit, and the devastating captions to his drawings, were uproarious. In one red-covered exercise book which he gave as a gift to a friend, he gave the teachers names: Psyche, complete with the school badge of a stag but with a face bearing warts and a caption 'Spare Us, Oh Psyche', a commentary on the teacher with the deadly aim with the ball in his gown. His fascination with deformities was rife throughout John's drawings. Psyche's mate, with bulging eyes and warts, was balding, while another drawing of the Psinging Psychies featured six men with deformities in their faces. 'The Wife' was captioned 'My Little Glad' and the woman had a deformed eye. There were wart-ridden features all over a character nicknamed Rigo. 'Typical Hairy Hairless Smell-Type Smith', a dig at the teacher who was notorious for his odour, had a teddy boy hairstyle and a desperate caption: 'Ooh, mate, HELP! Phew, mate.'

There was even a drawing of himself headed: 'Simply a Simple Pimple: short-sighted John Wimple Lennon'. He drew himself as learned, studious, and wearing his horn-rimmed spectacles, with thick bushy hair and holding a dripping candle. But the clincher of the drawing was that he had claws, not human hands, and drainpipe trousers. Nick O'Teen, described as an Irish madman, was drawn smoking with both hands and a cigarette in his mouth. A man and a woman were depicted in bed and in church, saying, 'I do', while another couple were wheeling a pram with seven deformed children.

'I DO'

John's vision of a church wedding. This is one of many cartoons he gave to a fellow art student

John's grasp of word-play was imaginative even at fifteen. He was shaping his sense of the absurd, his lampooning of hapless victims, his keen awareness of the ridiculous and – always – a tilt at authority. This would become the hallmark of his character later, with his two books *In His Own Write* and *A Spaniard In The Works*, which were acclaimed by critics as signalling a great new literary wit. But at fifteen, students and teachers at Quarry Bank had to assess poems like this:

> Owl George ee be a farmer's lad
> With mucklekak and cow
> Ee be the son of 'is owl Dad
> But why I don't know how
>
> Ee tak a fork and bale the hay
> And stacking-stook he stock
> And lived his loif from day to day
> Dressed in a sweaty sock
>
> One day maybe he marry be
> To Nellie Nack the Lass
> And we shall see what we shall see
> A-fucking in the grass
>
> Our Nellie be a gal so fine
> All dimpled wart and blue
> She herds the pigs, the rotten swine
> It mak me wanna spew!
>
> Somehaps perchance ee'll be a man
> But now I will unfurl
> Owl George is out of the frying pan
> 'Cos ee's a little girl.

Even the teachers, hard-pressed to smile at Lennon, laughed. They passed John's *Daily Howl* around the staff room, and enjoyed being lampooned. They admired John's spoof on the weather forecast: 'Tomorrow will be Muggy, followed by Tuggy, Wuggy and Thuggy', and his send-up of Davy Crockett, entitled 'The Story of Davy Crutch-Head'.

While John clearly defied grammar school, there was ample evidence later in life that he reflected on those years at Quarry Bank with a hint of affection. In 1967 a Quarry Bank pupil, Stephen Bayley, wrote to John. This was at the height of the controversy surrounding the Beatles and drug-taking and when their milestone-making new album, *Sgt Pepper's Lonely Hearts Club Band*, was released. Scarcely expecting a reply, the boy asked a few questions about the songs and added a postscript about John's old school and its innovations, like the addition of Russian to the curriculum.

John's handwritten reply demonstrated his interest in the school no matter what he said; his patience for anyone who genuinely was inquisitive about his work and opinions; and his waspish wit:

Dear Stephen,

As Quarry Bank was never a very *high* school, the changes (?) sound OK. How about sending me a copy of that magazine? All my writing has always been for laughs or fun or whatever you call it. I do it for that first. Whatever people make of it afterwards is valid but it doesn't necessarily have to correspond to my thoughts about it. OK? This goes for any books, creations, art, poetry, songs, etc. The mystery and shit that is built around all forms of art needs smashing, anyway. It must be obvious by today's trends. Enough said.

The song of Mr Kite is taken almost word for word from an old theatrical poster including the Hendersons.

Is Mr Burton* (English) [sic] still there? If so say hello. He was one of the only teachers who dug me and vice versa.

Russian, eh? Not in my day. How we've progressed. Don't tell me they let you into Calder as well** for experience and lessons. I think they asked me years ago rather vaguely if I would like to go back and look but I saw enough of it when I was there. I have fond memories, not too fond though. I have the same trouble as you in writing, but the answer is: just let it roll.

Love
John Lennon

P.S. I don't want to start a rush of letters from little Quarrymen so play it a bit cool as they say in Swinging London. But do say hello to any of those teachers – not quite the right word. Even Pobjoy who got me into art school so I could fail there as well. I can never thank him enough.

* John meant Philip Burnett, the progressive English teacher with whom he had a good relationship.
**Calder (Calderstones Park) is the girls' school next door to Quarry Bank where Lennon often trespassed to chat up the girls.

Quarry Bank produced many eminent public figures, among them William Rodgers and Peter Shore, who went on to become socialist cabinet ministers; trade union leader David Basnett; actor Derek Nimmo; and prominent industrialists including the chairman of Ford, Europe. William Pobjoy looks back on Lennon's days at Quarry Bank with a smile, but he was irritated by one aspect of John's perverse attitude to schooling. 'I think he was against school, not Quarry Bank, because he said during the Beatles period: "Look at me now, I've travelled all over the world and done these interesting things. I'm so well off and there are people who taught me at Quarry Bank who are *still there*!" He seemed to think that to still be here in one place was a sign of failure. At that time it obviously didn't enter his head that there might be such a thing as vocation, where material matters were of little account. But I think he probably changed later on.'

The sentimentalist inside Lennon did change his over-the-shoulder look back at his old school. One day in 1965 Aunt Mimi, out walking in Woolton, met Mr Pobjoy, who asked how he was. The answer to the question was obvious, for Beatlemania was at its height: John was a world-famous star. But she astonished the former headmaster by saying: 'John's scared to come back to the school, but he sleeps with a picture of it over his bed.'

At Quarry Bank John travelled quickly from his earlier desire merely to emulate the cheeky Just William: he was titillating girls with obscenities when he went to hang out in Calderstones Park. Rose Lane School nearby had a fair proportion of belligerent pupils, and John would enjoy a confrontation with a few of them in a café, or on Allerton Road, where both he and his mob and the Rose Lane crowd would have skived off lessons. He was rarely involved in actual fights, mostly backing off when fisticuffs were near. 'He regarded fighting itself as a waste of time, but if anyone set on him he could take care of himself,' says Michael Isaacson, who left the school a year ahead of John to go to art college.

One day, Isaacson returned to Quarry Bank from art college to collect some of his old drawings. Bumping into John in the art room, Michael asked how he had fared in his O-levels and John told him the bad news.

'You should try to get into art school – I'm having a marvellous time drawing nudes,' said Isaacson.

'Cor, that sounds good,' said Lennon.

4
ELVIS!

'Let me get it out of my system, Mimi'

It cannot have been a coincidence: John's hell-raising final two years at Quarry Bank coincided with the arrival in his life of a force that was to be his *cause célèbre*, his saviour, his lifeline. To John Lennon at fifteen, the arrival of two films was virtually a mirror-image of his own outlook on life.

Rebel Without a Cause, starring the mumbling, sharp, resentful hero James Dean, was youth's first tilt at the establishment, its first statement against such cosy pictures as *Oklahoma* and *A Star Is Born*. And *Blackboard Jungle* was even more important, for it reflected schoolboy aggression and catapulted a new music into the world. The music was electrifyingly urgent; the message of the film might have been written for Lennon and his cronies at Quarry Bank. But the star, Bill Haley, wouldn't do. He had no real charisma and his personality totally lacked the tough directness of his driving songs like 'Rock Around The Clock'. Still, the die was cast; the old guard of what was then called the hit parade, including ballad singers Jimmy Young, Tony Bennett, Dickie Valentine, and Tennessee Ernie Ford, now had a deadly rival. The infant was called rock 'n' roll.

In 1956, when John Lennon was sixteen, the film which was dramatically to re-route pop music was shown in Britain. *Rock Around the Clock*, starring Bill Haley and the Comets, disc jockey Alan Freed, the Platters and Freddie Bell and the Bellboys, was not a strong movie, even by those days' standards. It had no story line, and was merely a vehicle for the bands to play this new music called rock 'n' roll. In America, the film went unnoticed. In Britain, it began what is still called the generation gap.

This new music, loud, irreverent rock 'n' roll, thundered through the cinema halls of Britain. Parents looked on in horror as their sons and daughters – but mostly sons – identified with this clarion call to confrontation. The best news of all, for young people, was that adults thought it wasn't 'music'. It wasn't, indeed, mere music: it signalled a new approach to growing up. Rock 'n' roll was the new international anthem of youth.

American teenagers emulated their big heroes of the screen, the mumbling Marlon Brando and the gaunt, haunted James Dean, by adopting jeans and T-shirts. In Britain, a much more definite uniform was adopted. It was called the teddy boy outfit, so described because of its vague similarity to Edwardian fashions.

Greasy hair was one of the major requirements of a ted. It had to be shaped like an elephant's trunk at the front, coming down on to the forehead and – crucially – a DA (duck's arse) at the back, with side whiskers extending well down the face. Very tight trousers, called drainpipes, bright socks, perhaps luminous, thick crepe-soled shoes (called 'brothel creepers') and a long drape jacket were *de rigueur*.

Pop music may have been fey until this point, but it was at least a little escape from the drudgery of school work. And in a house with no television, the nightly listen to Radio Luxembourg, broadcast then as now on the difficult-to-tune 208 metres from deep inside Europe, was mandatory for schoolchildren. The BBC broadcast light music. Luxembourg was well ahead of the game, playing non-stop pop. Its poor reception somehow added to its clandestine magic.

Lennon did not have to wait long for his Pied Piper. It was from this station one night that he heard Elvis Presley's earth-shaking new anthem for rock 'n' roll, 'Heartbreak Hotel'. 'After that,' John told me in 1962, 'nothing was the same for me. He did it for me, him and Lonnie Donegan.'

Elvis's weapon was a triple ace. His robust voice was powerful, virtually beyond plagiarism; his songs, with the world-wide chart topper 'Heartbreak Hotel' quickly followed by 'Don't Be Cruel' and 'Hound Dog', were revolutionary. They grabbed every listener by the ears as well as the hips. And then there was the way he looked.

Elvis was an Americanized version of the teddy boy. For him, the uniform was not necessary but he was quickly christened King of Rock 'n' Roll because of his look, his leer, his loudness, and his rudeness: his hip swivelling was the talk of the critics who branded him as a danger to morality. Sexuality oozed from him. For anyone remotely concerned with teenagers at that time, Presley was the partisan demarcation line: make up your mind, whose side are you on? It was them and us, the kids and the adults. The more adults bemoaned Presley's arrival, the more the newspapers screeched about the new music of youth, the more Lennon and thousands of sixteen-year-olds like him loved it.

Aunt Mimi remembers the period well. 'It was Elvis Presley all day long. I got very tired of him talking about this new singer. I was particularly upset because suddenly he wouldn't let me into his bedroom. If I opened the door, he'd say: "Leave it, I'll tidy it up." He became a mess, almost overnight, and all because of Elvis Presley, I say. He had a poster of him in his bedroom. There was a pyjama top in the bathroom, the trousers in the bedroom, socks somewhere else, shirts flung on the floor.'

Mimi's voice would boom up the stairs: 'There's going to be a change in this house. We're going to have law and order.' Throughout his life John would use the same sentence to tease Mimi about the 'Elvis period' as he reflected on it. 'And of course,' says Mimi, 'when John said it, later on, we would just both burst out laughing about the past. He was lucky to get away with what he did. It was because I'm a book lover and a bit of an artist myself, so I understood his attitude. What he wouldn't come to terms with was that I had a house to run. Oh, he *was* a mess and a problem in those years. Elvis Presley! If John's Uncle George had been alive even he certainly wouldn't have understood the bohemian bit.'

The anchor of Elvis, his music and what he represented, marked John's life as significantly as Lennon was to mark millions of young lives only ten years later. There was to be one vast difference between Presley and Lennon: the American rock giant was a physical phenomenon who rarely spoke, and when he did it was an unimportant mumble. Elvis called nearly all strangers 'sir' as a mark of polite nervousness. John was to combine an intuitive grasp of fundamental rock 'n' roll ethics with highly cerebral leadership. He probably never called anyone 'sir' in his life.

But in the mid-fifties the personal pull of Presley, quickly followed by Little Richard, Jerry Lee Lewis, Buddy Holly, the Coasters, Carl Perkins, and the Everly Brothers, meant liberation for the academic flop that John Lennon had become. It also perfectly fuelled his inherent resentment of authority.

If Presley was John's clarion call to stand up and stand out, Lonnie Donegan was, in 1956 when John was sixteen, just as great a catalyst for his life. This time the hero was not just a distant, masculine figure propelling rock 'n' roll into millions of teenagers' brains. Donegan, clean-cut and formal, in suit and tie as befitted his jazzy background, was nobody's idea of high fashion. He was nasal-voiced, played guitar and banjo, but mesmerized a nation with a curiously British interpretation of the songs of the great American folk singers Woody Guthrie and Huddie 'Leadbelly' Ledbetter. Donegan, who emerged from the traditional jazz ranks of the Chris Barber band, galvanized British youth into his music, named skiffle, with a record called 'Rock Island Line'.

Donegan's influence on British pop music has been incalculable. He had a basic three-chord style, easy to copy, and the line-up of his group at the time (one other guitarist, upright double bass, and drums) inspired hundreds of thousands of young people to make do-it-yourself music. The sound was unimportant. What was crucial was that it wasn't difficult; the guitars were props, allowing the singers to be actors. Here was do-it-yourself rock 'n' roll for thousands of young people. Donegan's cute little songs, like 'Putting On The Style', 'Does Your Chewing Gum Lose Its Flavour (On The Bedpost Overnight)' and 'Cumberland Gap', became the anthems of sixteen-year-olds everywhere. Skiffle groups, formed in schools and clubs, played as much for fun as for money.

Lennon, then a bellicose schoolboy, went for skiffle like a homing pigeon. Jazz audiences already knew of skiffle, because splinter groups formed from the bands led by Chris Barber and Ken Colyer played mostly in London clubs and a few knowledgeable provincial clubs like Liverpool's Cavern and Iron Door. All Lennon knew initially was 'Rock Island Line', which even the B.B.C. was playing. He thought its acceptance by *that* bastion of respectability, which even Aunt Mimi acknowledged as tolerable listening, was the key to his breakthrough. 'All the boys of my age are getting guitars,' he told Mimi. 'Could you lend me the money to get one?'

John was seeing more of his mother and asked both Julia and Mimi to buy him a guitar. Every afternoon, on her daily visits to Mendips, Julia would be asked, but she did not want to override Mimi's authority by installing John with a guitar under her roof. John alone was enough of a responsibility for her sister. Julia could see, anyway, from his interest in her banjo playing, that with a guitar in his hand his studies at school, already a cause for concern, would plunge into irretrievable disaster.

John, faced with the two women in his life not helping him get a guitar, decided to send away for his first model himself. From a mail order advertisement in the *Daily Mail* he ordered a £5 10s model, 'guaranteed not to split', and was canny enough, at this stage, to have the guitar posted to Julia's address where he would run less risk of a scolding. His musically-minded mother was less of a risk than Mimi. He took it to Mendips eventually, telling Mimi that Julia had got it for him.

Armed with the cheap guitar, which he would occasionally leave at Julia's in order not to push his luck with Mimi, John concentrated heavily on all the pop music sounds he could hear on Radio Luxembourg. Buying records was generally out of the question: they cost six shillings. But he did invest in a 78 r.p.m. record of Donegan's 'Rock Island Line'.

The person to whom Lennon quickly sold that record, for two shillings and sixpence, once he had played it to death on Julia's old record player, was to be one of the players in the group that John formed at school. Rod Davis, a studious, successful, A-stream student at Quarry Bank, met Lennon only because he too lived in Woolton. At the forty-five-minute prep sessions after each day's classes, students got together in classrooms according to the house they were in. As Davis and Lennon and his inseparable partner Pete Shotton were in Woolton, they met on most days. The record Lennon persuaded Rod Davis to buy had a damaged centre hole: Davis felt conned when he realized why John wanted to sell it.

Inspired by the Donegan craze, Rod Davis had bought a Windsor banjo for £5 from his uncle. Excited about his purchase, he said to a classmate, Eric Griffiths, 'I went and bought a banjo yesterday.' Rod Davis was surprised to be told that Lennon and Griffiths already had guitars, and that Pete Shotton was learning to play the washboard, an integral part of any skiffle band's line-up. 'Why don't we have a practice on Thursday?' said Griffiths. 'We're going to start a skiffle group.'

Rod Davis had known John Lennon and Pete Shotton since they were all about six. He remembered him as the scourge of St Peter's Sunday School classes. 'He arrived looking resentful at having to come on Sunday mornings,' says Rod Davis, 'and he chewed gum throughout the lessons. It just wasn't done to chew gum at the Sunday School.' Eventually John and Shotton were invited to leave, although Mimi insisted that he was confirmed, at his own request, at the same church. 'Religion was never rammed down his throat, but he certainly believed in God, all through his childhood, and he asked to be confirmed,' she says.

But the only religion that seriously grabbed Lennon at the age of sixteen was music. Even William Pobjoy, headmaster of Quarry Bank, noticed the passion with which young Lennon, the terror of

John's obsession with
deformities is evident
in this witty drawing,
done when he was
eighteen

the school, was interesting himself in skiffle. It was, he reflects, good to see him feeling positive about *something*.

Mr Pobjoy was also surprised, and pleased, that making music seemed to be encouraging a generous side to John's nature; some schoolboy entertainers, however amateur, would ask for money to play at school dances and other functions. 'But John would always be most polite, and certainly not ask for money, when he offered the services of his group,' says the ex-headmaster, who retired in 1982. 'Some boys asked outrageous fees but John was really grateful for the chance to play free.' Pobjoy pointed out this attribute to those teachers who were despairing of him.

Inevitably Lennon and Shotton were the pilots of the skiffle group. After a few weeks of practice, with John hammering out 'Rock Island Line' and 'Cumberland Gap' as his *tour de force* songs and Shotton playing the washboard with thimbles – the accepted percussion for all skiffle groups of that period – Lennon felt in full swing.

Now that this 'new music' of Lonnie Donegan and Elvis Presley was the talk of the school, particularly in the C stream into which Lennon had plunged, the official formation of a school skiffle group was the next move and John its obvious leader. When John told his mother of his group, she suggested practices were held at her house after school. The first line-up was John (guitar), Rod Davis (banjo), Eric Griffiths (guitar), and Colin Hanton (drums). The first rehearsal was in Eric Griffiths' house in Woolton. Later they would play in Julia's bathroom, with one player standing in the bath to get the tinny echoey sound of amplification. 'John's mother really enjoyed us playing and encouraged us a lot,' says Rod Davis. 'She obviously preferred the banjo to the guitar so I got on well with her. I was always impressed with the fact that she played banjo with the back of her nails.

'John was the undisputed leader for two reasons. First, he knew one more chord than the rest of us. His mother's banjo playing had given him the edge – she used to teach John some banjo chords, and they used to tune the top four strings of his guitar to banjo intervals, forget about the bottom two strings, and play banjo chords on the guitars! It was all right for me – Julia would help me tune my banjo properly. So I'd probably be the only one in tune. I think everything was in C – I remember having terrible trouble playing F chords on the banjo.

'Secondly John was keen on singing and the rest of us were never particularly good at vocals. We joined in choruses but he sang lead.' The earliest songs were 'Don't You Rock Me, Daddy-

O', 'Love Is Strange', 'Rock Island Line', 'Cumberland Gap', 'Freight Train', the big hit made famous by Chas McDevitt and Nancy Whiskey, Johnny Duncan's 'Last Train to San Fernando', and 'Maggie May'.

'John used to belt the daylights out of his guitar and was forever breaking strings,' says Rod Davis. 'When this happened, he'd hand me his guitar and I'd have to change the string for him because I was better at it than him. While I was changing it, he'd borrow my banjo, so he's actually played my banjo quite a few times.' Today he guards the instrument as a priceless memento.

The first name for the group was the Blackjacks. They hit upon the uniform for their much-hoped-for public performances: black jeans, with green stitching and plain white shirts. Two new recruits to the band alternated on playing tea-chest bass; Ivan Vaughan, who had gone to Dovedale Primary School with John but went on to the posh Liverpool Institute when John joined Quarry Bank; and Nigel Whalley, who went to Bluecoat Grammar School, but who knew John from his Sunday School days. In a rare show of allegiance to his school, John quickly changed the name to the Quarry Men, the line-up of which was erratic, and at one time included a bass player, Bill Smith, who was in John's class. But he did not arrive regularly for rehearsals and soon left. Eventually, the bass-playing role fell to Len Garry.

The fact that Nigel Whalley and Ivan Vaughan were not at Quarry Bank made their regular inclusion in the line-up difficult to arrange, anyway; but Nigel, highly organized and ambitious for the group, said he would try to get them some bookings. He persuaded shopkeepers in Woolton to put notices, free, in their windows: 'Country, Western, Rock 'n' Roll, Skiffle, The Quarry Men, Open for Engagements.'

John named the group the Quarry Men partly as a tongue-in-cheek dig at the school in which they had been born, and partly because the name had a ring of skiffle about it, anyway. 'Quarry Men Strong Before Our Birth' was the school song, sung lustily by most boys at the end of term. Lennon and Shotton, when they were not smiling or making up rude words to the school song under their breath, quietly admired its sentiments. John saw the adoption of the school song within the name of the group as a means to an end; it gave them a stamp of credibility. And he was to foster the 'means to an end' rule throughout his life. It was Lennon who thought of the name and he told the others. That was that.

Slowly but encouragingly, occasional engagements were secured for the Quarry Men by Nigel Whalley. Childwall Golf Club, St Barnabas Church Hall at Penny Lane and St Peter's Youth Club were among the earliest. The group had made its public début playing on the back of a lorry at a carnival in Rosebery Street, Liverpool 8.

John's beer drinking had its beginnings during these days. Payments for Quarry Men concerts at Conservative dances and youth club parties were only a few pounds, but of equal attraction to John was the liberation of an evening out, the chance to chat up girls outside his normal Woolton beat, and drink, often 'on the house' as he was a performer.

The teddy boy movement was gaining ground by the time the Quarry Men secured some bookings. At dances, teds would ask the group to play some rock 'n' roll instead of the comparatively mild skiffle. The request hit a chord inside the ever-restless Lennon, who had adopted a bit of a teddy boy look with the beginnings of 'sidies' down his face and tight jeans which were as near as he could get to the obligatory drainpipe trousers. The Quarry Men entered several skiffle contests, failed to win or get a position at any one, and John was particularly taken aback by a group from Rhyl which won the Carroll Levis Discoveries night at the Liverpool Empire. 'They were really putting their act over, the guitarist was all over the stage and really full of a show,' recalls Rod Davis. 'We were really purist by comparison. John learned a lesson from that night. He said: "You've got to put it over a bit to do rock 'n' roll." In his mind, if not in the minds of the others, that was going to be the route to success. If Lonnie Donegan had provided the *will* to play, Elvis Presley was still the foundation upon which his musical attitude was based.

'None of us thought of it going any further than a good school lark that earned a few bob,' says Rod Davis. But Lennon thought differently and swung the songs towards rock 'n' roll. 'Jailhouse Rock' and 'Blue Suede Shoes', Lennon favourites, took him way beyond the purism of the early skiffle sounds, and gave full reign to his increasing stage personality. His mother taught him, in one week of solid tuition after school, the chords to a hot Lennon favourite, Buddy Holly's 'That'll Be The Day'. It was the first song John learned to play and sing accurately. There was growing dissent in the group about the increasing rock element from John. Nigel Whalley secured the Quarry Men a coveted booking at a jazz stronghold in Liverpool city centre, the Cavern in Mathew Street. Lennon disliked jazz fans because they were, he thought, elitist. Here, in a club which tolerated skiffle because it was a jazz offshoot but which banished rock 'n' roll as the trashy sound of youth, Lennon bit off more than he could chew.

Rod Davis argued on stage with him that the idea of doing rock songs would be unacceptable to the audience, and anyway that wasn't the original idea behind the Quarry Men. John maintained that as he was the only singer in the group, he had a right to decide what would be sung; anyway, the skiffle repertoire was restricting and boring. It was time to move on. And so the jazz crowd, dressed, as Lennon later sneeringly described them, in their 'G.C.E. sweaters', jeered and booed as Lennon went through his rockers. Davis said to him: 'We shouldn't be playing rock 'n' roll on stage at the Cavern of all places, John. It's a jazz place.' He was also concerned that John didn't know the words to many of the rockers he was putting forward. He was making up any words as he sang along. But Lennon totally ignored Davis's opinions and announced the songs as he wanted them: Presley's 'Jailhouse Rock', 'Don't Be Cruel' and 'Heartbreak Hotel' were more exciting than the restricting skiffle repeats.

The £5 guitar was not standing up to the strain of all these public performances. 'He kept bothering me for what he called a real one,' says Mimi. 'I wasn't too ready to provide it because I thought he should be getting on with his school work a little more seriously. But he kept on and on: "Let me get it out of my system, Mimi."

'I said: "All right, get it out of your system."'

One Saturday morning she took him along to the famous musical instrument shop, Hessy's, off Whitechapel in Liverpool. 'There were guitars hanging all around the room and John didn't know which one to choose for the best. Finally, he pointed to one and the man took it down and he played it and said, "I'll have that one." What I do remember is John nodding his head to me and me paying the £17 there and then for it. He was as happy as could be on the bus home. The Spanish-styled guitar had steel strings which quickly made John's fingers sore from his many hours of strumming, in his bedroom, to the exclusion of homework and to the continuing irritation of Mimi.

Finally, when she could no longer stand his foot tapping on the ceiling, Mimi ordered him into the porch at Mendips. It was to become his refuge and where, coincidentally, he preferred the acoustics, with the echo. On one occasion when he was banished there by an impatient Mimi she boomed the words: 'The guitar's all very well, John, but you'll never make a *living* out of it.'

At sixteen, John Lennon stood out as no ordinary schoolboy or teenager. Within the Quarry Men, the only disagreements were about skiffle versus rock 'n' roll. He was getting used to using his fists in a fight: being in the C stream, the going was rougher than in the academically higher streams, and he would not hesitate to punch when there was a verbal battle that couldn't be resolved. At home, the tension between him and Mimi increased as she tired of the regular morning phone calls from the headmaster's secretary, relaying John's latest misdemeanour. He was getting used to the prospect that he would have to battle his way through life, a fact confirmed by the punch-ups he saw in boozy audiences when the Quarry Men played at dances, particularly in the rough area of Garston.

Strangely, the most crucial decision in his professional life was to happen as a result of one of the most genteel events the Quarry Men played. It was there that he first met Paul McCartney.

The group was drifting between engagements and had fared poorly in talent contests when they secured a booking for the afternoon of 6 July 1957, as the music attraction at St Peter's, Woolton, garden fete. The weather was sunny and perfect for the Quarry Men – on this occasion John Lennon, Pete Shotton, Eric Griffiths, Colin Hanton and Len Garry on tea-chest bass – to perform their limited repertoire on a raised platform in the furthest field from the church. John, seizing Woolton's big day as an occasion when he could 'come out' and make an impression, dressed in full teddy boy regalia for the first time: tight drainpipe trousers which left nothing to the imagination; a jacket with heavy padding at the shoulders; blue and white checked shirt and – vitally – greased-back hair.

The Elvis Presley imitation fell stonily on Mimi, who began his day with a scolding. She reminded him that his school reports were appalling and for a grammar school boy to be adopting such a personality was a repudiation of all the standards she had been trying to instil into him. Lennon, never rude to his aunt but intransigent and defiant when it came to asserting himself, simply walked out in mid-morning and teamed up with Pete Shotton, ready for the afternoon's big appearance. John, who realized that the big garden fete audience could mean an important day for the group, steeled himself by buying bottles of light ale from the Woolton off-licence and getting mildly inebriated, but not drunk. All his life, drink was to be a recurring problem. He enjoyed it to relax, or celebrate, but he could never take much before feeling the effects. And when John got merry, he became aggressive.

That fateful sunny Saturday Aunt Mimi did not know John was taking his Quarry Men to the Woolton fete, and John did not realize she would be going to the fete with her sister. 'It was a gorgeous day, with all the young women in their backless dresses and summer frocks,' says Mimi. The chief attraction was the band of the Cheshire Yeomanry; the Quarry Men had to walk the gauntlet of stalls selling home-made cakes and fruit and vegetables, past the children's sideshows, before they could take the stand. The vicar, the Rev. Maurice Pryce-Jones, was doing the rounds and welcomed the band that was to provide the afternoon's skiffle, a particularly trendy attraction for a church event.

'Well, when I got there and stood talking to young people over a cup of tea, there was suddenly this loud beat – bang, bang, coming from the bottom field. It shook everybody up,' says Mimi. 'All the young people left their stalls and proceeded down to the field. I said: "Where are they going?" and my sister said: "There must be a band, let's go."'

The sight that greeted Mimi as she neared the band platform transfixed her. 'I couldn't take my eyes off him,' she said. It was the first time she had seen, and heard, John in full cry with the Quarry Men. 'There was this grin all over John's face and then he spotted me walking towards him and his expression changed a bit. I don't know why – I was pleased as punch to see him up there.' But Lennon, in his mildly alcoholic haze remembering the row that morning about his teddy boy attire, feared the renewed wrath of Mimi. He began to busk the words to the song he was singing: 'And Mimi's coming down the path, oh oh.' The songs played that day included 'Cumberland Gap', 'Railroad Bill', 'Maggie May' and 'Come Go With Me'. On that song John characteristically – and irreverently, for a church affair – changed into the more suggestive: 'Come little darling, come and go with me.' It was a lyrical tactic he was to employ to devastating, often hilarious, effect later in his life, as a writer.

John's shock at seeing Mimi was softened when she led the applause as the group finished its set. But that was not to be the only significant part of the day. Among the audience, unknown to John, casting a keen fifteen-year-old's eye on the music which he regarded as very primitive, was a boy from neighbouring Allerton: Paul McCartney. He and John had a mutual friend, Ivan Vaughan, who lived in a house immediately behind Mendips and had attended Dovedale Primary School with him. When John went to Quarry Bank Ivan had gone to the Liverpool Institute, the posh grammar school alongside the art college. Ivan became friendly with McCartney who was another Institute student. Realizing Paul's interest in rock, Ivan thought it would be good if he heard the Quarry Men and met John. 'You've got to come and meet this guy John Lennon,' Ivan said to Paul. 'You'll get on well with him . . .'

Paul stood with Ivan watching and listening as John stood on the stage, even at the age of not quite seventeen a commanding figure, undeniably the leader. Musically, John and the Quarry Men exuded more energy and enthusiasm than talent, but it was infectious enough. What impressed McCartney as much as anything was that these schoolboys, only a little older than him, had actually got a group together. His talent as a guitarist, coming from a musical family, was prodigious compared with John's; still, it had no outlet.

Ivan Vaughan led Paul across to the church hall after the Quarry Men finished playing. There, introductions were made. As Paul recalled later in a warm and amusing foreword to John's first book, *In His Own Write*: 'At Woolton village fete I met him. I was a fat schoolboy and, as he leaned an arm on my shoulder, I realized that he was drunk. We were twelve then [*sic*] but in spite of his sideboards we went on to become teenage pals. Aunt Mimi, who had looked after him since he was so high, used to tell me he was much cleverer than he pretended. . . .'

But that day at Woolton fete it was the clever young McCartney who held the aces. First, John was floored by the fact that Paul could actually tune his guitar, thus correcting the banjo tuning that John had inherited from his mother. Secondly, McCartney was able to demonstrate a stunning knowledge of the words to a favourite of John's beloved rock 'n' roll: Paul wrote down the words to Eddie Cochran's 'Twenty Flight Rock' from the film *The Girl Can't Help It*. Next, he ran through other rockers and floored John with what, to the skiffler trying to become more adept in musicianship, was the performance of a virtuoso.

John Lennon had never had an inferiority complex. He was a sixteen-year-old schoolboy hell-raiser, a defiant challenge for his caring Aunt Mimi, and had so far not needed to project himself beyond a punch-up, always backing off when the going got really tough or dangerous. But that day in July 1957 was to prove a watershed for John. The meeting with Paul McCartney had come just before he left Quarry Bank School, sadly failing all his O-levels. John didn't show signs of worrying much about that. He had a chip on his shoulder about formal education and 'pieces of paper that say you're bright'.

But the Quarry Men, for all their amateurism, were important to John. With school success slipping away he desperately wanted to stamp his personality on something, anything, that would mark him out as a success. The skiffle group was obviously going to have to grow or go. That night, as he sobered up after the evening performance at the village fete, long after Paul McCartney had cycled home to 20 Forthlin Road, Allerton, the leader of the Quarry Men was tortured by a question. Should he invite Paul McCartney to join the group? A better guitarist than John, and with a better knowledge of rock 'n' roll songs, he was going to be a formidable performer. Lennon's leadership might be threatened. The alternative was to shun competition and plod on with the Quarry Men, going the same aimless way as thousands of skiffle groups all around Britain.

At first the decision was tough, but eventually it proved logical that he should offer Paul McCartney the chance to join. First, he would have a powerful, talented ally in the swing to break away from skiffle and make it a rock 'n' roll band. Secondly, he had enough confidence in his own dominance to believe that he would have the edge over a boy two years younger. Thirdly, the group needed new blood.

It was Pete Shotton who passed the news to McCartney. 'John wants you in the group,' he said to Paul as they cycled one day over Allerton golf course. McCartney was cool but pleased. It would be two months before he could get into the Quarry Men, he said; he was going to scout camp.

5
THE ART STUDENT

'I want to be rich and famous'

For the art college's vital day of judgement on him John's carefully groomed appearance and his sober demeanour complemented the kind recommendation of William Pobjoy. He was accepted as a student at Liverpool College of Art. The soot-blackened building was just around the corner from Liverpool Institute where Paul McCartney, his brother Michael, George Harrison, and John's old friend Ivan Vaughan were studying.

When he went for an interview John took an impressive portfolio of his Quarry Bank work. This corroborated Mr Pobjoy's generous description of Lennon, to the college principal, Mr Stevenson, that the boy deserved a chance. Mimi went to the college with him for the interview; as on all bus journeys with her, he travelled alone upstairs on the bus while she sat downstairs – a typical teenage embarrassment at being seen out 'in the care' of a relation. 'He'd hardly been into town before that, certainly not on his own,' says Mimi. John dressed soberly for the big day, wearing Uncle George's old brown jacket, plus a shirt and tie. 'He was himself, not nervous, quite confident,' says Mimi; 'he was never one to *show* his feelings, even then.'

The interview went successfully. John was told that he would be expected to work hard on his own initiative, and he started college in September 1957.

As John entered college the Quarry Men continued, but with less momentum than when he was at Quarry Bank. The pace of things was reduced because Pete Shotton had left Quarry Bank to become a police cadet, with Nigel Whalley holding things together with regular bookings. But all of them were preoccupied with getting used to new daily environments; John had the additional distraction of girls at college. No more did he have to climb the walls of Calderstones Park Girls' School, near Quarry Bank, to eye the schoolgirls, chat them up, and make rude signs to them. At Liverpool College of Art, in the autumn of 1957, there were pretty girls in every room. The beatnik period was under way: it meant teenage assertiveness and individuality in tandem with the recent youth explosion that had come with Elvis Presley, Lonnie Donegan and skiffle, James Dean, and the surly style of a great new young film actor, Marlon Brando, in *The Wild One*. It was a perfect period for the individualism in John Lennon to grow.

One student who got to know John from his first days at college was Phyllis McKenzie. They travelled on the number 72 bus together every morning from Woolton to Canning Street, near the college in Liverpool 8. Although John didn't care much about it in the early days of these journeys, Phyllis was the closest friend of another student, Cynthia Powell, whom she had known since they went to the Secondary School of Art together at the age of twelve.

Lennon could not be ignored on that bus, recalls Phyllis. He was scruffy, often in a black leather jacket, and always travelled upstairs so that he could smoke. John held his Woodbine between his first two fingers, with all four fingers curling around it, using the thumb as a support. It struck Phyllis as strange.

'He might have been scruffy but he was always clean,' says Phyllis. 'And he was not mean – he'd usually offer to pay my fare, eight old pence, just because he knew I was, like him, a hard-up student at the college.' As the months went by and he realized Phyllis was Cynthia's best pal, he became wary of talking to her, lest whatever he said should be repeated. 'He used to say I was his rival for Cynthia's attention.'

Art college was legendary to any young person in Liverpool. 'You just knew you were in for a good time,' says Michael Isaacson, who left Quarry Bank a year before John and was installed at art college when Lennon arrived. 'But it was tricky going in and establishing yourself because a lot of people there were a lot older than grammar school boys like John and me. The Korean War was on at the time and there were a lot of older men who had returned from Korea and got a grant.' The procedure was for all new entrants to go into the painting school for their first year and then go into specialist areas like illustration, sculpture, graphic design, or lettering.

'John had a tremendous amount of confidence, even then,' says Isaacson. 'Most of us spent the first few months, or maybe the first year, wondering what we should do and trying to be industrious in our work. Not John – he went straight in, played his part to the limit, and gathered people around him, and looking at him, from almost day one.'

There was an unlikely rapport between Lennon and Michael Isaacson, just as they found at Quarry Bank. 'I wasn't a pushover and he knew that and probably liked it,' says Isaacson. 'He knew I was good at art, and I drew cartoons not unlike the doodles which he did whenever he had a spare moment. Also, I decided not to join his teddy boy or beatnik element but to stand apart. My trick was to be the cleanest guy there. I found a shop in London Road where they made incredible silk brocade waistcoats. I didn't have much money but I bought lots of these in different colours, and I looked like something out of Wyatt Earp. John looked totally the opposite. We used to eye one another and size each other up. He admired my individuality.' John always had respect for people who were different.

'When John was on his way to join art college, I knew things would happen when he got up to his tricks and I looked forward to the years ahead with Lennon. He was a terrible guy, actually, but I liked him.' Other students say Isaacson despised John and they clashed, but he denies that: 'Of course I frowned on everything he did, his work and his attitude, but his responses were always beautiful, so we did get along fine. When you look down on someone, you can do it with total disrespect, or with respect.'

Lennon's recognition of Isaacson rose when he realized Michael's prowess. A year older and demonstrably more ambitious, Isaacson quickly became the art college artist who 'got printed', extensively at first by the Liverpool University students' union magazine and later, at the age of eighteen, by the *Liverpool Daily Post.* 'John was certainly aware of me. He commented on my success and said, "You're successful because you bloody well want to be, aren't you?"'

Isaacson's most animated clash with Lennon came, not unexpectedly, on the subject of music. Isaacson, who coveted leadership whenever it was available, took it upon himself to run the art college music club and provided a staple diet of jazz, notably the trendy sounds of Miles Davis and the Modern Jazz Quartet.

Lennon, who by the time he entered college was deeply into all things Elvis, confronted Isaacson one day in the music room. Eyeing the records by artists whose names he had never heard of, John said: 'What a lot of fucking shit you play. Why don't you play something proper – like Little Richard, Chuck Berry, Elvis Presley?'

Isaacson's retort was a challenge: 'What do *you* know about it? Most of the people here like this. If you really want to do something, bring your group to the art school dance and prove yourselves. I'll put you on and give you a break.' The group did play, and Isaacson says they were a shambles, with a poor sound, and deservedly got a thin reception.

The dominating characteristic at college inside everyone with ambition was a burning desire to get out of Liverpool. 'Lennon told me quite candidly even at that age, that he wanted to be rich and famous. That was the drive inside all of us at that time and that's why Liverpool in the late 1950s and early 1960s was such an exciting place. We all wanted to get out of the city as soon as possible, and be wildly successful.' Isaacson went to London, became a successful political cartoonist for the national media, and eventually formed his own advertising agency.

Reflecting on Lennon, he says: 'I think if he had not become successful he may well have become more than just a wayward bum. He might well have become a really nasty piece of work. It's all hypothetical, but I fear the worst could have happened. If he hadn't become famous his anger could have been vented in another direction. Where his energy was channelled into creative music, it would have gone into something destructive instead of creative. He was strictly an all-or-nothing kind of guy.'

None of the students who attended college with John recalls him as a profound person. He was more physical than cerebral. He had little time for lengthy discourse on anything beyond music and girls, notably Cynthia Powell, who had the most electrifying effect on him once she had become as besotted with him as he was with her. Once John had secured her love, his possessiveness about her was overpowering. Although he followed his own roving eye, the slightest move towards another man by Cyn brought forth John's fury and cross-examination. 'She was very pretty, Bardot-like, and I enjoyed looking across the canteen at her,' says Michael Isaacson. Another student, Ann Mason, says Cynthia was attractive enough to have been the girlfriend of many others at the college, but her passion for Lennon was incredible. 'It was certainly surprising that a girl like Cynthia had been caught by this shit called Lennon,' says Isaacson. 'They looked at each other adoringly. They were totally fixated.'

Ann Mason's link with John was not romantic, but she was unique in having, as her boyfriend for one afternoon, another student named Stuart Sutcliffe, who came from Prescot Grammar School and was John's closest friend, and, for a much longer period, Geoff Mohammed. John recognized in Stuart's gentleness the reality of his own personality. The difference was that John's quiet studious nature was submerged beneath an outward veneer of ruggedness, which often manifested itself in raw aggression. Stuart was the opposite; quiet outside, tough inside. This tension was to lead to Stuart's blinding headaches which would later prove fatal. But when they were together Lennon and Sutcliffe found a rapport which neither, in their teenage simplicity, needed to explain.

At college, John was forging strong musical links with Paul by having daily lunchtime sessions in Arthur Ballard's room; John had also developed a good non-musical friendship with another student who found it hard to concentrate on his work.

Geoff Mohammed was five years older than John, of much bigger build, and came from Manchester. His father was Indian, his mother French–Italian. Geoff was dark-skinned, good-looking, and for most of the time clowned his way through the classes. It was his irreverence for orderly work, and failure to complete his work, together with his great sense of humour, that drew John to him.

'I never had much time for John,' says Ann Mason, Geoff's one-time girlfriend. 'I despised him because he didn't work hard. He was a terrific tearaway but he had this strange thing about him: he was either going to land up as a great, or in the gutter. It wasn't because of anything he actually did, because his art work was rather poor. But there was this strange destiny about him. Geoff Mohammed had the same quality.' Geoff died a few years before Lennon, having left college to become a security man at the Whitworth Art Gallery back in his home city of Manchester.

Ann remembers her ex-boyfriend as 'intelligent, philosophical and far more sensitive than John'. He also had a neat line in self-deprecating fun. Aunt Mimi remembers that John went home one day roaring with laughter at a story about himself and Geoff who had been in a café where there were a lot of black people. The dark-skinned Geoff had them all laughing uproariously as he opened the café door and shouted: 'Right, all foreigners OUT!' This sense of the ridiculous appealed to John: in 1959, on the day they both received some money from their college grant, they went out together into the city and returned dressed in identical clothing

— dark green suede shoes, dark grey trousers, and fawn donkey jackets. They were also boasting about having been to the barber's for a shave, an unnecessary extravagance for hard-up students. It was an innocent example of doing anything to make an impact.

'I was afraid of John because he could be so caustic,' says Ann Mason. 'I was never on the receiving end of his sarcasm. Maybe I was protected by being Geoff's girlfriend. People found John very amusing at times, but there was always this underlying fear that he might turn his wit around and use it against them. What made the partnership interesting between Geoff and John was that John respected Geoff, but Geoff in turn wasn't afraid of John as some were.' He was keen on palmistry, which also fascinated Lennon.

When Geoff had a row with Ann Mason, he and John went out for the night and got drunk. Everyone at college knew by the sight that greeted them all in the college canteen next morning; the two of them had returned late at night and filled the canteen with stuff they had stolen from the trendy Bold Street area of the city – street nameplates, signposts, posters, parking meters, and even parts of cars and bicycles. They were admonished by the college principal but both quietly laughed. The prank – and the emotional release it had given Geoff during a heavy row with his girlfriend – was well worth the rebuke, and the hangover.

At the art college some students were serious about their work, others there mostly for the enjoyment of it all, letting their career take its own direction. John enjoyed art and was talented in an unorthodox way, particularly as a caricaturist, but he was not prepared to let art get in the way of his determination to press on with his rock 'n' roll

Most lunchtimes, in Arthur Ballard's room 21, guitarist Len Garry from the Quarry Men would join Paul McCartney and George Harrison from the Liverpool Institute next door. About twenty students would finish their canteen lunch and form the audience as the musicians spent an hour playing Buddy Holly and Everly Brothers songs, finishing off every day with Lennon singing the old British variety favourite, 'When You're Smiling'. He would inject the names of college teachers into several of the songs, in a sardonic send-up that amused all the students.

John eased himself into college life with a central characteristic that was to mark his life. He *used* every moment. He manipulated every minute he was given to make it work to his advantage. Even the teachers who riled him, like the strong, colourful Welshman

John's sharp facial features dominate these drawings by Stuart Sutcliffe of his best friend. 'Stuart drew these at my mother's house three months before he died,' says Astrid. 'He never drew likenesses, always impressions.'

Charles Burton, who regularly picked on Lennon for his artistic inadequacies, had their value to John. They would crop up in his songs, used as target practice.

'He was an original, and being one myself, I could single him out as a true individual,' says June Furlong, who enjoyed a strangely intuitive relationship with Lennon from his first weeks in the art college. 'I'd seen him sitting in life class, or outside the pub Ye Cracke, and I can remember saying to myself about this seventeen-year-old teenager: "Where will your original talent take you? This is no ordinary boy student . . . he's going to do something unusual." '

June Furlong was a twenty-seven-year-old nude model whose class in room 71 John attended twice weekly during the day, and occasionally in the evenings if he wanted to return with any of his friends like Stuart Sutcliffe, Geoff Mohammed, Tony Carricker, or Dave Davies. To some, drawing a nude model while still only a teenager might have been the source of much nudging and winking. Occasionally, John would say to his friends when drawing naked June: 'Christ, I wonder what Mimi would have to say about *this*.' But that light joke was merely to emphasize the stern background from which he came. Most of the time, John was an earnest and conscientious member of June's nude life class. 'He was a completely charming and one hundred per cent decent person. Nobody alive could pull a fast one over him, but if he realized you were genuine and interested in talking intelligently to him, about art or anything else, he would talk to you for hours.' And we did,' says June Furlong. 'He had no time for flippancy in conversation.'

He fascinated her. Their friendship was purely platonic, but during the sessions when he would be drawing her, their conversation would strike the most personal chords. 'He hadn't got it all together, mentally, when I first met him, but there was this. . .well, originality is the word, there was this total originality about him. I could see some potential in his mind, although his drawings were just average. John could just hold his own in art, and that was that. He wasn't anywhere near his closest friend, Stuart Sutcliffe. Stuart was not just good, he was great, but he had a streak in him which appealed to John. He lived every day as if it was going to be his last. The teachers all knew he had a rare talent, but they had to hold him back and try to channel him. "Yes, OK, Stuart. It's excellent work, but take it easy. Less output and more plan of thought," Charles Burton told him.'

But it was precisely that non-stop drive that endeared Stuart to

John. And they both had this in common; they were determined to capitalize on what they were good at – for Stuart art, for John music.

'I could see from the first few times I met him that here was a bloke who wasn't prepared to play life from the sidelines,' says June Furlong. She sits in her house in Falkner Street, just five minutes' walk from the college, where she was born, where John Lennon visited her, and remembers the college's most famous student with fondness. 'Always, he either wanted to be in the scrum half, or he wasn't going to be involved in the game. I'd say that when he entered a room, or started a class like the life class, his attitude to everyone was: "What's going on here, what's this, who's that?" And that's how he quickly got to know all the people around him, in his groups, their strengths and their weaknesses, their hang-ups, their difficulties and the obstacles. His sarcasm with the weak was very cutting.'

Lennon wanted his own way in most things and didn't relax his pressure until he got it. After the evening life class sessions he went through the phase of insisting that some students joined him in going to the Liverpool Empire to see comedy acts like Robb Wilton; Wilson, Keppel and Betty; Morecambe and Wise; and the famous drunk comic, Jimmy James. The more traditional the comedian, like Robb Wilton, the more John enjoyed mimicking them. He would roam about college next day repeating Wilton's famous phrase: 'The day war broke out, my missus, she says to me: "What are you going to do about it?" ' Despite his outlandish behaviour, and assertiveness as a rock 'n' roll trailblazer, John was quite normal in his taste for traditional British humour.

Stuart Sutcliffe was not among those who went to the variety shows with John and the other students. He was not particularly interested in the stage, a fact that might at first have ensured that John and Stuart would be able to sustain only a casual, art college friendship. 'But I've never seen two teenagers so close as those two,' says June Furlong. 'John, as an extrovert personality, used to attract a lot of blokes who were not extroverts. He didn't have to have a lot in common with his best friend to consider him his best friend.' He expected a vast amount of loyalty from his friends, but gave a lot in return. Underneath an exhibitionist exterior, Lennon had a fermenting brain. Stuart Sutcliffe was a quiet, intellectual thinker. With his spiky hair and lithe physique, he didn't have to make any effort to be vulnerably attractive to women, whereas John kept working on his looks. Stuart, a runaway artistic talent whom all the teachers reckoned would be a

'John and Stuart loved our days at the seaside and had lots of pleasure drawing pictures on the sand,' says Astrid, who took this picture on the beach at Ostsee, near Hamburg, in July 1961

star student in the years ahead, possessed the brooding authenticity that John secretly yearned for. In John, Stuart saw a speedy brain and a demonstrative style that he could never summon. The pair were inseparable and whatever other male friendships John forged, nothing compared with Stuart. 'That was his only friend,' says Aunt Mimi. 'He was the only other boy he really enjoyed being with for long periods of time.'

Stuart's nude drawings of June were stunning. 'I wonder what happened to them,' muses June Furlong today. 'He liked me in one particular pose, and he did several.' Normally, she did not bother to inspect students' interpretations of her poses, but Stuart's were so good that she took a particular interest in all his work.

Lennon, fully heterosexual though he was, had taste and respect for her nudity. His twice-weekly sessions in the life class during the week were augmented by his wandering over from Stuart's nearby flat at Gambier Terrace in the evenings from seven o'clock until nine. 'I was his foil for a while,' says June. 'I was attracted to him, not in a physical way but in a Liverpool way. He was a positive Liverpudlian, and there was this streak of iron and steel in his character, every moment. Look at anybody who's made it, and if they came from Liverpool, it's partly *because* they came from Liverpool. John hadn't the artistic talent, but to speak to, whether he was joking about the strictness of his Aunt Mimi, or whether he was on about last night's show at Liverpool Pavilion, he had this *edge*.'

Lennon always reacted firmly to the person he faced or the treatment he was given. Confronted by a fool asking cretinous questions, as he often was during Beatlemania, John was the most scathing, often vitriolic, adversary. But treated sensibly, engaged in serious conversation by anyone who was genuine and an enthusiast about his own craft – which didn't necessarily mean enthusing over music – John was a powerful, discerning conversationalist. 'He was a great sender-upper of other students,' says June Furlong. 'If he came across one who was crude or stupid or a bit of an upstart, he'd play on that. But I've never met anyone who could move so fast in detecting what made people tick.'

6
ROCK 'N' ROLL

'Be careful of that John Lennon'

Always speedy at analysing situations, John realized that while art college might not be crucial to him as a place to learn art, it offered other tremendous benefits, such as his deep attachment to Cynthia and his friendship with Stuart; and the infectious atmosphere in the college's Liverpool 8 district, which made it equivalent to Paris's Left Bank, was a perfect escape route for John from the genteel middle-class environs of Aunt Mimi's Woolton. The pubs of the college area, Ye Cracke, and the Philharmonic and the Jacaranda coffee bar at 23 Slater Street, were places to hang out and become an adult. Mentally, Lennon was always ahead of his years and sought out people who would travel with him as speedily as possible. And a fourth benefit was the 'fix' he was to get at lunchtime from sessions with Paul in Arthur Ballard's room.

Pop music was steadily taking over his life. In the months that followed their first meeting at the Woolton church fete, a teenage empathy had developed between John and Paul. The reluctant art college student and the more studiously rounded, conscientious academic from the posher Liverpool Institute (the 'Inny') next door had a friendship based solely on music. Lennon was increasingly nervous about letting Paul into the Quarry Men, but it became a *fait accompli* in the light of Paul's runaway talent.

George Harrison was a different matter. Another Liverpool Institute scholar, he was three years younger than John but a gifted and accurate guitarist considering his age. Paul would bring him occasionally to the lunchtime sessions at the art college, and John was impressed with his skill. George quickly decided that the older, irreverent, and altogether adult John Lennon was great.

Lennon and Cynthia became irritated by George's constant presence as he waited for them to come out of college together at lunchtime. With the insensitivity of youth, George did not realize that a passionate love affair needed privacy.

'Hi John, hi Cyn,' George would say.

'Oh hi,' John would say, coolly turning right quickly and increasing his and Cynthia's pace towards Gambier Terrace.

The loving couple regarded George as a bit of a hanger-on but tolerated his youthful lack of understanding. Harrison hero-worshipped Lennon at this stage. John, who eventually invited him to Menlove Avenue when Mimi was in, eventually had good reason partly to reciprocate and respect the teddy boy taste of young George, the son of a bus driver. When George had left her house, Mimi told John she disapproved of his mode of dress. 'He had a *pink* shirt on! And *winklepicker* shoes!' recalls Mimi. 'I wasn't having any of *that*.' That rejection was enough to clinch the acceptance by John of George as a fully-fledged Quarry Man.

Paul's mother, Mary, a nurse, had died from breast cancer on 31 October 1956, nine months before he first met John Lennon; Paul was fourteen then. Paul's father, Jim, had two sisters, Auntie Jinny and Auntie Millie, who went into the McCartney family house at 20 Forthlin Road, Allerton, every Monday to cook the 'Sunday' roast dinner. Paul's background was similar to John's in that he was living without a mother, but his father was a major influence on his life. A cotton industry salesman, Jim McCartney was a kindly man of firm British values. He was also an accomplished pianist who once ran his own traditional jazz band, so that the McCartney home was full of the most fashionable sounds of the period. Jim's favourite song was 'Stairway To Paradise', and young Paul was weaned on a diversity of sounds ranging from musicals to hot jazz.

The major difference in Paul's and John's attitude to making music lay in McCartney's background. While Lennon had to fight every inch of the way to get Mimi to see he was serious about playing, eventually persuading her to buy him a guitar, McCartney was actively encouraged. Family parties became singalongs with Jim at the piano, and he also played trumpet in various bands. Paul and Michael were sent every week for piano lessons round the corner in Mather Avenue, and when Paul warmed to the sounds of pop on hearing the Everly Brothers, Lonnie Donegan, and Buddy Holly, he had no trouble whatsoever in getting a guitar from his Dad. 'He was only too pleased,' says Michael. 'He made it look hard because he had to pay for it, and that was his way of making Paul appreciate what he was doing. But really, he was knocked out that his eldest son was getting into music. The only thing that bothered him was Paul's partner, John the ted!'

Paul's background was much more working-class than John's; his father, a widower at fifty-three, had a tough time raising two young sons. In fact, of all the Beatles who eventually emerged, John was the one from the most affluently middle-class home. But McCartney – whose surname John perversely mis-spelled as McArtrey for several years – was such an asset to John's confidence in learning music that any differences in background quickly became submerged by the joy of musical togetherness. 'Paul was very serious about his guitar,' says his brother Michael. 'He demanded to know every facet of it, every conceivable variation. Chords he hadn't heard of, or couldn't learn from a book, he'd make up. He was heavily into rock 'n' roll, of course, but not to the exclusion of other music. He never turned away from a thing just because it wasn't Elvis Presley or Little Richard, much as he liked them.' That catholic taste was to be both the strength of the Beatles and the cauldron of the songwriting partnership of John and Paul, as well as an artistic contrast and melting pot for them in the years ahead.

John always conceded Paul's instrumental superiority, and never made any claim for his own ability as a guitarist. Paul had his own pressures at home; his father regarded Lennon as an undesirable influence on the life of his son, who, far from needing encouragement down the teddy boy road, 'ought to have his sights on a decent career, like entry into a teacher's training college, or accountancy.'

But to Paul, a kindred rock 'n' roll spirit like John was the catalyst he needed. To John, Paul deserved respect not just for his prowess but because he had also actually started writing his own songs. A few months after meeting, John and Paul had engineered a way to meet secretly together, with no interruptions from other students; when Jim McCartney was out at work, they would safely install themselves in the living-room at Paul's home and start playing and writing songs together, often daring to smoke tea from a pipe, and indulging in what became known as 'afternoon sagging off school'.

It was an electric partnership at the time between two personalities that at first sight looked destined to clash. John was, at seventeen, caustic, cynical, assertive, and brash. Paul was, even then, more quietly diplomatic and certainly more facially attractive to girls. He was an academic swot who lived an orderly life.

Two Liverpool lads in the front room of a council house writing music that was to shake the world. At Paul's home in Forthlin Road, Allerton, in September 1962, a bespectacled Lennon and the left-handed guitarist McCartney grapple with the chords and the words, written in Paul's exercise book, to 'I Saw Her Standing There'

He wanted to please his widower father. Theoretically, Lennon should have loathed him, but both realized that, at that moment in life, they needed each other for a mutual passion: making music.

Michael McCartney, two years younger than Paul, enjoyed observing the afternoons which were to give rise to the most significant songwriting partnership in modern popular music. Sitting in the McCartneys' home in Forthlin Road, he 'saw this extraordinary-looking ted coming down the road, with long sideburns and wearing skin-tight dark blue jeans with a polo neck sweater and winklepicker shoes'. The McCartneys, Michael avers, had such a conservative upbringing that within days of being introduced by Paul to John their father warned both his sons: 'Be careful of that John Lennon. He could get you into trouble.' For Paul and Mike, the warning had the effect that parents everywhere risk: 'Paul and I were immediately drawn to John like moths to a flame because of what Dad said.' It was a remarkable parallel with John's bond with George Harrison, fired by Mimi's condemnation.

Brotherly love was one thing, but the braggadocio of Lennon was quite another: Michael McCartney grew to hero-worship John, for all his outward spunk and all his inner softness. 'Young as I was, and certainly later during the Beatle years, I decided he was a "pretend hard" man. He was a performer, all his life, and from his toughness right through to his teddy boy looks, he wasn't really either. It was just that, whatever he adopted, John did it with more reality than anybody else.' The smouldering fire inside John's mind did not allow him to go the whole way in any direction for very long. Teddy boy, beatnik, peacenik, poet – all were mantles to be adopted for periods and then discarded, victims of his chameleon-like personality at various points in his life. But as an eighteen-year-old playing truant from college his intuition and desperation to convert the hobby of music into something worthwhile made him work feverishly on his partnership with Paul.

It was a matter of expediency. By the skin of his teeth he'd got into art college with no credentials from school, and now he was pretty sure that art would not offer him a career. With Mimi bearing down on him, and a bleak future pretty well assured, Lennon clung to music, and McCartney, like a life raft.

He had plenty to offer Paul, though. McCartney had a wider grasp of music, and particularly its variety of styles from ballads to jazz, but John compensated for his technical inferiority with an almost indefinable, animal quality that screamed rock 'n' roll. Paul was supremely talented; John was an unrepeatable original. If music had not pulled them together, there would have been no reason for John Lennon and McCartney to have developed any bond of friendship. But both realized, even as teenagers, that they needed each other if their music was to flourish.

'I saw it, but our Dad didn't want to know,' says Michael McCartney. 'When John came round to the house, as far as Dad was concerned it might just as well have been the Devil. Yet there would be a double-edge, because Dad would realize that, musically, there must be something there in John.' Sometimes he would verbally condemn John's appearance. 'John didn't dare reply, because he respected my Dad as a good bloke who was looking after Paul and me. But once, Paul said something in defence of John and my father said: "Bloody hell, you will *not* have your trousers as tight as his. They're teddy boy trousers and not only will you not wear them in this house, you won't wear them, full stop. It's a bad thing." ' A diplomat, Paul knew when a boat should not be rocked. He took far fewer chances with his father than John took with Mimi. The afternoon meetings and the chance to sing and practise a few tunes and write a few lyrics, as well as hone hits made famous by Eddie Cochran and the Everly Brothers, were too precious to fritter away by alienating his father completely. George Harrison's council house at 25 Upton Green, Speke, was to prove an alternative refuge for the three of them, but Paul's Forthlin Road home was their favourite, partly because it was closer to Woolton and meant travelling a shorter distance with their guitars.

Mimi approved of Paul as a 'nice polite boy', but John knew that even asking permission to play rock 'n' roll there would be regarded as a heinous crime. The tactic adopted to arrange meetings was that Paul would coolly enquire of his father what time he would be home, most days, and strategically inform John that it was safe for him to arrive at a prescribed time for their two-hour 'sagging off school' sessions.

On some afternoons when plans had been laid by John and Paul, young Michael would be paid two shillings as the incentive to 'go to the pictures, see what's on at the Gaumont'. This was Paul's ploy to guarantee privacy for the songwriters, but not only to make music.

'Hold on,' said Michael, 'you never give me anything for nothing. What's happening?'

'Well,' said Paul, 'John's coming round and. . .girls, well, you know what girls are, don't you, Mike? But you're a bit young. You do things with them that you don't understand. It's big boys' stuff, this.'

'Oh,' said Michael, 'I think I'd better stay. I can't take the money off you!' Michael faced a dilemma: whether to stay and wait for the girls to arrive, or take the money from Paul and head for the cinema in Allerton. Paul always ended such a discussion by threatening to go elsewhere with John, which would have denied his young brother both the money *and* the chance to see the action. Michael took the money and vanished. On the whole Michael was happy enough just to be allowed to take photographs, a burgeoning hobby, when the two musicians got together.

One of the first songs written by John at these songwriting sessions was 'One After 909', and another was the unrecorded 'Winston's Walk'. Sometimes when he entered Forthlin Road he would wear the black horn-rimmed spectacles which he had managed to persuade Mimi to buy him, rather than be saddled with wire National Health-style glasses which ironically, later in his life, he was to make fashionable. 'He'd never be seen with specs on if he could avoid it,' says Michael McCartney. 'But without them he was as blind as a bat. He'd walk down the path to our house, squinting, and whenever I saw him walking outside art college he'd hardly be able to see you. People used to think he was being off-hand or rude, not saying, "Hi", but it wasn't rudeness. He just couldn't see.' Glasses were too 'sissy', John would tell me years later when the Beatles story was at its height. He wore contact lenses and we would hunt for lost lenses together on bedroom carpets and in dressing-rooms from Cheltenham to Munich and New York.

Just as his friendship with Paul blossomed and bore creative fruit, with tentative songwriting and a style taking shape that merged ballads and music with a beat, another powerful relationship was fast developing in John's life. He was getting to see more of his mother. She lived only a short bus ride from Woolton, in Spring Wood, where she had set up home with John Dykins (Twitchy). Julia, often called Julie by neighbours and friends in the street, had a twinkle in her eye, and a style and vivacity, which was at odds with the seriousness of these post-war years. Her handing over to her sister Mimi of the raising of her son had been a painful but rational decision, based on her uncertain home life with John's father Fred away at sea. Vitally, Aunt Mimi and Uncle George were not short of money, but were not ostentatious with what

George had earned through his hard work as the Woolton dairyman. Paul McCartney's exaggerated claim that John's family 'almost owned Woolton at one time' can be seen as a comparative judgement. Certainly Mimi and George were better off than any other Beatle's parents. 'John wanted for nothing,' says Mimi proudly. 'But he was never spoiled. I wanted him to learn the value of money.' She would make him mow the lawn at Mendips for five shillings. 'He'd do it when he came home from school or college, and do it quickly and not well. As soon as he'd finished a bit of lawn and he thought he could get away with it, he'd come in with his hand out,' says Mimi.

John's reunion meetings with his mother were becoming more and more frequent, but he had little time for her man. John spied a weak streak in him because he gave him too much pocket money for no reason. John viewed this as courting popularity with Julia's son. As a sign of weakness and insecurity, he despised it. But he took the money: it came in useful to upgrade the cigarettes he normally bought – when Twitchy gave him a windfall he would buy Senior Service instead of the lower-priced Park Drive or Woodbines.

Because she missed his company so much, Julia over-compensated John whenever they were together, at teatime after school *en route* to Mimi, and at weekends when he would spend whole days with her. She was more of a friend than a mother-figure, and had an infectious sense of fun. She dressed colourfully and was the first and only woman in her road to wear trousers – which in the early fifties was rare for women. Julia loved music and wanted to know every move John and the Quarry Men were making.

When John was waiting at her house in Spring Wood one warm July evening in 1958, Julia was paying a visit to Mimi for the traditional cup of tea and chat. The sisters had totally different temperaments, but Julia loved Mimi for her bookish intelligence and worldliness, while Julia's sense of humour and warm perso-nality were adored by Mimi. Julia went to Mimi's on most days, and nodded knowingly at the catalogue of problems in bringing up John with which Mimi would regale her.

On some nights Mimi would walk Julia to the bus stop two hundred yards away. But that night Mimi said, 'I won't walk with you tonight, Julia – I'll see you tomorrow.'

Julia's words were to be prophetic: 'Don't worry.'

Julia crossed one side of the dual carriageway, stepped through the hedge to cross the second half towards her bus stop, and was sent spinning into the air by a car. She died instantly, aged forty-four.

A policeman broke the news of the accident to John and Twitchy at the house in Spring Wood. They went together to Sefton General Hospital which, ironically, five years later, John would joyfully re-visit to see his wife Cynthia with their son, Julian, who was born there. It wasn't until they reached the hospital that the horrifying truth was given to John by a doctor: 'I'm sorry, but your Mummy's dead.' Twitchy was no help: he broke down in tears.

John was appalled: the woman he was coming to discover as his best friend had been cruelly snatched from him when he was seventeen, and just as his life was becoming structured by the routine of college, its camaraderie, and the growing importance of the Quarry Men, Paul McCartney and Stuart Sutcliffe. His father's absence had been capped by his mother's death. His early tears were replaced by silence on the subject.

Mimi was distraught. 'It was a terrible, terrible shock to me. One minute she was sitting here, having a cup of tea with me, the next' – Mimi snaps her fingers – 'she'd gone. I never told any of the family where she was knocked down, to save them the pain. They drove past the spot every day. It wasn't just a case of my sister dying in a car accident, either – I'd got her little boy, so our relationship was very special. We'd never quarrelled about John and who should have him. She found a new man and I wasn't interfering with her life. After all, she'd had a rotten deal with that other thing [John's father, Fred]. When she went with the new man, I said that to think of another man providing for him shoes, clothes and food and perhaps grudging it later on – it's not fair. Nobody was going to have the chance to look sideways at one of ours. And Julia agreed. So as John got older, he naturally got to know his mother better and everything was happy. He was broken-hearted for weeks. He just went to his room, into a shell. First his Uncle George, now his mother. I was in a state.' Julia was buried in Allerton Cemetery as Mrs Lennon.

The agony was prolonged by a court case. The car which knocked down Julia had been driven by an off-duty policeman who stood trial, but was acquitted. The scars in John's young life were beginning to mount: the Blackpool tug-of-war between his parents; the death of lovable Uncle George; the self-inflicted abysmal failure of his schooldays; and now, at the emotionally crucial age of seventeen, the loss of his mother, so suddenly, was crushing.

John's hurt ran deep but he did not allow it to be seen. He bottled up his sadness at Mimi's home, and at college there were only a few occasions when, sitting alone in class, students would notice him becoming uncharacteristically quiet or, shortly after Julia's death, the tears welling up. Ann Mason, girlfriend of John's friend Geoff Mohammed, says: 'Most of us knew his mother had died, but he shied away from talking about it. We knew it wasn't a subject to be discussed.' Twelve years later, John was to articulate the pain of his mother's loss with poignant songs called 'My Mummy's Dead', 'Mother' and 'Julia'. But the immediacy of the tragedy was too much for a teenager who had already absorbed enough traumas.

Lennon sought early refuge in drink. The atmosphere of the Liverpool 8 district dominated by the art college and the Institute was conducive to behaving like an artist, poet or writer. Lennon found comfort in the pubs of the area and on many afternoons returned to Arthur Ballard's classroom drunk, accompanied by Geoff Mohammed. Most students and teachers, knowing the reason behind John's behaviour, turned a blind eye to his wildness.

Only one person fully understood John's suffering. Paul McCartney had been similarly hit by the loss of his mother two years earlier. Few words were spoken between John and Paul about Julia's death. 'We didn't say anything about our mothers' deaths, but I did notice a quieter, more serious John for a while afterwards when he came round to our house,' says Michael McCartney. 'Suddenly, though, Paul and John had a bond that went beyond even the music.'

The Quarry Men – later briefly called Johnny and the Moondogs – continued throughout 1958 with a succession of line-ups, notably adding George Harrison on guitar. The rounds of youth club dances and social club events, particularly in the Woolton area where they had a name, kept them active. It was a useful diversion from college for John, still feeling desolate as the impact of his mother's death lingered. Later, during the Beatle years, John would muse on these uncomplicated years as a Quarry Man playing for a pint of light ale and a pie: 'We were doing it for fun then. Now it's a job.'

John's attitude to his college work was not endearing him to the teachers. Only Arthur Ballard, who supervised painting, saw him as having much potential, and developed a rapport with John partly through drinking with him in Ye Cracke at lunchtimes; this was the kind of language John understood, trading light ale for black velvet. John's poor punctuality in the morning, leaving for lunch with his eye more on making music with Paul and George in Arthur Ballard's room, or the canteen, than on college lectures, and erratic attendances in the afternoons, made him stand apart from most students and teachers. Dressed as a teddy boy, albeit a mild version, he was a marked man.

He added up to a dangerous ally for all but the brave, like the wild-eyed Geoff Mohammed, with his manic sense of humour and lightweight ability at art, and Stuart Sutcliffe, who could read John like a book. Indeed, Stuart was to write of John later, in a deadly accurate portrayal of the college Lennon:

> Sometimes a girl or boy would ask him about his sudden changes of mood, why he could be charming one minute and distasteful the next. His reply was always the same, if he bothered to reply. Usually when he did he felt no sympathy with his interrogator and would say: 'I hate you. Why should you like me, charm is only superficial and is easily exposed as having no concrete value.' Underneath the reserve that he piled upon himself at times like this, we knew there beat a human heart. A heart as kind and gentle as could be. He really hated hurting people and hated himself for doing so. He regarded people as conniving scoundrels, endeavouring to have a private view of his behaviour.

This was the cynicism of John Lennon stripped bare and placed in perspective by one who knew and loved him. Since the death of his mother there had been a few girl students with whom Lennon had a relationship – Annette and Thelma and Barbara and Beth. But now his character was firmly shaped. He would be a loner.

7
ROMANCE

'Don't blame me just because your mother's dead'

'Hey, John, I believe your mother got killed by a police car.' The cold, clinical way in which a girl student greeted John in art college on their return from a long summer holiday in 1958 stunned the crowd of students gathering to sign on in the foyer for the start of a new term.

John was sitting across the 'signing in' table, his legs dangling, his expression introspective. His reaction to the girl's greeting was as impassive as the remark itself was tactlessly stark. 'Yeah, that's right.' He remained insouciant.

Thelma Pickles was stunned. She was introduced to John by another student, Helen Anderson, who was established as a mate of John's. And Thelma did not know how to react to the embarrassment that the girl had caused her by speaking so brusquely about such a sensitive subject.

But Thelma need not have worried. 'I couldn't believe John's reaction. He didn't register anything. He didn't choke on it. It was as if someone had said, "You had your hair cut yesterday," or something like that.'

In the next six months Thelma came to understand a little more about the mind and emotions of John Lennon, to whom she was immediately drawn that day. Tony Carricker, one of John's pals, was sitting with him on the table in the college foyer. 'But my eyes definitely set on John. Tony was prettier, more handsome, with dark hair and dark eyes, but John was so powerful. When he was in a group like that, the focus of attention went to him. He had a presence. I found him very striking from that moment on.'

A year younger than John, Thelma was to figure in one of his

93

most torrid teenage love affairs before he met Cynthia. Their friendship blossomed in a spectacular conversation one day as they walked after college to the bus terminus in Castle Street. In no hurry to get home, they sat on the steps of the Queen Victoria monument for a talk. 'I knew his mother had been killed and asked if his father was alive,' says Thelma. 'Again, he said in this very impassive and objective way: "No, he pissed off and left me when I was a baby." I suddenly felt very nervous and strange. My father had left me when I was ten. Because of that, I had a huge chip on my shoulder. In those days, you never admitted you came from a broken home. You could never discuss it with anybody and people like me, who kept the shame of it secret, developed terrific anxieties. It was such a relief to me when he said that. For the first time, I could say to someone: 'Well, so did mine.' '

At first Thelma registered that he didn't care about his fatherless childhood. 'As I got to know him, he obviously cared. But what I realized quickly was that he and I had an aggression towards life that stemmed entirely from our messy home lives.'

Their friendship developed, not as a cosy love match but as teenage kids with chips on their shoulders. 'It was more a case of him carrying my things to the bus stop for me, or going to the cinema together, before we became physically involved.' John, when she knew him, would have laughed at people who were seen arm in arm. 'It wasn't love's young dream. We had a strong affinity through our backgrounds and we resented the strictures that were placed upon us. We were fighting against the rules of the day. If you were a girl of sixteen like me, you had to wear your beret to school, be home at a certain time, and you couldn't wear make-up. A bloke like John would have trouble wearing skin-tight trousers and generally pleasing himself, especially with his strict aunt. We were always being told what we couldn't do. He and I had a rebellious streak, so it was awful. We couldn't wait to grow up and tell everyone to get lost. Mimi hated his tight trousers and my mother hated my black stockings. It was a horrible time to be young!' Lennon's language was ripe and fruity for the 1950s, and so was his wounding tongue. In Ye Cracke, one night after college, John rounded on Thelma in front of several students, and was crushingly rude to her. She forgets exactly what he said, but remembers her blistering attack on him: 'Don't blame me,' said Thelma, 'just because your mother's dead.'

It was something of a turning point. John went quiet but now he had respect for the girl who would return his own viciousness with a sentence that was equally offensive. 'Most people stopped short,'

Thelma Pickles photographed during her intense relationship with John which began at Liverpool College of Art in 1958

says Thelma. 'They were probably frightened of him, and on occasions there were certainly fights. But with me, he met someone with almost the same background and edge. We got on well, but I wasn't taking any of his verbal cruelty.'

When they were together, though, the affinity was special, with a particular emphasis on sick humour. Thelma says categorically that John and she laughed at afflicted or elderly people 'as something to mock, a joke'. It was not anything deeply psychological like fear of them, or sympathy, she says. 'Not to be charitable to ourselves, we both actually disliked these people rather than sympathized,' says Thelma. 'Maybe it was related to being artistic and liking things to be aesthetic all the time. But it just wasn't sympathy. I really admired his directness, his ability to verbalize all the things I felt amusing.' He developed an instinctive ability to mock the weak, for whom he had no patience.

In the early 1950s Britain had National Service conscription for men aged eighteen and over who were medically fit. John seized on this as his way of ridiculing many people who were physically afflicted. 'Ah, you're just trying to get out of the army,' he jeered at men in wheelchairs being guided down Liverpool's fashionable Bold Street, or 'How did you lose your legs? Chasing the wife?' He ran up behind frail old women and made them jump with fright, screaming 'Boo' into their ears. 'Anyone limping, or crippled or hunchbacked, or deformed in any way, John laughed and ran up to them to make horrible faces. I laughed with him while feeling awful about it,' says Thelma. 'If a doddery old person had nearly fallen over because John had screamed at her, we'd be laughing. We knew it shouldn't be done. I was a good audience, but he didn't do it just for my benefit.' When a gang of art college students went to the cinema, John would shout out, to their horror, 'Bring on the dancing cripples.' 'Children often find that kind of sick humour amusing,' says Thelma. 'Perhaps we just hadn't grown out of it. He would pull the most grotesque faces and try to imitate his victims.'

Often, when he was with her, he would pass Thelma his latest drawings of grotesquely afflicted children with mis-shapen limbs. The satirical *Daily Howl* that he had ghoulishly passed around at Quarry Bank School was taken several stages beyond the gentle, prodding humour he doled out against his grammar school teachers. 'He was merciless,' says Thelma Pickles. 'He had no remorse or sadness for these people. He just thought it was funny.' He told her he felt bitter about people who had an easy life. 'I found him magnetic,' says Thelma, 'because he mirrored so much of what was inside me, but I was never bold enough to voice.'

'Thel', as John called her, became well aware of John's short-sightedness on their regular trips to the cinema. They would 'sag off' college in the afternoons to go to the Odeon in London Road or the Palais de Luxe, to see films like Elvis Presley in *Jailhouse Rock* and *Kid Creole*. 'He'd never pay,' says Thelma. 'He never had any money.'

Whether he had his horn-rimmed spectacles with him or not, John would not wear them in the cinema. He told her he didn't like them for the same reason that he hated deformity in people: wearing specs was a sign of weakness. Just as he did not want to see crutches or wheelchairs without laughing, John wouldn't want to be laughed at. So he very rarely wore his specs, even though the black horn-rimmed style was a copy of his beloved Buddy Holly.

'So in the cinema we sat near the front and it would be: "What's happening now, Thel?" "Who's that, Thel?" He couldn't follow the film but he wouldn't put his specs on, even if he had them.'

Even then she was attracted to his 'very straight, lovely, Romanesque nose' which was accentuated by his habit of tilting his head back. The stance became a crucial hallmark of John's stage posture as a Beatle; it was generally thought to be part of his arrogance, a defiant declaration of his domain. In fact, the stance was caused by his short-sightedness. 'He'd take ages to see things in a room,' recalls Thelma. 'He'd say: "Who's that in that corner?" when it was someone he should have recognized immediately.'

It was not a big step from cinema visits and mutual mocking of people for John and Thelma to go beyond the drinking sessions in Ye Cracke. 'It wasn't love's young dream, but I had no other boyfriends while I was going out with John and as far as I knew he was seeing nobody except me.'

On the nights that John's Aunt Mimi was due to go out for the evening to play bridge, Thelma and John met on a seat in a brick-built shelter on the golf course opposite the house in Menlove Avenue. When the coast was clear and they saw Mimi leaving, they would go into the house.

'He certainly didn't have a romantic attitude to sex,' says Thelma. 'He used to say that sex was equivalent to a five-mile run, which I'd never heard before. He had a very disparaging attitude to girls who wanted to be involved with him but wouldn't have sex with him.

' "They're edge-of-the-bed virgins," he said.

'I said: "What does that mean?"

'He said: "They get you to the edge of the bed and they'll not complete the act."

'He hated that. So if you weren't going to go to bed with him, you had to make damned sure you weren't going to go to the edge of the bed, either. If you did, he'd get very angry.

'If you were prepared to go to his bedroom, which was above the front porch, and start embarking on necking and holding hands, and you weren't prepared to sleep with him, then he didn't want to know you. You didn't do it. It wasn't worth losing his friendship. So if you said, "No", that was OK. He'd then play his guitar or an Everly Brothers record. Or we'd go to the pictures. He *would* try to persuade you to sleep with him, though.

'He was no different from any young bloke except that if you led him on and gave him the impression you would embark on any kind of sexual activity and then didn't, he'd be very abusive. It was entirely lust.'

The art college in the late 1950s was a hotbed of promiscuity. 'There was much weeping in the loo,' says Thelma. 'At sixteen we were very ignorant; it was very much hit and miss. Suddenly there was a pregnancy explosion, and five students were pregnant in one year. They had to leave college. It was a social stigma, no matter what circle you came from – working-class, middle-class, or whatever.'

John never talked about the dangers of pregnancy. 'He wouldn't care. It wouldn't enter his mind to think about it.'

Thelma was John's girlfriend for six months. 'It just petered out,' she says. 'I certainly didn't end it. He didn't either. We still stayed part of the same crowd of students. When we were no longer close, he was more vicious to me in company than before. I was equally offensive back. That way you got John's respect.'

Her memory of her former boyfriend is of a teenager 'very warm and thoughtful inside. Part of him was gentle and caring. He was softer and gentler when we were alone than when we were in a crowd. He was never physically violent with me – just verbally aggressive, and he knew how to hurt. There was a fight with him involved once, in the canteen, but he'd been drinking. He wasn't one to pick a fight. He often enraged someone with his tongue and he'd been on the edge of it, but he loathed physical violence really. He'd be scared. John avoided real trouble.'

One day in the lettering class at college the uncouth rebel who looked unkempt, who delighted in disruptive behaviour and acting the fool in class, and who needed nursing with loaned ruler or paintbrush, became a source of fascination for another girl – Cynthia Powell. The story of their unlikely mutual attraction has already been told. At home, over tea one day, John said of Cynthia: 'Do you know what, Mimi, there's a girl sending me chocolate biscuits and coffee in the canteen at college.'

Mimi said, 'You don't accept them, do you?'

'If she's fool enough to send them,' said John, 'I'll eat them.'

The girl from the posh side of the Mersey seemed at first sight the least likely partner for the college troublemaker. She spoke very softly, neither drank nor smoked, and behaved decorously. She had had a strict upbringing with her two older brothers. Like John, she lived with one parent, her strong-minded mother, Lilian. Her father had died of cancer two years before she met Lennon; also like John, she was seventeen when she lost a parent.

It would be easy to analyse their mutual attraction as Cynthia the mother substitute and John the swaggering teenage tough guy, Cynthia's concession to dangerous living. But from the time they got together, it was more than just another fling for them both. It wasn't long before John and Cynthia were spending afternoons and nights at Stuart Sutcliffe's flat. It was a dangerous affair, demanding lies of both John and Cynthia: she would tell her mother that she had stayed at a girlfriend's flat for the night, and John would concoct a story for Mimi about playing with the Quarry Men too far away to get home. Neither Lilian Powell nor Aunt Mimi were to know of the affair, still less the intensity of it, for many months.

Cynthia's memory of John during their earliest days together is of a 'rough diamond with a heart of gold'. There were only two problems about him, in her view: his ferocious temper and his incredible jealousy if any other man should go near her. In true chauvinistic style, he considered it all right for him to dabble with other girls, as long as Cynthia did not discover it. Today, she smiles at the fact that she was kept under strict surveillance by him while he had other girlfriends. 'But it didn't matter. What mattered, in my eyes at that time, was that while John was with me, I was blind to anything else. He gave me his everything when he was with me, and I didn't need any other assurance.' In a small community such as Liverpool 8 at that time, secrets were hard to keep but Lennon did pretty well. His absence from college lectures and the lack of interest by the tutors in disciplining him gave him *carte blanche* to vanish at all sorts of odd hours to consolidate his trysts.

Just as he scorned the physically afflicted, John mocked people who were conventional, toed the line, and didn't join in his flouting of authority. Cynthia Powell, the epitome of middle-class Hoylake, was in that category. She was among the smartest dressed of the girl students, with pale pink twinsets and fancy embroidered collars. She was as polite as John was aggressive, and was not among the girls who joined Lennon's table during lunch in the canteen. There were different camps. 'I was in his camp of boys,' says Thelma Pickles, 'because I was a bit of an arty beatnik. Cynthia was dainty and sweet. We used to take the mickey out of her, but John always said he fancied her. He called her Miss Prim, and he said to me: "It's a pity she's a bit posh", implying there was a gulf he would never be able to overcome. He was certainly always attracted to her from the first time he saw her in the canteen.

'It wasn't that John thought *she* had any feelings of superiority. He just recognized her different background, because she was from over the water. It was *our* inverted snobbery. When she walked into the room, he'd say: "Don't talk like that, 'cos Cynthia's here." He meant we had to be on our best behaviour.'

John was acutely aware of one other girl at college who was besotted with him. 'She sat weeping over him,' says Thelma, 'but instead of feeling sorry for her and giving her a kind word, he'd put her down verbally.' John could not tolerate such a public display of emotion. He despised the girl for *showing* what he considered as a weakness. What weaknesses *he* had he either kept well hidden or exploited, as in the case of cripples.

Thelma Pickles heard when she was temporarily away from college that John and Cynthia had become as closeasthis. 'I was startled but pleased. I thought she'd be good for him, temper his aggression. I knew she'd have to tailor herself into looking like Brigitte Bardot for him, and I remember reflecting on the fact that he'd teased her so much about being so proper. I remember thinking: "He's got what he wanted – again." '

Cynthia believes that most of the staff and tutors were frightened of John. This led to mutual disrespect, as John could not stand weakness. 'He was constantly being told off for coming in late. If it hadn't been for Arthur Ballard, who acted as his guardian, I think some terrible things might have happened between John and the teachers. I heard Arthur Ballard saying to the others: "Look, he's not a bad lad, he's going through a bad patch. He's talented." '

But his greasy, quiffed hair, with the DA at the back, contrasted with most of the other students' long hair. His scruffy black trousers, with tight 'drainies' altered by Helen Anderson, and his shiny black jacket, made him look utterly different from the traditional bohemian student look of casual jacket, with leather elbow pads, or duffle coat. Eventually John demurred and, in another change which surprised students, came to school regularly in his Uncle George's brown tweed jacket and grey trousers.

'All the changes in dress, and particularly that teddy boy period, were a throwback to his younger days,' says Cynthia. 'At Dovedale and Quarry Bank, he told me he felt he had to look tough and hard. It was his wall against the world, in case somebody picked a fight. So he dressed in a tough way. When he first went to college, he felt as if he had to be on guard. Most of the students weren't tough or aggressive, but he'd come from a tougher school background. Woolton was a genteel area but he didn't want to be regarded as a genteel lad, so he played a hard role. It was his friendship with Stuart and then with me that changed him and made him realize there was no need for that acting at all.'

Nothing could deter Cynthia. Her work suffered as she spent every minute at college thinking of him, or seeking him out. She had plenty of conventional reasons for saying 'enough is enough' and dumping John. He could not take his drink and once, when a fellow student was rude to him at a party at a tutor's house, Lennon dragged him out to the street and pinned him to the ground within seconds, thumping him. 'I was dancing with Stuart Sutcliffe upstairs when the row began. We wondered where John had gone but were soon told there was a fight,' says Cynthia. 'It was the drink again – he had a very small capacity before he became aggressive. The slightest thing would have him in a terrible temper.' To a prim girl from the Wirral, he was quite a visual spectacle as he slouched into lettering class twice weekly, battered guitar slung nonchalantly across his shoulders. His fingers were permanently stained by nicotine from the twenty cigarettes he got through most days, most of them scrounged tersely ('Gimme a fag?') from the nearest student. The profile of John as an undesirable was completed by big ugly callouses on his fingers, the effect of his guitar picking.

The effect Cynthia and John had on each other was immediate. Within about a year, John had dropped even his teddy boy posturing. He took to an 'arty' look, wearing scarves, ordinary black jackets and trousers, and combing his hair more traditionally. That was his concession to Cynthia's conventional appearance and also an indication that their love affair was giving him fewer reasons to make a dramatic visual impression. He was growing up. Cynthia's change, for John, was much more radical. Aware of his fanatical enthusiasm for Brigitte Bardot and Juliette Greco, and a more pouting expression than she naturally showed, 'Cyn' took to wearing black fishnet stockings with seams, tighter skirts, and suspender belts. All three features were requested by John. Crucially Cyn, who had arrived at art college with reddish-brown hair, gradually lightened it until she was dyed a beautiful golden blonde. The transformation was complete: John had secured his Brigitte Bardot look-alike. For Cynthia, it was not just a pleasure but a political move, too: no more would John be able to drool to others in the canteen at lunchtime, at the sight of another student named Joni Crosby: 'Cor, doesn't *she* look just like Brigitte Bardot?' Cynthia, infatuated or in love, was acutely aware of what she perceived as competition.

During these teenage pre-Beatle years, Cynthia was the only person in whom John would confide his deepest feelings. Three people figured in his conversations with her about his home life, besides the omnipresent discipline of Aunt Mimi. There was Uncle George, whom John missed terribly and said so. He would proudly tell Cynthia when he was wearing one of George's old jackets. They did not fit but he did not care. His father was a taboo subject: John had this vision, which he gave to Cynthia, of a great seafaring man, with a wonderful singing voice, 'a hero in the distance' whom he could not see because he had to go away for important work at sea. It clearly troubled John but he had closed his mind to his father's existence. Thirdly, of course, there was his mother and the pain of her recent accidental death.

'He didn't talk about his Mum to anybody but me,' says Cynthia. 'It shattered his life. He often said how terrible it was that he'd lost her just at the time she was becoming his best friend. I could see the feeling welling up deep inside him, then he would say something like that, and close down. I'd say: "Come on, John, I want to know all about you." And he'd shake his head as if to say no. It was obviously too painful for him to open up very much. I'm sure that's why he went completely crazy at college and why the combination of drink and anger made him so aggressive. It was a bitter rage. When he became successful as a Beatle he was a different person altogether. The aggravation was restrained. He became gentle. He still drank but he didn't get so aggressive.'

John's jealousy and possessiveness about Cynthia was almost overpowering. When she could not stay the night with him he insisted she stayed in Liverpool until the last train left Central

Station at 11.20 for Hoylake, getting her home just before the critical midnight hour. 'He always made me get that last train home to make sure he was the only man I was seeing that night.' After college, they would adjourn either to Stuart's flat or the cinema, or go for drinks. 'He wanted total commitment and I was pleased to give it,' says Cynthia. 'If I as much as looked at another man, he would go mad and say: "Who's *he*?" in a moody voice.' With her daily allowance of eight shillings, Cynthia plied John with cigarettes – the cheapest varieties, Woodbines or Embassy – because he was usually broke. 'He wasn't mean, just always broke from spending his cash on black velvet, the mixture of Guinness and cider which was the students' cheap way of getting drunk quickly: four pints most lunchtimes. But he was very moral – he pooled his money.'

Cynthia is philosophical about affairs which John had before and during his college days. 'When John was with me, it was total commitment. Whatever he did outside our relationship didn't seem very important. We were together such a lot of the time that whatever other affairs he had once we met couldn't have amounted to much because I was with him most of the time. He kept me in Liverpool as late as I dared stay. It wasn't as if he wanted to get rid of me. Later on, during the Beatles' very busy period and when he was away a lot, it was a different matter. But love is blind.'

Once their betrothal was clinched, and they couldn't bear to be apart, John and Cynthia decided it was time they met each other's families. 'After a few months, I went up to Mendips and got on fine with Mimi. The only thing that was kept secret from her was that John and I spent some nights together in Stuart Sutcliffe's flat. She must have thought I was a nice young girl. Little did she know.' After tea of eggs and chips and bread and butter, John and Cynthia and Mimi would sit talking before, eventually, Cynthia would go and stay with her best friend, Phyllis McKenzie, who also lived in Woolton.

The trips by John to Trinity Road, Hoylake, were less frequent: he clashed with Cynthia's mother on their first meeting. 'He ran out of the house after he and Mum hadn't got on well. It was all very tense, that first meeting. I ran after him and found him halfway between the house and the station. He wanted to get back to Liverpool quickly. But I persuaded him to return and patch up the argument for my sake. Mum wasn't mad about his appearance and made it clear to him. She'd much rather I'd chosen a clean-cut office type. John only went across to the Wirral three times.

The early days of romance, as seen
by John. He drew this Christmas
card for Cynthia in 1958

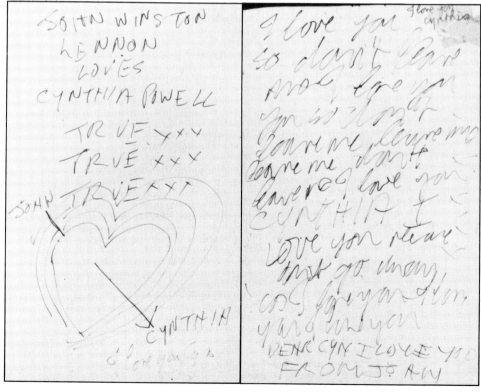

DEAR CYNTHIA
ALL I WANT
FOR CHRISTMAS
IS YOU CYN
SO POST EARLY

I LOVE YOU
I'M GLADY's I LOVE
OR I'D GO MAD
I'M ALREADY THO'
HEE HEE!!! I love you
I love you XX XXX
XX XXXXXX XX XXX
XXX XXX XXX XX
XX XXX XX XXX
I love you
MERRY CHRIMBO from John

I love you mum mum mum cyn.

DEAR CYN.
I LOVE YOU I LOVE YOU
I love you I love you I love you
I love I love U I do I love U
I LOVE YOU LIKE MAD I DO
I DO LOVE YOU YES YES YES
I DO LOVE YOU CYN YO. I LOVE
I love you Cynthia Powell
John Winston Love C. Powell
Cynthia Cynthia Cynthia
I love you I love you I love
you for ever and ever is N
great? I LOVE YOU LIKE
GUITARS I LOVE YOU LIKE
ANYTHING LOVELY LOVELY
LOVELY LOVELY CYN LOVELY CYN
I LOVE LOVELY CYNTHIA CYNTHIA
I LOVE YOU. YOU ARE WONDER
FUL I ADORE YOU I WANT YOU
I LOVE YOU I NEED YOU DONT
GO I LOVE YOU HAPPY XMAS
MERRY CHRIMBO I LOVE YOU
I LOVE YOU I LOVE YOU CYNTHIA
CYN CYN CYN CYN CYN CYN
I'S LOVED BY JOHN JOHN JOHN
JOHN JOHN I LOVE YOU
Love John

HAPPY
CHRISTMAS
CYN
WITH ALL
MY LOVE
JOHN
XX XXX
XX XXX
X XXXX
X XXX X
X XX X
X XX X
XX

I HOPE IT WON'T BE THE LAST

He was destined never to get on well with Cynthia's mother, not even during the most joyful days of Beatlemania. When she lived at his Weybridge mansion, he regarded her as an intruder.

The year 1959 was a significant one for John. First, he made a tentative move from Mimi and Woolton, and went to live with Stuart in Gambier Terrace, in a house with an impressive view of the Anglican Cathedral which was then being built. To describe Stuart's home as a flat would be an exaggeration; it was a room with a shared toilet in a large Georgian house. There were mattresses on the floor as beds, paints and kettles and all the trappings of student living spread chaotically around the floor. Its appeal to John was its very disorderliness, and also the fact that it was a haven for him and Cynthia to sleep together. 'Even though both our families knew we were seeing a lot of each other,' says Cynthia, 'in those days kids were not as open about their lives together. John and I took the view that with Mimi and my Mum, what the eye didn't see the heart couldn't grieve over.' She made no move to leave her Hoylake home, but her mother noticed an increased number of nights when Cynthia said she was staying at Phyllis's home in Woolton. Cynthia's alibi was perfect. But Mimi was furious about his departure to 'dirty' Gambier Terrace.

'Please Cynthia, try to get him to move out of that place. It's filthy and it's unhealthy.'

'There's not a lot I can do, Mimi,' said Cynthia. 'He wants to be with Stuart.'

John rubbed salt in Mimi's wound by technically not leaving Mendips: he would return there every few days to collect and deliver dirty and clean shirts, underpants and socks. Mimi consoled herself that at least she saw him regularly and made sure he got a square meal.

Living with Stuart had another stabilizing effect on John; there was his company, and conversations long into the night with the male friend he admired more than anyone, plus Stuart's encouragement to John to try his hand with painting. In return for the casual art lessons, John tried to teach Stuart bass guitar. He was never a good player, but John loyally brought his mate into the Quarry Men and later into the early Beatles. Even if he couldn't play well, and disguised the fact by turning his back on the audience so they couldn't see his inadequacies on the guitar, Stuart had a major redeeming quality which John liked: he looked mean and moody, and the girls liked him, complete with his adolescent spots. Stuart's quiet vulnerability made him something of a heart-throb. Visually, if not musically, he was an asset to the group at a time when they needed all the fans they could get. To Stuart, the music was light relief from his intensive work as a painter: at college he was known as a workaholic.

Cynthia remembers that, at this stage, John was totally consumed with music. 'It was his complete conversation outside college and a lot of the time in college, too. He couldn't get enough rehearsal time in and he seemed genuinely keen on the partnership that was developing with Paul McCartney.' Locations for rehearsing the hits of the day, particularly the prophetically titled Buddy Holly hit 'It Doesn't Matter Anymore', were getting better. Despite his mother's death, John remained in touch with Twitchy, and he, Paul and Cynthia would use Twitchy's house in Spring Wood for jam sessions and songwriting when they wanted a change from Paul's home. 'If Twitchy was in, he'd let us in. If he wasn't, we'd break in through a window, raid the larder, and leave after a jam session lasting two or three hours in the afternoons and early evenings,' says Cynthia. 'John suffered Twitchy all right. They were polite to each other, that's all. But his house came in useful. That's the way John would have seen it.'

Paul — then, as now, highly organized with fine attention to detail — carried an exercise book in which he wrote down the words to the songs he and John were working on. This year, too, they formally shook hands on an agreement that was to inscribe their names together in the history books. They agreed that, from then on, whether a song was written individually or together, they would have both their names stuck on them as songwriters, thus: 'Lennon–McCartney'. It was a touching manifestation of togetherness at a time when neither knew how significant the partnership would become, or how much rancour would result ten years later.

'It was a beautiful period,' reflects Cynthia, looking back. 'It wasn't just a musical convenience that put them together. By the time I saw them playing at the college or at Twitchy's they were friends, at one with each other. They seemed to have been friends for many years. It was intuitive. George, being younger and not writing songs, didn't have the communication with them, but John and Paul couldn't stop playing together, practising the chords of the latest Elvis Presley song, the Everly Brothers, and getting the confidence to try writing their own words. I sat there, on these "away days" of rehearsals, absolutely mesmerized. Their harmonies were so beautiful. John had this image of being the toughest boy in college but his music showed what all of us knew was underneath. He had a gentleness that needed to come out, and it did in those songs.'

Cynthia saw music come to be Lennon's salvation. Mimi might have thought she was punishing him by banishing him to the porch when she tired of his guitar strumming; but John relished it, because the acoustics were better than inside the house. The college lunchtime sessions with Paul and George only once attracted a crowd of any size. In the canteen, students who saw him during lectures as the wild one were astonished at the music that came from him. A typical programme would be 'Peggy Sue', 'Good Golly Miss Molly', 'Rip It Up', 'All I Have To Do Is Dream', and always, as a finale, 'When You're Smiling', sung by John in a cackling, Goon-like voice.

'He didn't like an audience for these sessions with Paul,' says Cynthia. 'But luckily for the big audience he didn't have his glasses on so he couldn't see how many people had gathered round. I remember several of the students saying: "My goodness, this is a different John Lennon." They'd see him walking round with a battered guitar and thought he was trouble. Suddenly, at the sight of him playing soft melodic music, they realized that inside him was so much more.'

Money, fame and ambition for the Quarry Men were still secondary to John's love and lust for Cynthia and a rarely admitted desire to please Mimi. 'I don't think that at nineteen John had the faintest idea he would be rich or successful, or even hoped for it in the same way that some people hope to win the football pools,' says Cynthia. 'Paul was a keen schoolboy but John wasn't like that. He was just happy doing what he wanted. He was carefree.' Underneath that indifference, though, was a conventional wish. As the Quarry Men earned a few pounds from their engagements, John would love the pleasure of giving Mimi a bundle of notes, erratically. 'He'd give her £10 or so from time to time. I saw the expression on his face that almost said: "Look, we've *made* it!" Even though they hadn't made it at all, he wanted Mimi to think he was doing something well. "There's the money for my keep," he'd say to his Auntie.'

Every student who was with Lennon at art college has a different anecdote about him. But they all agree on one central point: if John had not emerged successfully with the Beatles, he could easily have gone seriously off the rails. Cynthia says that if he had not had Paul McCartney to cajole him, and their son Julian to motivate him to make some money, and still later Brian Epstein as Beatles manager to push him, 'he would have ended up a bum. . . . It's hard to say that now, after what happened, but he wouldn't have cared that much. I'd have gone out to work, he wouldn't have any qualifications whatsoever because he was falling foul of the art college, and Mimi would have pushed him in all sorts of directions. He would have needed to learn a trade, or go back to school again, and I can't see him concentrating. He'd have gone downhill.'

8
HAMBURG

'Have a drink. We've been chucked out of college'

Predictably Lennon failed his lettering examinations. Even the combined faked papers from Cynthia and Thelma could not save him. His disorderliness at college, his swearing and contempt for the teaching system had all but resulted in his being expelled. Arthur Ballard came to the rescue and gained a stay of execution for Lennon, partly because of John's association with the brilliant Stuart Sutcliffe: this, it was claimed, redeemed Lennon as far as his ambition was concerned. Geoff Mohammed was thrown out of college and John and he were to be seen celebrating in a city coffee bar. Michael McCartney walked in to find the pair in jubilant mood: 'Hey, Mike, come on in and have a coffee. We've been chucked out of college!' It was not technically true in John's case, but it might well have been. Lennon was not the sort of nineteen-year-old who returned confidences or even the compliments of Arthur Ballard. His attendance at college became more and more erratic. He regarded himself as a 'visitor' rather than a permanent student.

Luck came to John's rescue; within a few weeks of facing expulsion he would visit Germany as a musician, an event which was to mark his entire life.

Days were now spent mostly drinking coffee in the Jacaranda, a club not far from the college in Slater Street. The *Sunday People* newspaper focused on Stuart and John's shambles of a room – with its stolen Belisha beacon and macabre, empty coffin as part of the furniture – in an exposé entitled 'This is the Beatnik Horror'. John, free of the shackles of Mimi's home, felt physically and mentally liberated. He could now enact all the fantasies of the world to combine rock 'n' roll with all that being an art student meant, without producing much art.

The 'Jac' was a coffee bar run by Allan Williams, a Welsh-born hustler with a keen eye on the pop scene. He proved to be an important stepping stone in the Beatles' success story. Through his affinity with Stuart Sutcliffe, whom he admired, Williams found himself constantly harangued by Lennon for a few sessions for the Quarry Men in the basement of the 'Jac' when regular groups like Cass and the Casanovas, Derry and the Seniors, and Rory Storm and the Hurricanes (featuring Ringo Starr on drums) failed to show up or were not available.

Williams relented. John dragged Stuart into the group on bass guitar (he had bought the instrument with the money he had won in an art competition). Within days, Stuart's delicate artist's fingers were in shreds. Lennon now believed that rock 'n' roll was the only avenue open to him, for he started to look moderately tidy for the sessions that Williams fixed. The band wore black polo-necked Marks and Spencer's sweaters, dark blue jeans, and white plimsoll shoes.

It was against this background of a fading interest in art and increasingly bohemian living, accompanied by life with Stuart in a flat of their own, that John slowly became more aggressively ambitious for his group. He pestered Allan Williams for dates and eventually landed one at the Grosvenor Ballroom in Seacombe. It was a notorious local bloodbath where gangs went not for music or dancing, nor to find women partners, so much as 'have a scene' with rival groups: 'a scene' meant a punch-up. The band playing rock 'n' roll from the stage would have a tough job making itself heard and not getting involved in the trouble. Although he would be one of the first to run at the sight of real danger to himself, John enjoyed being on the precipice overlooking a battle. The rock 'n' roll music he loved was anyway full of assertiveness, and a spot of bother seemed appropriate to the combative stance and sound of Elvis Presley. In his mind, John was moving well away from skiffle and such soft music as the Everly Brothers' 'Cathy's Clown' and mellow ballads like Cliff Richard's 'Travelling Light'. (John was later to describe Cliff Richard to me as the epitome of all he hated in British pop. 'He's so bloody Christian I can't stand him and his lot.') Rock 'n' roll was a clarion call for John, an act of such defiance that a change of name for his group was now on the horizon.

The momentum of the group was now quickening. Paul might have been the better musician, singing the more acceptable, poppier melodies ('You Are My Sunshine', 'Home', and 'You Were Meant For Me') while John went for the slightly more abrasive, beatier stuff like 'Ain't She Sweet'. But Lennon remained firmly the leader. When name changes were discussed, to try to steer them away from Quarry Men which was 'too skiffly and restricting', said John, his own name would invariably be mentioned as an alternative. Long John Silver, a parody on his name and a character in a favourite childhood story, *Treasure Island*, was quickly rejected. It was almost as corny as the pop music of Cliff Richard and Frankie Vaughan and Craig Douglas which John was now trying to debunk!

Stylistically, no pop act came near Buddy Holly in John and Paul's affection at that time. The light beat of Buddy Holly's distinctive songs was a perfect progression from skiffle. John was attracted by the name of Holly's backing group, the Crickets, and played around with names to emulate that. It was Stuart who first came up with the Beetles, as a 'play' on Crickets. It appealed to John who, in a masterly example of his skill in word-play which was to stay with him throughout his life, later modified the spelling to Beatles, to incorporate the word 'beat' which was fast becoming conversational currency in Liverpool, with its proliferation of rock groups that no other city could match.

John continued to pester Allan Williams for more work. They secured a drummer who, even though he was thirty-six, was very competent on the instrument which all groups regarded as vital. Tommy Moore, a fork-lift truck driver, was a fine player and technically the best John, Paul, and George had in those years. What he lacked in youthful exuberance he compensated for by improving the tightness of their sound. John had little patience with the slow-moving personality of Moore but saw him as a means to an end, of raising the group to a higher musical level than the other groups on Merseyside.

The Quarry Men's last performances under that name were at a club in the Liverpool suburb of West Derby run by Mona Best, mother of the Beatles' future drummer, Peter. In August 1959 they played at the opening of the club, and over the next three years were to play there about a hundred and twenty times, going through various name changes along the way until they finally reached the Beatles. The problem in filling the drum chair was not easily solved by John, Paul, George, and short-lived guitarist Ken Brown. So difficult was it that, when they entered a Carroll Levis talent contest in Manchester towards the end of 1959 under the skiffle-like name of Johnny and the Moondogs, John, Paul, and

George were without a drummer at all. Their appearance was a failure.

The Allan Williams and Jacaranda connection, as well as Williams' control of another club where the Beatles played, the Wyvern Social Club, later called the Blue Angel, at 108 Seel Street, was to be important in the Beatles' next phase. Larry Parnes, a famous name from London, had a reputation for creating top British pop stars and giving them names that evoked a positive image in a pop scene that was mostly spineless. After discovering Tommy Steele in the 2 I's coffee bar in Soho, Parnes had gone on to launch such luminaries as Marty Wilde, Vince Eager, Duffy Power, Johnny Gentle, and Dickie Pride. It was a pop stable with Elvis Presley stereotypes, painfully British in its imitative stance, and people laughed. But in the late 1950s Parnes was a name to be noted by anyone with an eye on making headway in the pop music world.

Through Allan Williams John's group, then known as the Silver Beetles, secured an audition with Larry Parnes in Liverpool. The winning group would accompany another Liverpool singer from the Larry Parnes stable, Billy Fury, on a nationwide concert tour. The Silver Beetles failed that audition, but were offered something equally attractive – the grand sum of £18 a week to accompany one of his lesser-known singers, Johnny Gentle, on a tour of the far north of Scotland. John and Stuart were ecstatic. They would find it simple to skip college for one week. Paul was equally determined to make the break from his studies for school exams. He had an uphill job persuading his father that the break would rest his brain and be beneficial, but with the aid of his brother Michael he clinched it. With Tommy Moore, George and Stuart, the Silver Beetles set off from Liverpool's Lime Street Station, and for a week enjoyed for the first time the life of hotels, autograph hunters, and importantly, non-Liverpool audiences. The money proved barely adequate but the freedom from home and school was wonderful, particularly for the wanderlust in John, who did not have parental security as a backdrop to his life.

Two people were to be the butt of John's cruel streak on that Scottish tour. Curiously, neither was prepared to join in his verbal jousting or retaliate, and since John preferred fighters to pacifists, they were easy targets. He got a special delight out of taunting Stuart, whose attempts to keep up with the music were simply beyond his capabilities. It didn't seem to occur to John that it was he who had dragged a reluctant Stuart into playing bass in the first place. Now, Stuart was verbally pummelled by his best mate for not coming up to scratch. More cold-bloodedly, Lennon had no patience whatsoever for Tommy Moore. When the group van, which singer Johnny Gentle was driving, had a bump with a car, and Moore was taken to hospital, it was Lennon who went to his bedside and insisted that he got up in time for that night's show.

Scotland had a more profound effect on John than on the other four. Tommy Moore left the Silver Beetles immediately on their return, feeling the age gap too much and the prospects not too rosy. Paul and George went back to the Liverpool Institute, while John's art college days were sliding into disarray. While he was away in Scotland, Cynthia had heard of his failure in lettering. Nothing could redeem his all-round lack of art college application. It was at this time that he hit his worst patch with Mimi, too. 'What was I going to do with someone who had no certificates from school and who appeared to be going the same way at college? I didn't stop worrying,' says Mimi. 'I'd say: "You must think about getting a job instead of messing about with the guitar, John. Concentrate on your studies. You know you're good at drawing."

'And he always replied along the same lines: "I'll be OK, I don't need the bits of paper to tell me where I'm going." '

Rock 'n' roll as a livelihood was clearly established in his mind by now, though he was less sure about how he would manage it. He increased the pressure on Allan Williams to get them work. Weekly sessions at Mona Best's Casbah Club, and the support work at the Jac, as well as the occasional accompaniment of a stripper in the New Cabaret Artistes Club, were not enough. Fresh from the taste of a proper concert tour in Scotland, John was fired with a hunger for engagements almost nightly. Allan Williams was now more convinced of their potential. They were even rivalling Derry and the Seniors and Gerry and the Pacemakers as local favourites. Before long, Allan Williams was getting the Silver Beetles engagements at the Grosvenor Ballroom in Seacombe and at the Neston Institute. The teddy boy movement plummeted to its nadir at some of these halls. Boozed-up teds were infuriated by the fact that the band on stage was highly fancied by the 'birds' they had brought along, and they took it out on the musicians. The aggression usually stopped short of fist fights, but not always. John, faster with his reflexes than anyone in the group, had come to the rescue of the physically slighter Stuart one night. A group of teds set on Stu and kicked him in the head after a dance. Lennon set about Sutcliffe's assailant with a ferocity rarely seen. It was as if John needed a good excuse, like the battering of his best friend, to show even himself the strength he now had at twenty. Though there was a lot of blood, and Stuart went home with a gashed forehead, it could have been much worse without John's retaliation.

Most of John's energy was not used for punch-ups, however: it was going into his passionate love affair with Cynthia; his songwriting sessions with Paul; the night-time shows whenever they came up; perfecting his mean, Elvis-like looks; and into trying to get more work for the group, which he now feared was probably going to be his only real hope of making money. Not surprisingly, he pestered Allan Williams more than anyone. 'Al, get us some work.' 'Al, what's next for us?' John would say when they played the Jacaranda. 'What have you got lined up for us next?' Williams was as enthusiastic as they were, but he had a roster of other bands to protect. Williams was to relinquish his link with the group and Brian Epstein eventually became manager of the Beatles. Fourteen years later Alan Williams wrote a book about his experiences with the Beatles, entitled *The Man Who Gave the Beatles Away*. After reading it Lennon, in a classic example of his rapier-like wit, referred to Allan as 'The Man Who Couldn't Give the Beatles Away'.

A strange quirk of fate led John, Paul, George, and Stuart from struggling through £10-a-night dances in Liverpool to kicking their act into blistering, world-breaking energy in Hamburg. Allan Williams was again the man who caused that trip to happen.

The Royal Caribbean Steel Band, his regular act at the Jacaranda, went to Hamburg and wrote to him saying there were great opportunities for British pop groups there. About the same time, the Silver Beetles had dropped the 'Silver' because John felt it was too twee and reminded him of the absurd suggestion that he should call himself Long John Silver. From a show in June 1960 they were styled as the Beatles. Other groups in Liverpool, who traded under more thrusting imagery (the Seniors, the Pacemakers, the Hurricanes, the Searchers) laughed at the corniness of merging the still-new word 'beat' with something else. It had no precedent but then neither had John Lennon. He was as perverse about the decision to change the name permanently to Beatles as he was in many other directions.

It was the Beatles, then, that Allan Williams sold, during a visit to Hamburg to follow up the attractive-sounding letter he had received from his beloved steel band. His first call was to a club on the Reeperbahn, then as now a neon-flashing street teeming with sex shows, clubs, bars and prostitutes. The manager of the Kaiserkeller club, one Bruno Koschmider, hired the Beatles and they were booked for their first shows there in September 1960.

It was just as well for John: college was a write-off. He was never formally expelled like his best mate Geoff Mohammed, because Arthur Ballard, his faithful mentor, was lobbying for him to be moved on to a new section called the Faculty of Design. But Ballard's pleas were falling on obstinate, more conservative ears. Other tutors now regarded Lennon as definitely more trouble than he was worth. During this period of debate about whether John was to remain an art student the Hamburg offer came in and clinched it: he was off, and told everyone so. Even Mimi had no argument against John's proud claim that they would be earning £100 a week each. 'I feared the worst,' says Mimi. 'But of course, he was getting older by then, not a child, so it was not so much a question of telling him what I thought as advising him. I couldn't see any future in going to Germany but he told me the money would be good.'

Before they went, they needed a drummer. At the Casbah Mona Best's son, a handsome, mean, moody-looking boy named Peter, had often sat in with John, Paul, George, and Stuart. He was rather more introverted than John and Paul, and they had little in common beyond the music, but that was enough: he was a good, lusty drummer. Other forces were causing ripples in the group. Paul and Stuart were starting to clash. The perfectionist inside McCartney had no patience with Stuart's thinly veiled attempts to play bass guitar properly, and Paul was constantly criticizing his playing. With George improving all the time and functioning strongly as the lead guitarist, individual roles needed defining more clearly. John was a competent rhythm guitarist, but there was no need for two. McCartney fancied the bass playing role himself, instead of Stuart. There was also jealousy for Lennon's attention. McCartney could not understand why John, as hard a man as one could wish to meet, could be so stupidly loyal as to have his incompetent best friend in the group against his better judgement. Stuart was also competition for the attention of girls, a fact the vain Paul did not like. On several fronts, then, Stuart Sutcliffe was bad news to Paul McCartney.

But for the Hamburg trip, expediency was essential. Peter Best lacked a sense of humour but had been hugely popular with the girls at his mother's coffee bar. He was in.

There was a problem finding John's birth certificate, which was essential to get a passport for the German trip. The problem in getting documentation for Paul, George, Stuart, and Pete was worrying enough for Allan Williams. In the case of Lennon, with no parents to sign the papers, and the vital birth certificate only found at the last moment, it was touch and go. He also won the difficult battle of persuading the parents of every member of the group that they would be safe and that a profitable trip lay ahead in Germany for the band, which was, he assured everyone, full of potential.

And so on 16 August 1960 the Beatles' first journey to Hamburg began. This was the trip that was to convert John Lennon, aged nineteen, Paul McCartney, aged eighteen, and George Harrison, aged seventeen into world beaters. The Hamburg Experience, as they later called it, was to teach them not only to hurl themselves full-bloodedly into making a great show; it was to teach them survival, and introduce them to stimulants in the form of pep pills.

Parting from Cynthia was painful. For two years John and Cyn had hardly been out of each other's company – and even then only a twenty-minute train journey away – and the thought of separation for an unknown time in a foreign country was worrying for Cynthia. As four months elapsed, Cynthia's feelings for John increased. He kept a simple promise, and hardly a day went by without a letter from Hamburg arriving at Hoylake. Envelopes were emblazoned with all the messages of teenage love: kisses and hearts, codes like SWALK (sealed with a loving kiss), 'Postman, postman, don't be slow, I'm in love with Cyn so go, man, go.' John's loving verse would almost obliterate the address. Inside, John would tell her of how much he wanted her – particularly sexually – needed her and missed her, but also how well the Beatles were doing in Hamburg, despite the fact that Bruno Koschmider was exploiting them, working them hard and giving them living quarters consisting of three filthy rooms containing only camp beds and blankets. He also said the washing and toilet facilities were appalling and that their rooms were situated behind a cinema screen, the cinema having been converted from an old theatre. Cynthia still worried about the girls available to John in promiscuous, dangerous Hamburg – 'the love and warmth of his letters made me feel wonderful and miserable at the same time,' she says candidly.

Immediately John went abroad, Cynthia realized that she and

John did not have photographs of each other. So she took to going to a Woolworth's photo booth every week. Carefully combing her hair, she dressed in her finest and turned on her most seductive pout for John to receive a picture of her. That, she hoped, would dissuade him from the German blondes who were worrying her.

With one of these photographs, Cynthia asked John to send in return pictures of himself from a coin-in-the-slot machine. The result was an unmistakable stroke of Lennon. He mailed Cynthia pictures of himself in grotesque poses: his face would contort, he would pretend to be a hunchback, his eyes would leer maniacally, and he would try to make each picture more sick than the last. Despite this, from the scores of letters she received from Germany Cynthia decided that John's aggression was waning. He was more ambitious for the Beatles, more enthusiastic about their success, than anything else, she says. 'I could sense his feeling that it was all starting to happen for him. It was just as well, as there was nothing much for him to come back to in England, as far as work was concerned.'

The Indra club, which they played almost immediately on their arrival, was a small and seedy basement. The audience was only about half a dozen strong, but the opportunistic promoter who had booked them, Bruno Koschmider, was scarcely a man with whom Liverpool teenagers would argue. He had a limp, a crooked nose, and all the authority that came with having fought in the war with the German Panzer Divisions. His idea in booking the Beatles was to inject some life into the place, and to try to get them to do for the Indra what their Liverpool rivals, Derry and the Seniors, had done for the Kaiserkeller: swell audiences and thereby raise the bar takings.

The Indra had previously been used as a strip club, and had a tiny, cramped stage. The Beatles' performance was stifled, and when a woman in the flat above the club complained to the police about the noise, Koschmider decided that the energy of the group would be better used in his much larger Kaiserkeller club. Derry and the Seniors had played there to packed houses; in Germany there was no admission charge but patrons had to buy drink, and plenty of it, which had a boisterous effect on many of them, resulting in fights. Here was born the full-blooded, almost animal-like rock 'n' roll in John Lennon.

Koschmider had heard Allan Williams trying to instil a touch of show business razzmatazz into the Beatles' act. Allan had often told them 'to make a show', to attract customers. Soon, the forceful Koschmider was using the phrase 'Mak show, mak show' to the boys all the time. Lennon, more than the other four, realized the *carte blanche* he was being given to perfect a wild stage personality. Besides, the demands Koschmider was making on them were physically punishing, so something more than music was essential. The contract called for the Beatles to perform from eight in the evening until two in the morning, with the occasional fifteen-minute break. What this amounted to was about six sets of forty-five minutes each. The schedule taxed the group's repertoire to its limit, and the chance of varying from set to set was minimal. It was little wonder that they tired of 'Roll Over Beethoven', 'Be-Bop-A-Lula' and 'Long Tall Sally'.

Survival was everything to John and the others. From the tough audiences, beer would arrive on stage together with an occasional request for a song. Hamburg John, often drunk but never incapable of delivering a power-crazed blast of rock 'n' roll to 'the bloody Krauts' as he called them, revelled in the challenge of it all. For a group of teenagers fresh from Liverpool, the violence as the waiters jostled with drunken customers, gangsters and prostitutes in the audience, and the hilarious language barrier made it all larger than life. Customers who got out of hand were often threatened by the bouncers with coshes and flick knives. John said later: 'I grew up in Hamburg, not Liverpool.' But the key to the Beatles' endurance lay in their first serious use of stimulants, in the form of pep pills.

Preludin was a mild stimulant which John and the others acquired mostly from the waiters, and in John's case, not surprisingly, from a barmaid girlfriend. Basically they were slimming pills which had to be taken with beer to have the right effect: they stirred the brain and the body into such activity that, until the effects of the pills wore off after twelve hours, the pill-taker could not bear to be still. Adrenalin poured from the system. Conveniently, the pills killed the appetite for food.

One effect of Prellys, as John and the Beatles christened them, was to give them a false confidence. After a few weeks John had grown to dislike the innate aggressiveness of the Germans. His waspish wit, born on Merseyside, was to be sharpened to perfection in Hamburg as the easy targets of nationalism and inhumanity during the war dawned on the super-sensitive John that hid beneath the loudmouth. 'What did you do during the fucking war? Bloody Krauts, Heil Hitler, back to your tank,' he would shout from the stand to nobody in particular, when he knew that amid the din nothing could be heard. John totally refused to learn German, though Paul and George and Stuart managed a few words and Pete Best had an O-level in the language. For John the Hamburg Experience, like hundreds of other very important periods in his life, was to be absorbed, used, then disposed of.

Hamburg was a hard baptism but there were side benefits. The young teenage girls who went to the clubs and the Reeperbahn cafés looking for men were attracted by the five good-looking, comparatively innocent young British lads. The girls warmed to John, Paul, George, Stuart, and Pete as a refreshing change from the tired businessmen and sex-starved sailors. There was not a lot of time for much besides working, sleeping, and playing cards – usually 'brag', a variation on poker. John, like the others, had the occasional relationship with girls during his first four-month visit to Hamburg. But to paint a picture of five teenagers wallowing in scenes of orgies and depravity – which has regrettably become part of the Beatles mythology during those years – is to fall victim to rumour and exaggeration. They dabbled with girls from time to time, but work, music, Prellys, and sheer exhaustion were by far the most important factors in their lives.

One girl, particularly, was to make an indelible impression on the Beatles, especially on Stuart and John. Astrid Kirchherr, born in 1938, the daughter of a sales director of Ford Motors in West Germany, was at first sight the least likely fan to visit the tacky Kaiserkeller club in which the Beatles played seven nights a week. Her visit there, and her subsequent closeness, particularly to Stuart and John, came through her boyfriend, Klaus Voormann. From childhood, and particularly during her teenage years, Astrid had taken a keen interest in art and had designed and made all her own clothes. Her friendship with the Berlin-born doctor's son had blossomed at a private art academy, Hamburg's Meisterschule. Klaus was crazy on rock 'n' roll and, as an illustrator, kept saying how much he wanted to design pop album covers. Astrid's emergent talent lay in photography, and she switched to studying that after first entering the college for dress design.

Klaus lived in a room in the house occupied by Astrid and her mother in the middle-class Hamburg suburb of Altona. Astrid's father had died when she was seventeen. When the Beatles arrived in Hamburg she was twenty-two, with an air of cool, independent assertiveness that perfectly matched her riveting good looks. Her cropped blonde hair, pure white skin, and big expressive eyes put John once again in mind of his goddess, Brigitte Bardot.

It was a row with Klaus that took Astrid to the Reeperbahn one summer evening in 1960. A few days earlier Klaus had walked out after their argument, gone to the cinema, and then drifted into the

The elegant love match: Stuart Sutcliffe and Astrid Kirchherr at her
Hamburg home in November 1961, just five months before Stuart died.
Stuart's clothes uncannily anticipate the uniform Brian Epstein was to
devise for the Beatles much later

seedy St Pauli district of Hamburg. Nice people never went there, still less inside the Reeperbahn clubs. But Klaus, hungry for the sounds of rock 'n' roll was drawn to a noise coming from a street called the Grosse Freiheit. He went downstairs in search of the sound and, once inside, unknowingly sat next to the Beatles who were watching the group on stage. They happened to be another Liverpool group, Rory Storm and the Hurricanes, featuring Ringo Starr on drums.

Klaus's first memory of that night is vivid, 'I couldn't believe the look of the boys whom I sat next to, and there wasn't much conversation as they couldn't speak German. But the sound when the Beatles eventually went on stage was amazing.' When John tore into rockers like 'Sweet Little Sixteen' and 'Roll Over Beethoven', the combination of teddy boy hairstyles and their music bowled over the enthusiastic Klaus. He wanted to talk to the group, judged Lennon to be the leader, and, when the session ended, asked John about designing album covers, which was his ambition. Lennon beckoned Klaus in the direction of Stuart, saying: 'Show it to him, he's the artist in the group.'

The next evening Klaus Voormann returned to the club to see the Beatles' full session. As an artist, as much as a rock 'n' roll fan, he was particularly fascinated by Stuart's appearance, for despite his lack of musical prominence he looked like the artist he was: scrawny, fragile, James Dean-like, with moody dark glasses, winklepicker shoes, and an air of shyness.

Klaus did not consider for a moment that in persuading Astrid to visit the club, three nights after his discovery of it, he would be marking the end of his own love affair. But immediately the leather-jacketed Astrid entered the Kaiserkeller with the Beatles on stage, her eyes fell on Stuart. The magnetism she radiated, all elfin-chic with a detached beauty that lifted her a million miles from the Reeperbahn scrubbers they had been used to, attracted Stuart.

Astrid's effect on the Beatles was enormous. On their four further visits to Hamburg in the two years that followed she was to offer them much more than the warmth, eggs and steaks and chips which they desperately missed, and total commitment as their closest German friend. She was to invest them with style and point them in a direction that would stir the world.

Her own firm leanings were towards the 'exis', who formed most of her friends at the Meisterschule. Derived from the existentialists, they were in the forefront of the avant garde. They believed firmly in rejecting universal values, and stamped their own imprimatur on everything from appearance to opinions: in art, fashion, music, and in personal behaviour the 'exis' were fiercely independent. Most of all, they wanted to define youthful freedom.

Stuart and Astrid were together, surprisingly without any resentment from Klaus, within a few nights, and both Astrid and Klaus and another friend, photographer Jürgen Vollmer, were to become part of the Beatles' coterie, inseparable from them when they played the club, and during the day too. Astrid persuaded her to let them take their photographs, and within a few weeks Stuart had moved into the Kirchherr home. Astrid's mother worried about his thin frame and decided he needed food and care.

Astrid and Klaus were the first intellectual Beatles fans. Before they arrived John and Stuart had enjoyed a long-standing special relationship, and Paul and John both felt passionately about music, but as a unit they came together only for blazing rock 'n' roll. Now Astrid and Klaus introduced them all to her home, to her friendly mother who spoke not a word of English but loved cooking them egg and chips. And Astrid gave them a glimpse of her style, mirrored in her all-black bedroom with its floor-to-ceiling silk sheets and huge mirrors which screamed individualism.

Today Astrid remains in the Hamburg she loves, her memories of Stuart and John indelibly etched in her mind. She carries her attachments to them both, for both John and Stuart gave her their guitar plectrums which she wears in her pierced right ear, as earrings. Her reflections on John and Stuart as twenty-year-olds, and the interaction of the Beatles before their meteoric rise to fame, are tempered with her visible love for the two.

'When I first met him,' she says, 'John had this knowledge of everything that surrounded him, because he had particularly high intelligence. But he didn't have much experience, and he was so *nosey*. He wanted to keep finding out everything. He had an innocence and didn't stop investigating, asking questions – about art, about clothes, about the German people, who fascinated him. Of course, he would take the mickey out of us: "Bloody Krauts", and all that. But I thought of him as a gentle, sentimental boy who was in such a hurry to find out about everything. Stuart was the same, but really he had a deeper natural intelligence than John. When they were together, it was very powerful for them both.'

No serious photographer had been near the Beatles. When Astrid took them to pose for her in the parks and fairgrounds they were 'incredibly excited', she says, at the results. 'I did big prints showing their expressions naturally, not asking them to pose, and they went crazy. They'd never seen anything like these in their lives. Jürgen Vollmer came down to take pictures of them too. He was fascinated by their appearance.' Indeed, one picture of Lennon standing in a Hamburg doorway was chosen by John fourteen years later as the cover for his 1975 album, *Rock 'n' Roll*.

Astrid says her clique dressed mostly in suede or velvet clothes, always black with white collars, and she often wore a short leather skirt. 'They'd never seen anything like the way we looked.' Still less had they witnessed a hairstyle like Klaus's. Tired of the fast-scissored traditional formula of Hamburg hairdressers, and looking for something that would emulate her own sense of the eccentric, Astrid had cut Klaus's hair herself for years. She *never* combed his hair backwards, always out from the side, and it was always longer than the accepted length. 'The Beatles were dressed like teddy boys, with these very, very pointed shoes which we in Hamburg had never seen before. We were fascinated with those, just like they were with our things,' says Astrid. 'And their very tight trousers and little tiny grey jackets. They didn't have many clothes, of course. And their hair was combed back with side-boards, like teddy boys.'

Stuart, the first to have his hair cut and styled by Astrid, faced John's scorn when, one night, he arrived at the club for work with what later became known as the Beatle haircut. 'John collapsed laughing,' Astrid says. 'He didn't have the guts to say, "Hey, that looks great", which is what he really thought. John was a complicated person when it came to showing his feelings like that: he hid his emotions. Because he could not bring himself to say what he really thought, he would cover it up and in doing that he would hurt people.' Shy Stuart was an easy target. The situation was not helped by the obviously strong love affair that had bloomed between him and Astrid.

'Stu at that time was really mad on her,' remembers Paul McCartney. 'We all fancied her a bit but it was, kind of, you know – "Hands off, I'm serious." I know you lot, you just like her, OK, but I mean this one, for me. . . . And anyway, she liked Stu. They hit it off very well and we used to chat with her friends. There was Klaus and Jürgen and Astrid, who were like the gang, and they used to have a couple of other mates of theirs who were from art school. They used to hang around the club, and got to like our band particularly because we were sort of different, too, from all the other groups. We were a bit more into the black leather and black polo sweaters. It was a different look at that time, like new wave or punk later. Astrid and her friends were great. They were

At the time of John's twentieth birthday, in October 1960, George, Stuart and John are pictured at a funfair at a Hamburg park where they often played to boost their income

like a different race of people because they dressed very differently. They dressed in all the black leather and black polo necks, and she had blonde, short-cut hair. She looked really great. I think all of us thought she looked great. But Stu. . . .'

Paul, always more conscious than the others about his appearance, was the next to ask Astrid to style his hair. 'He asked me what started me in cutting Klaus's hair. I told him I couldn't stand my boyfriend having greasy hair swept back, and the same with all my friends at art school. The boys did the girls' hair, and the girls did the boys'.'

John was the last Beatle to succumb to the Beatle cut. Only Pete Best declined, retaining his quiff and teddy boy aura that attracted the girls. 'John was the same with the collarless jackets which I designed and Stuart was the first to wear,' recalls Astrid. 'They all laughed when Stuart went in wearing one, and John always said he fancied my leather pants and jacket. But it took all of them to adopt the jacket before John could be bothered. He was defiant about clothes and appearances. He didn't like to be led, you know – for someone else to have thought of something before him.'

Astrid and Klaus had been together for two years, but she and Stuart became serious after two weeks. 'It was very hard for all of us. Klaus liked Stuart a lot, and Stuart had a conscious hurt about falling in love with me and hurting Klaus. John and Stuart had no problem about our love – we were in a sense all together, laughing at the same jokes, and John and Stuart had the same sense of humour, very black, very sick.'

It was Astrid, then, who injected a sense of style, in hair and clothes, into the Beatles. It wasn't just a question of how they looked, and what they wore, she would tell them at the club and at her home: it was their general presence, the way they moved, off stage as well as on it. The message got home years later when, as international stars, they acknowledged their debt to their Hamburg days and to Astrid.

If John and Paul got together as opposites, then Stuart was John's foil in an utterly different way. 'They had similar outlooks on life, and attitudes,' says Astrid. 'John really loved Stuart, in the best sense, but Stuart was never made aware of that love and worried about it. John always had to be the hard man, teasing Stuart about his looks, his bass playing, his singing, anything. Stuart took it all, and, being highly intelligent and sensitive, never replied much. John would know how far he could go. But something deep inside John stopped him from putting his hand on Stuart's shoulder and saying: "Hey, I love you." Which he did. I think John regarded Stuart as a mental rival.'

Stuart was less reticent about his friendship with John. Most of the time, when they were not working, John and Stuart were together. 'At first Stuart was very tight about talking because he was together with four boys who acted very rough. But when Stuart became loose, he talked to me about his love for John, how John was the only one in the group he could relate to. Stuart knew he was not a musician and only came into the group for John. Stuart was a genius and would have been a very, very great writer and painter.'

While John was heavy on Stuart from a paternal standpoint, Paul waded in with the impatience of a long-suffering perfectionist who was exerting his ambition and ability. Paul was playing the piano frequently between belting out 'Long Tall Sally' and other Little Richard rockers. When Stuart stepped forward with his tiny physique to take a singing solo with the Elvis Presley ballad 'Love Me Tender', McCartney would berate him. Paul didn't like the slowness of the song after the rockers, says Astrid. It is more likely that the ballad-loving Paul was just looking for a good excuse to dig at Stu.

But while Stuart would take John's knocks for his weak singing, Paul's digs cut more deeply. Stuart felt very inferior, with reason. 'He knew he couldn't play, and criticism coming from Paul was more than he could take,' says Astrid. 'John had persuaded Stuart to play bass guitar but he knew in his heart it was ridiculous. He was simply not a good player. Paul played bass better than Stuart, Paul played piano better than Stuart and John, and Paul played guitar as good as John, and Paul played drums. His heart and soul were in music. Paul used to have a lot of arguments with Stuart. He didn't like his singing much. But Paul was in a difficult situation. John was the leader, up there on stage. However good a musician Paul was, John just gave off this feeling of being the leader. And John wanted Stuart in the group. It was bound to lead to tension.'

Paul remembers Stuart as 'a great fellow, a very good painter who used to get picked on by us generally'. On the clashes, Paul says: 'One of the main problems was: he wasn't that good on bass. So what you had to do, if you were having a photo taken, was tell Stu to turn away, do a mean moody thing looking over his shoulder, 'cos you didn't want anyone to see what he was actually playing. 'Cos anyone who knew would realize he couldn't play it. He just used to turn his amp down and sort of make a bass noise. It was quite good. But he didn't know what key we were in half the time. He just put a lot of bass on it and sort of bluffed and stamped a lot, you know.'

An insight into the twenty-year-old Lennon comes from Astrid's memories of her drug experiences with him. 'I was always close to John,' she says, 'but he never allowed anyone to get inside him. Only when we took the pills did he open up about himself.' And to set the record straight about the pills, she says: 'Drugs? It was just a big laugh. The stories that the Beatles were all doped up during their visits to Hamburg is so much rubbish. We were young kids. George, particularly, was a baby of seventeen. We could only afford to drink beer, which was the cheapest, and then one of us discovered these little pills called Preludin. They were pep pills so that when you took them you felt no hunger. We called them slimming pills. We discovered that when you took them and drank beer, you felt great. You didn't get drunk but you got all speedy and talked away like mad. They were fifty pfennigs each and my Mummy used to get them for us from the chemist – you had to have a prescription for them, but my Mummy knew somebody at the chemist.

'We had maybe one and a half for the whole night. They'd last for seven or eight hours. And it was from those pep pills that I had my best talks with John. He and I would take them and then go out of the club for a long talk. The pills would make a person feel more relaxed. When John took one, he lost all his inhibitions.

'He would talk about his feelings and the things he liked. He'd say: "Oh, I want to tell you so much how I feel. I love you and I love Stu." Without the pills, he would never have given me this honesty. He would have choked up at telling the truth. And so most nights John would say: "Come on, Astrid, let's take some beans and talk." But to say he was kept going by pills in Hamburg is really rubbish. He was kept going by something deep within himself,' says Astrid forcefully.

Beatles mythology says that the five young men on their Hamburg trip wallowed in a sea of orgies and carried on as depraved sex maniacs, drug addicts, and alcoholics. John, Paul, George, Stuart, and Pete have been painted as five Liverpool louts rampaging through the Reeperbahn red light district, high on pep pills, using prostitutes all the time. Astrid, who was closer to the group than anyone, says adamantly that the stories are inaccurate, and have grown over the years into sheer fantasy. 'Prostitutes!' she laughs. 'First, they were too frightened to go anywhere near them, and secondly, they didn't have the money. Thirdly, and most importantly, they didn't need them. There were girls in the club sitting around waiting for John or Paul or George to go and sleep with them. But there were no sexual orgies. They all had their little affairs in Hamburg, but in 1960 even teenagers had a totally different sexual attitude towards one another. The girls were not prostitutes, they were seventeen or eighteen years old, and official-ly couldn't get into the club until they were eighteen. They were salesgirls or workers or students like me.

'The Beatles were five sweet, innocent young men, and they couldn't believe girls were falling in love with them. Yes, they had the occasional affairs, but definitely there was nothing wild about their behaviour.' In the popularity stakes, Paul was the most popular with the girls in the audience. 'He was always so neat and clean and the girls loved that,' says Astrid. But among the student friends whom she brought along John and Stuart carried the honours. 'We all thought they had more style,' says Astrid. It was John who christened Astrid and her friends the 'exis'.

On their relationship, the subject of much speculation by Beatles watchers, she says, 'He was attracted to me, and me to him, but it was more mental than sexual. We would hold hands occasionally but he would find it hard even to do that, because he would never, never have done anything to hurt his best friend Stuart. John always called me the German Brigitte Bardot and he admired my long blonde hair and small waist. I used to dress in the style he found fantastic – he went on and on about my black leather gear.

'I loved his mentality, not because I thought he was a sexy boy. That was reserved by me for Stuart, whom I adored and fancied right from the start. John was pleased for Stuart. Also, John told me he had left his girlfriend at home in Liverpool, so that was that.'

Alone among the Beatles, John would trudge to the Hamburg post office every week to send back to Cynthia the £35 he eventually earned at the Star-Club. 'I couldn't believe what he was doing,' says Henry Henroid, one of the club's booking agents who often walked with John to the post office. 'I said, "If you do this every week, what do you live on?"

'He said, "Oh I can earn a few marks by playing for this stripper round the back street in the afternoons." It was incredible – very responsible behaviour for a boy of that age. All the musicians seemed to booze their money away. John had to get it back to Liverpool quickly.'

John's obsessive 'noseyness', as Astrid describes it, was especial-ly evident at her home. He raided her book collection, taking a particular interest in works by the Marquis de Sade, and looking for any connection with sadism. 'You read books like *that?*' he said to Astrid once. 'It's dirty!' She reminded him of his own tendency to learn the rudest words in the German language, to augment what she described as 'John's most basic version of Hitler Deutsch'. 'He loved poking fun at the Krauts, shouting "Where's your tank?" at audiences. I told him about Jean Cocteau and books I'd read, whenever I met him, and he wanted to know everything. I'd end up buying them for him, in English, which was not easy to find.' Classical records formed most of Astrid's collection, with the odd Nat King Cole thrown in. Paul often went straight for her Stravinsky records, but John would shout: 'Take that off.'

Routine for the Beatles during their first Hamburg visit was totally bound up with work. They would collapse into bed around dawn after all-night sessions, sleep until midday, and often be collected by Astrid in the early afternoon for the ten-minute drive to her home. Nostalgic for British breakfasts, which Astrid or her mother cooked, they tucked into bacon, eggs, beans and toast at their whim. John struck up a particular affection for Astrid's mother: 'George and Paul just shook her hand and said hello, that was all. But never John. He always kissed her and put his arms around her. My Mummy admired John most after Stuart.'

Astrid smiles at aspects of the John Lennon she knew so closely. He choked up at the mention of the death of his mother two years before he went to Hamburg. 'John was rough and sweet and gentle all together, I often used to wonder if this was a mixture of his emotions at losing his mother and the fact that his father wasn't there during his childhood. If you asked him a question he would answer, but without being asked he wouldn't tell you anything about himself, unless he had taken a pill. You had to work very, very hard to get deep thoughts from inside him. But if you asked and you were sincere, as I was, he'd pour them out. "Yeah, most of my friends grew up with a Dad and a Mum," he'd say. "I missed all that."'

Because music and success meant much more to him than to Stuart, John adopted a fiercer, more penetrating character in Hamburg. Realizing that it was a heaven-sent make-or-break city for them to knock their act into shape, his humour was blacker even than during his Liverpool Art College years. 'Stuart shared the sick sense of humour,' says Astrid, 'but his was much happier than John's, which was always mean and cruel. I never knew why.'

Postcards and letters to Mimi would be conventional, and tell nothing of the exhausting test that was Hamburg. He told her nothing of the money problems, either; the £100 a week they expected fizzled into more like £15 a week each, says Paul McCartney. 'They were always broke, always,' says Astrid.

'John used to have his dreams about being as famous as Elvis Presley. George would say it would be OK to be as popular as Cliff Richard, that would be a start! Stuart said: "When I'm a famous painter, I'll buy you a Rolls-Royce." I said, "When I sell my first picture of you all to *Life* magazine I'll buy you a new leather jacket." '

John did indeed grow up in Hamburg, but the experience was to be more valuable to him than profitable. Word about the lively British teenagers' energetic appearances at the Kaiserkeller, and their indefatigable improvement in the face of the demon promoter Koschmider, soon spread around the tough city. Peter Eckhorn, a reputable promoter who ran the rival, bigger Top Ten club, invited the band over to watch another British act, Tony Sheridan, who worked as a solo singer. Unknown to John and the other Beatles, Koschmider had a friend who told him the fateful truth: the Beatles had appeared on stage with Tony Sheridan in a jam session, which was strictly forbidden under the terms of Koschmider's iron-fisted contract. He also feared that, like Tony Sheridan before them, the Beatles intended to leave the Kaiserkeller for the more sophisticated surroundings of the Top Ten club. In Hamburg, inter-club warfare was almost as intense as the fights that broke out inside them.

Koschmider struck back at the Beatles for their truancy in a devastating way. He called the police. George Harrison, aged seventeen, was arrested and jailed for a day for being under age while working in a foreign country, and deported home. Paul and Pete Best were ordered by Koschmider to leave, after allegedly causing a small fire to some sacks by using candles in their tacky digs behind the cinema screen in the club. John Lennon, unscathed but broken by the anti-climax of it all, wended his way home alone, leaving Stuart to the comfort of Astrid's home. They had become engaged, and Stu wanted to pursue painting in Hamburg.

John was penniless. The dreams of riches had been illusory. They had not made nearly so much money as expected, and what Deutschmarks they had earned had gone on clothes, beer, fags, and food. Dejectedly, he had drifted across on the ferry from the Hook of Holland to Harwich and by train to Lime Street Station and taxi home to Menlove Avenue.

Cynthia was at once pleased and sad at his return. Mimi, once more vindicated by the unlucky turn of events, had the additional irritation of having to pay his cab fare. 'What happened to the £100 a week you mentioned?' she asked John.

John's reply was to typify his sharp retorts as the Beatles story got into its stride later. 'Spent it all, Mimi.'

He was contrite, recalls Mimi, but with all her spirit she respected the streak in him that was to strike terror into the hearts of those who asked him 'damned stupid questions'.

'Once his mind was set on something,' says Mimi, 'nobody and nothing could shake him. He was down but not out.'

9
LIVERPOOL

'Right then, Brian, manage us'

Returning to Liverpool ignominiously from Hamburg, penniless and with an uncertain future, was bad enough. Going back to Aunt Mimi after experiencing the liberation of Gambier Terrace, the illicit nights with Cynthia, and Hamburg's wildness, was stultifying for John. With his best friend left behind, in love with Astrid, Lennon was at one of his lowest psychological ebbs during December 1960.

There were two consolations to add to the physical improvements of being back in a comfortable house, with Mimi's cooking and Cynthia's faithful knock on the front door, which came within a day of his return.

Both were musical. First, he was now equipped with a Rickenbacker guitar, a much sought-after Club 40 model which was his pride and joy. Secondly, less tangibly, the reputation of the Beatles' huge impact on Hamburg audiences had spread back to Liverpool's burgeoning beat scene. Derry and the Seniors had put the word about that the Beatles had taken the Kaiserkeller by storm and had only been ejected from Germany by an act of spite.

They had improved their act beyond all recognition in Hamburg, developing an almost manic energy and a repertoire twice as big as when they left Liverpool. Yet John knew that while he was a dominant leader on stage, he was not pushy or organized enough to give the group its thrust. His own ambition, to be bigger than Elvis, was unshaken. He had a new aggression after Hamburg. What he needed now, for his band so curiously called the Beatles, was a stroke of luck.

The twist of events throughout early 1961 and the rest of that year was to put the Beatles on the fastest-moving escalator to fame and fortune in the history of entertainment. Throughout his school and college years, and in the fights at the ballrooms and clubs of Liverpool and Hamburg, John had relied intuitively on fate smiling on him. It was as if someone was watching over him, baling him out of disasters in every step of his twenty years. Now, having flounced out of college, blown it in Hamburg where their name was being sullied by Koschmider as unreliable, and having to persuade Mimi that all would come right, John was irritable.

The biggest problem was, as ever, getting work for the Beatles in an increasingly competitive Liverpool beat scene. They sought refuge back at the Casbah in West Derby, where Mona Best welcomed her son's group with a triumphant poster on the door of the cellar in which they played: 'The Fabulous Beatles Are Back!' The coffee, snacks and Cokes were a far cry from the beer and Prellys of the Kaiserkeller, but in Liverpool, in December 1960, the Casbah was a haven for four young men facing the spectre of failure. Nor was there much joy at the Jacaranda, where Allan Williams was licking his own Hamburg wounds. But it was then, in that coffee bar, that the Beatles met the man who was to mark their career so forcefully.

Bob Wooler was a twenty-eight-year-old ex-railway clerk turned disc jockey whose knowledge of the mushrooming Liverpool beat group scene was encyclopaedic. John and Paul found a receptive ear in the man who was to be a vital link in the chain that ensured they got work. Wooler, with his unequalled grapevine knowledge of which group was coming up, sensed that the Beatles' Hamburg experience had made them special. He got them a date for £6, first at Litherland Town Hall where promoter Brian Kelly was amazed by their fiery energy. 'On their first appearance I was completely knocked out by them. They had a pounding, pulsating beat which I knew would be big box office. When they had finished playing I posted some bouncers on the door of their dressing-room to prevent some other promoters, who were in the hall, entering. I went inside and booked them solidly for months ahead.'

The Litherland dates became important for the Beatles, but Wooler was yet to deal his ace to them. He urged Ray McFall, owner of the Cavern club, a dingy, dank cellar and stronghold of traditional jazz at 10 Mathew Street in Liverpool's city centre, to give them a try. Lennon was ecstatic at the chain of events that was slowly but surely unfolding through Wooler.

Cynthia was still at art college. As far as Mimi was concerned, so was John. But in his mind he had quit college the day he set out for Hamburg, and had returned hell bent on music as a career. Until he was successful, he decided, it was best not to rock any boats with Mimi.

Wooler's memory of John in that desperate year of 1961 is of a hungry, difficult young man. He knew, says Wooler, that the Beatles were on the precipice of something, but worried that, instead of becoming successful, the scales might tip against them for want of both work and luck.

The Cavern, however, was to be the turning point for John and the Beatles. From their first appearance there the Beatles attracted not only their regular fans from West Derby, the area of the Casbah, but from Aintree and Litherland. Girls with beehive hairstyles from the typing pools nearby, in North John Street and Whitechapel, formed a new, quickly growing army of Beatles fans.

The Cavern, with little ventilation, appalling acoustics, walls dripping with dampness, stale air and cramped stage conditions, would tax even the most enthusiastic of young musicians. Its history was similar to dozens of cellar clubs in Britain in the late 1950s. It was a hotbed of traditional jazz featuring Liverpool's favourites, the Merseysippi Jazz Band and Manchester's Saints, with regular attacks from top London names such as Acker Bilk and Kenny Ball. The audiences were, in John Lennon's opinion, snobs against rock 'n' roll. He hated them for their superior attitude as trained musicians, their anti-pop attitude, and most of all because they always seemed to be well educated.

Over the next two and a half years the Beatles played the Cavern 292 times. They would play lunchtime and evening sessions, for a payment of around twenty five shillings a session. The Cavern was to represent, to John, something much more than success for the Beatles. He saw it as a crusade against jazz and all it stood for, 'with all those bloody musicians and their G.C.E.s'.

John told jazz singer George Melly, who had played the club with the Mick Mulligan Band: 'You lot kept us from getting into the Cavern and other places much earlier. All that jazz crap held us back.' Melly conceded this point to Lennon; once the steamroller of rock 'n' roll had gathered speed, the death knell of traditional jazz's boom years was sounded. Through Acker Bilk, Chris Barber, and Kenny Ball 'trad' had enjoyed a brief flirtation with pop success. But with rock 'n' roll groups, led by the Beatles, pulling in students, previously the jazz fans' natural audience, 'the game was up' as Melly succinctly puts it. Lennon relished the kill.

The tiny Cavern stage bulged with Pete Best's drum kit and cheap amplification, part of which had been 'permanently borrowed' from Liverpool Art College music room. Lennon's demeanour on that stage could be likened to that of a caged tiger: this was his domain. Here, he honed his short-sighted, head-tilted, legs-astride stance into a statement of defiance, much more than mere music. By the time that Lennon reached the Cavern, the Hamburg experience had galvanized his lithe, tallish frame into demonic energy.

Even now, the creative tension between John and Paul was rearing itself as they vied for the choice of songs. John made most of the announcements, taking the mickey out of the 'men in suits' who came. 'Shurrup, you with the suits on' became a regular Lennon message, especially to young teenagers who came during their lunch breaks from the insurance offices nearby. He mocked them for taking 'regular jobs'.

Among the regulars at the Cavern lunchtime sessions (admission one shilling) was Liz Hughes. She was a fourteen-year-old school-girl from Rock Ferry, across the Mersey, who saved the five shillings dinner money her parents gave her every week to spend on ferries and buses across to the city centre. Cavern sessions began at noon. At 11.45 precisely, dozens of Liverpool schoolgirls like Liz would eye the clock and get their belongings together to make a dash for it when the bell sounded. 'It was twelve-forty or even one o'clock before we reached the Cavern if we missed the first ferry,' says Liz. 'But it was worth it. Going to the Cavern and seeing the Beatles, the Big Three and later the Clayton Squares was almost like religion to certain kids of my age in those years.'

Today Liz Hughes and her husband Jim – another Cavern regular – are leading defenders of Liverpool's Beatles faith. They opened the Magical Mystery Store in 1978, and the Cavern Mecca in Mathew Street in 1981: this featured a Beatles museum and the re-creation of the old Cavern, complete with arches. As if in a time warp, Beatles music plays non-stop. Liz and Jim are the proud curators of what for millions was pop music's most important period.

Few women in Liverpool, outside the Beatles' family, can feel the warm nostalgia of that period with Liz Hughes' passion and intensity. She studied the style of John Lennon during the year that was, for him, the turning point of his life, the switch from potential bum to success beyond his wildest dreams.

'John always had this air about him,' says Liz. 'It gave all us kids the impression that if the audience had dropped dead, it would have gone right over his head. His attitude was as if he was saying: "I can take yer or leave yer. I'm here because this is something I wanna do, and I'm doing you lot a favour, not for the money."

'He looked as if he'd just stepped off the back of a motor bike. He usually wore dark clothes, crumpled trousers or jeans and a polo neck, but it was always unironed. They weren't in uniforms. It seemed that whatever caught their eye, or was on the back of the bedroom chair when he got out of bed, went on their backs. Except for Paul. He was the gentleman, the neat and tidy one who all the girls thought would be lovely to take home to their Mum. Paul played the part of the nice guy. But that John – he was the *animal*. The girls stood a bit back from him, a bit frightened. You never really knew which way he'd jump.

'I think John fed off Paul, but it was John who made most of the announcements. Paul would add to what John had said, but John made most of the first moves. They were obviously having a lot of fun. George was very quiet. A lot of the girls said he shouldn't be up there, he looked so embarrassed.' In the tiny dressing-room from which Bob Wooler would make his introductions of the Beatles, so much more majestically than for any other group, a few lucky teenage girls would huddle with the sweating Beatles after the session. They giggled at George's admission that he stuffed cardboard in the toes of his precious winklepicker shoes to ensure they remained pointed.

'Paul was safe and pretty, neat and tidy. George was so vulnerable. John looked like the sort of lad who would whip you up an entry, say thank you very much after he'd pleased himself, and ta-ra. All the girls were wary of him. He gave the impression of being so hard.'

What separated John, particularly, from all the other musicians who got on that three-feet-high Cavern stage, was his complete lack of professionalism. He would just stop singing or playing a song – dead – in the middle and start talking to Paul, for no apparent reason. He would light a cigarette, announce a new song, and carry on, with no explanation to the audience. 'It was like a permanent rehearsal. But he was someone you couldn't take your eyes from,' says Liz Hughes. 'My friend Deidre was absolutely crazy about him, but if he'd spoken to her, she'd have run a mile. That was a typical reaction. Her admiration was mixed with a fear of John. He was dangerous to all the girls, and that's what made him so attractive.

'The men in the audience took to him. He was a real man's

man.' Jim Hughes agrees. 'Some of the lads modelled themselves on him. They'd lounge around the walls of the Cavern trying to imitate his stance, the way he held a fag, the legs astride, the lot.'

The music was like nothing else heard in Britain at that time. John's favourite songs, giving full rein to his leathery vocal work which had been hardened by the Kaiserkeller, were included in a set which usually featured this repertoire, refined in Hamburg: 'What'd I Say', 'Boys', 'Will You Love Me Tomorrow', 'Wooden Heart', 'C'mon Everybody', 'Twenty Flight Rock', 'Hallelujah I Love Her So', 'Mailman', 'Red Sails In The Sunset', 'Crying, Waiting, Hoping', 'Over The Rainbow', 'Mean Woman Blues', 'Lucille', 'Hey Good Looking', 'Blue Moon of Kentucky', 'Love Me Tender', 'Corinne Corinna'.

But it was John's magnetism, and his merciless mickey-taking of anyone in the audience who proved an easy target, that gave them that edge. There was no alcohol in the Cavern, and the Coca-Cola the Beatles always had by their side was in bottles, for these were the days before cans. It was just as well, for one day, early in their residency at the lunchtime sessions, Aunt Mimi decided to visit the Cavern. John had still not told her that he had left college. His days were spent hanging round the record shops, playing at the Cavern, or meeting Paul wherever they could manage it, to develop their songwriting. Mimi, uncharacteristically lost for words at the sight of Lennon in full flight amid the sweat in such unsalubrious surroundings, could manage just eight sardonic words when he came off stage to take a break. She awaited him in the dressing-room.

'This is nice, John. This is *very* nice.'

John put his arm around her, but she stomped off.

The longer the Beatles dug in as the resident band at the Cavern, the more confident and more aggressively ambitious he became. Soon they were so popular that they played on Monday, Wednesday and Friday lunchtimes as well as on Wednesday and Sunday nights. It was a claustrophobic hell-hole but a massive breakthrough to Lennon; apart from Cynthia, this was the greatest anchor of his life so far. Even Mimi, who now knew by mid-1961 that he was channelling everything into a life in music, had to concede that at least he had a goal, however errant. He was also earning a little money.

The fans, who hung on their every song, soon developed unswerving loyalties. The roles were cast. John, the tough, abrasive, fiercely masculine leader whose quick mouth could wound in a flash, carried the male vote. Paul wooed the girls with his flashing

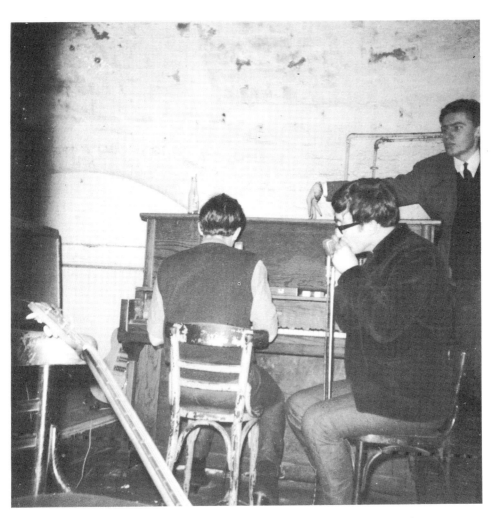

October 1962. Behind closed doors at Liverpool's Cavern Club John plays harmonica and Paul piano at rehearsal. McCartney's chair had been 'borrowed' from the Star-Club, Hamburg. Mike McCartney is standing by the piano

big eyes, comparatively immaculate dress, and romanticism set to music. George, enigmatic, shy, getting the music right, the apprentice electrician at Blackler's department store opposite Lime Street Station, was by far the best guitarist. And Pete Best at the back, on drums, had those sharply defined features but slightly sulky detached air that made him very popular with the girls. The contrasts, together with the electricity within the group, meshed perfectly.

Even in 1971, when the Beatles had split amid acrimony, Paul was admitting that his 'best playing days were at the Cavern lunchtime sessions'.

'We'd go on stage with a cheese roll and a cigarette and we felt we had really something going in that place. The amps used to fuse and we'd stop and sing a Sunblest bread commercial while they were being repaired. We used to do skits. . . .I'd do a Jet Harris impersonation because he'd played there. He fell off the stage once and I'd fall off it, too. You couldn't beat it.'

There was no contest between Lennon and McCartney for attention. They knew they attracted different people. Paul developed a warm friendship with the fans, while John tended to keep at a distance, retaining his slightly sinister mystique compounded by his increasing short-sightedness and refusal to wear glasses.

Before long, Lennon had nicknamed the crowd of schoolgirls who surrounded the stage most lunchtimes 'the Beatlettes'. Aged between fourteen and seventeen, the eight members of this elite clan shouted song requests, fetched the boys Cokes, and were the group's earliest known entourage. After evening sessions, the Beatles' blue Commer van, driven by Pete Best's friend Neil Aspinall, would even drop the girls at their homes to demonstrate to their parents that everything was 'above board' and that nothing was happening to their daughters, whatever the hour.

Hilary Williams, then a confirmed Beatlette of sixteen and now a Liverpool nurse, says that for all John's toughness he showed her and her schoolgirl friends a different side to his character at lunchtime or evening sessions. 'It was he who realized we were too young to have much money. The Beatles were each allowed one guest free in the club and John said we should be given that free ticket because we had been with them from the start. And one day he bought me a cup of tea for threepence. I couldn't believe it. Neither could my friends. "*What?*" they said. "Lennon, the big he-man, bought you a cup of tea? Why?" It was because he asked me how I could afford to keep coming, and I said I couldn't and I was broke that lunchtime. He just came up and put the cup by my side.'

John was palpably sexual, even to sixteen-year-old girls in 1961. But Hilary Williams remembers that he had a code of honour with her and her innocent friends. 'John would swear more than anyone else from that stage. If a string broke on his guitar, or if he was angry with the way a show was going, he'd curse all right! But in the 1960s, there were either decent, well-brought up girls, or there were tarts. He knew the Beatlettes were not tarts and treated us kindly and carefully.' Hilary Williams still has a rare memento of those years, a leather jacket she dared to wear on her Cavern outings. It still reeks of the unmistakable Cavern dampness, which the author experienced.

When the Beatles adjourned for beer to the Grapes, the pub just along Mathew Street from the Cavern, the Beatlettes and other supporters who were under drinking age would mournfully leave them and go into the Kardomah coffee bar in nearby Whitechapel. John and Paul would follow them later and buy them tea. Lennon's staple lunch would be a cheese sandwich followed by his own special weakness, red jelly. Hilary Williams said to her two brothers, who admonished her for bothering with the ruffians at the Cavern: 'They'll be famous one day, just you wait and see.'

For the schoolgirls who went to the Cavern and lived and breathed Beatles as a hobby, there was one major problem: Cynthia Powell. She was known to be John's art student girlfriend, and the very sight of her entering the Cavern made the possessive Beatlettes go schoolgirl crimson with a combination of jealousy and embarrassment. Outwardly, they were friendly to the twenty-two-year-old, but as they huddled together beneath the stage and in the Kardomah they could not contain their resentment. 'We called her Cindy to try to appear friendly, but it was no use,' says Hilary Williams. 'We couldn't compete. She had long blonde hair, and black leather, a real arty look, whereas we were dressed in denim. Looking back now, it's obvious she was a lovely girl, but at the time feelings were very strong against her. She'd got our John!'

When Cynthia went to the Cavern, John's behaviour changed. 'He swore less from the stage and was more gentle. There was even a rumour that Cindy was not his steady girlfriend but that he'd been out with another girl named Iris. Well, a few of us decided that was a cover-up to put us off knowing that he was serious with Cindy.' Hilary and other Beatlettes saw their defeat at the hands of

Cynthia avenged one night. After a Cavern session, Paul McCartney conscientiously drove the girls to their homes in the Allerton area. First to be dropped off, in Menlove Avenue, was John. 'It was two o'clock in the morning, very late. We'd all just been talking after a session,' recalls Hilary Williams. 'Cynthia came out of his Auntie's house and hit him over the head with a bread board. We all collapsed with laughter in the van.'

The Beatles' popularity in Liverpool spread like an epidemic throughout 1961. 'It was horrible when that happened,' says Hilary Williams. 'They weren't ours any more. Girls used to come in at lunchtime and in the evenings from Widnes, St Helens, and Aintree. They were the ones who started the screaming for John or Paul. The earliest fans never screamed. But the new ones took sides with whichever Beatle they fancied.'

Competition was intense among the groups. Although they had different sets of fans, there was a special rivalry between the Beatles and Gerry and the Pacemakers. 'There was this contest for who was the best band in Liverpool,' says Gerry Marsden. 'But the nice thing was, we never nicked songs from each other. For a start, the Beatles didn't have a pianist as we did, so that gave us more room for Jerry Lee Lewis-type songs. We watched the Beats, as I called them, and they watched us, but there was this unbreakable rule that we never nicked songs. It was all done very politely, as a swap: John would say: "Ere, can we have 'Jambalaya' if we give you 'Some Other Guy' or something like that?"

Gerry remembers Lennon as more outgoing than the other Beatles. 'He was always more involved in more things than the others were. It wasn't just the group to him during the Cavern and ballroom dates. He was interested in seeing whatever else was happening around him. I spent more time with John because he was always up and ready.'

The Beatles and Gerry and the Pacemakers shared the bill on scores of Merseyside dates, even combining forces, at one memorable, crazy night at Litherland Town Hall, to become the Beatmakers. 'After a show, it would always be John who'd be the first one to say, "Yeah", if I said, "Coming for a pint, then?" Paul or the others would more often say: "No, I'm just going to run through this song." '

Marsden, the former British Railways van driver, and Lennon, whose caustic wit was more than a match for Gerry's sharpness, became firm friends. That closeness developed in Hamburg, where

Gerry's group played the Top Ten club while the Beatles played the Kaiserkeller. 'So we never had a chance to see them on stage in Hamburg. We played the sets and met for drinks or meals afterwards.' Gerry went to the Cavern to see them immediately they returned from Germany. 'And I said to my brother Fred, who played drums with my band: "John and Paul are going to be big, big, big. Never mind what happens to the Beatles, there's nothing can stop those two." I couldn't believe how good they were. The energy, the way they shaped up to the microphone together, you know – Paul, the left-handed bass player, John standing there, couldn't give a shit, the *attitude* of the man. I thought: "They'll be the first band out of Liverpool to make it." '

Lennon was not even a great guitarist, says Gerry. 'John never claimed to be a great player: "I'm a cinema-verité player," he once said. Nor was he a good pianist, although he dabbled on it when there was no one around. But I could always tell a Lennon guitar touch, even when he was just strumming. It came at you from an angle. It wasn't like anyone else. And that voice! In the Cavern, on the stage at Litherland, he'd belt out "Memphis Tennessee" or any Chuck Berry songs and I'd say to myself immediately: "*That's* John Lennon!" Much more important than anything is to have a distinctive voice. It's more important than any other quality. It doesn't have to be fantastic in any way, or never sound flat, or never raunchy. It's got to be a voice on its own for rock 'n' roll, and John had that like nobody else I know. His vibration on stage was special, because he simply stood there, with this attitude: "I'm going to have a bloody good time, hope you'll join me." '

Gerry shared John's sick humour. 'He'd sit in a pub doing a drawing, which appeared quite straight, a doodle. Then suddenly at the back would be a pair of crutches. I'd fall about laughing, because he had this black macabre sense of sick humour. He was always taking the mickey out of cripples, or walking down the street around Liverpool he'd pretend to be one. I went along with it because I found it funny, too.' Once, in a Paris jazz club, a drunken John and Gerry did a crushingly accurate imitation of cripples. As the two men lurched uproariously around the club, the mostly sober audience sat back, flabbergasted at the sight.

Another who was at the Cavern one lunchtime was a girl named Priscilla Maria Veronica White. She was never the official hat check girl at the cellar but occasionally, when she was broke, Priscilla asked the doorman if she could be allowed in free if she volunteered to help with the cloaks.

It was John Lennon who remarked, 'Pretty girl, Brian,' to

Epstein one lunchtime, when Epstein had become their manager. And the girl went on to become, under the name Cilla Black, a singing star and comedienne in the Gracie Fields tradition.

Cilla recalls: 'I played truant from Anfield Commercial College to see the Beatles at lunchtime sessions. At that time I was singing with some of the local bands, billed as "Swingin' Cilla", on a semi-professional basis. But this was the first time I had my chance to sing with the Beatles.

' "What's your name, girl?" asked John.

'When I told him he yelled: "Do you hear that, lads? She's got a boy's name. This is Cyril who is going to have a bash at singing something with us."

'John went on: "What key do you sing in, Cyril?"

'When I said I had no idea – because I'd never had a lesson in my life! – he shouted: "Let's try a Yale!"

'The group had just come back from Germany and wore gear they'd bought in Hamburg. John's hair was much longer then than Brian Epstein ever let him wear it later on. It was brushed forward instead of back and he had an enormous pink leather hat over it. He had black leather pants on, lined with red satin, black T-shirt, black leather jacket, and high black boots with Cuban heels. I took one look and thought: "Oh, my God!"

'At the end of 1961 I was appearing with Kingsize Taylor and the Dominoes at the Tower Ballroom in New Brighton. The Beatles were on the same bill. I noticed a very smart man deep in conversation with John. John told me it was their new manager, but I just laughed because I thought this was another of John's jokes. Then he took me over and introduced me. It was Brian Epstein and he'd just signed the Beatles. Even then John was still doing his "Cyril" thing with me: "Come over here, Cyril, I want you to meet Brian Epstein."

'It was John who persuaded Brian to listen to me. He told Brian that he should sign me up. I did an audition at a club in Birkenhead with the Beatles backing me. I must have been dreadful because I was very nervous. Brian didn't say anything at all and I didn't like to ask him what he thought. Eight months later he signed me. I remember I used to be dead scared of John, although he was the one who had helped me most. He had this aura of super-intelligence. I hated being left alone to speak to him. Once he said: "What's wrong with you, girl? Don't you like me?"

'I confessed, "I'm frightened of you, John."

'He roared with laughter: "And I thought you were a snob!"

'After that we often talked. John loved coloured singers – many

October 1962. John launches into one of his imitations of deformity in a jokey backstage session at the Cavern. Paul gives a helping hand, Cavern owner Ray McFall joins in, and Cynthia watches the camera

of my own American favourites. He talked about his songs, but the memory which stands out is the way he admitted he longed to become a famous actor one day.'

John loathed crowds. He told me, in the midst of the Beatles' fans wildest scenes, when he was waving at thousands of them from a hotel balcony in Munich: 'I'd hate to be in the middle of that. I couldn't stand being hemmed in.' The seething Cavern crowds made him feel claustrophobic, too.

If Liverpool rock 'n' roll was a religion in the early 1960s, then the parish priest was Bob Wooler. Until the old Cavern was closed on 27 May 1973 to make way for an excavation shaft for an underground railway link, Wooler was able to take people down there and affectionately recreate those halcyon days. Today, the great Cavern compère is an institution among Beatles fans who marvel at his place in history, having survived the stifling, sweaty cubby hole they called a dressing-room which he shared with the Beatles. His memories of Lennon tempered by an historic punch-up with him, are warm and respectful. When the Beatles returned to Liverpool for the northern première of their film *A Hard Day's Night* in 1964, Wooler went to Speke airport and was greeted by a typical Lennon remark: 'Hi, Bob. Has anyone given you a black eye lately?'

McCartney was his perfect foil, says Wooler; both John and Paul realized that the group needed John's edge, but Paul was there to apologize when John offended people. 'I have rarely seen any one person embody youth so much as Lennon did in those years,' says Bob Wooler. 'He had aggressiveness, but not aggression. He would stand straddling the far left of the stage and look, unseeingly, into the audience because he was *so* short-sighted. It was obvious the applause was washing over him, but he loved it. He managed to give off this attitude of not caring two hoots, but deep down I know he did. He loved every minute. I told him he reminded me of the actor Kirk Douglas and he said that was rather high-sounding. He did have a cleft chin like Kirk Douglas and that was part of his appeal to the girls. But he was adored by both sexes.'

Wooler remembers John as a 'very black and white character who couldn't be bothered with people'. The identification of Lennon in black and white is significant: the Cavern was totally black and white in appearance and in atmosphere, and John often told his friends that he preferred the earthy simplicity of mono films and art to colour: it was partly because the film *Help!* was in unreal colour that he felt it ended up looking tawdry. 'In the Cavern,' says Bob Wooler, 'the shadows and the starkness helped the Beatles create a great drama from their music. It was love us or loathe us, but that's how we are, straight ahead, black and white.'

From his close encounters with Lennon, Bob Wooler's overall view is that there was so much loneliness in his life that the thing he most feared was showing his tears. As an example of John's vulnerability, Wooler recalls the day Aunt Mimi went to the Cavern lunchtime session. 'It was the custom, if a father like Jim McCartney or any close relative came to see the group, to dedicate a record to him or her,' says Wooler. 'But John insisted that no record should ever be played for Mimi or any of his mates. I think she would have loved it, but it might have given people in the crowd the feeling that John was a softie, and that image was never allowed to register.'

The problem for John, when the Beatles became famous, was that, never having believed in himself, he could not fully absorb what was happening. 'Paul's horizon had already been in focus, so he was ready. But John was really thrown by it all,' says Bob Wooler. Lennon, he says, had a love/hate relationship with the Cavern but often admitted that, because it was so difficult to play on account of its acoustics, it had played a big part in forcing the Beatles to 'play hard'.

Coincidentally, Liverpool Art College canteen, where they first played, was also a basement with arches. But, in a totally different sense, the ambition to climb out of that damp, sweaty, unlicensed catacomb that had no acoustics became John's greatest incentive for the Beatles. 'We couldn't get out of the place fast enough,' he said. He wasn't ungrateful for what the Cavern had done for them, but to John any form of regularity very quickly became monotony. This was the restlessness that was to mark his life, and make him so utterly different from his partner, Paul McCartney. Once a thing was rolling along, Lennon wanted to move on: a new kick, a fresh challenge, something a little dangerous. Thus the Cavern had to be escaped from.

Many people who were in Liverpool during 1961 could claim to have played a big role in giving the Beatles the thrust that enabled them to break out of the confines of the city into a London recording studio, with all that led to. Bill Harry, who saw most of their Cavern shows and had been at art college with John, encouraged John in his early writings, diverted Brian Epstein to the Cavern, which was to lead to a great partnership, and can claim to have been the first to publish John's words.

Harry saw the rumblings of a big beat group scene on Merseyside in 1960. With Stuart Sutcliffe, he was on the students' union committee, so it was inevitable that Sutcliffe would lobby for his best friend's band to get work. As a friend of Stuart's, Bill had been to the Gambier Terrace flat which Lennon shared with him. There he first became aware of John's weird sense of humour, his special way with words, and his ability to draw. 'We'd drink at Ye Cracke and then spend entire evenings at the flat in Gambier Terrace or at another student's flat in Huskisson Street,' says Bill. They played games, many of them invented by John. They sat in a circle, including Rod Murray and his girlfriend Dizzy who occupied the flat next to Stuart's. 'John suggested we create stories by saying whatever came into our heads. One person would reel off a few sentences, and the following person would continue unfolding the story. We laughed till the tears ran down our cheeks at some of the tales, particularly John's, which were often cruelly suggestive with references to spastics, cripples, and crutches.

'When Margaret Duxbury fell asleep on the bed, John suggested we get potatoes and use matchstick legs to make them look like spiders. We suspended them from the ceiling so that she'd get a shock when she woke up. All this made me realize that John had a macabre sense of humour and a creative turn of mind.'

It was that electricity from Lennon that connected with Bill Harry when he was about to launch, with great foresight, a newspaper called *Mersey Beat*. Bill had talked about poetry with John in Ye Cracke. Lennon said he wrote it occasionally and grudgingly showed some of his rough work to Bill. 'I liked it, particularly since it wasn't a pastiche of Beat Generation poetry which was all the rage with other students,' says Bill. 'It once again indicated his individuality. In fact, the group actually backed a beat poet named Royston Ellis. He'd been booked by Liverpool University to read his poetry there, and he later talked the Beatles into providing backing for his readings at the Jacaranda.

'In 1961, when I was preparing *Mersey Beat*, I remembered John's poetry and decided to ask him to write for the paper, beginning with a biography of the Beatles.' Bill was a fan of the group and saw them perform several hundred times.

'I met him at the Jacaranda for the copy and he shoved two pieces of paper torn from an exercise book into my hands. He seemed embarrassed by the piece. It was like no other biography of a band and I told him I'd be pleased to print it, which cheered him up no end.' In the piece, John spelled Paul's surname wrongly, calling him McArtrey, as he had done in letters to Cynthia from Hamburg. The humour and light touch of John's first printed work was a talking point among the local beat population; it read like this:

Being a Short Diversion on the Dubious Origins of Beatles
Translated from the John Lennon.

Once upon a time there were three little boys called John, George and Paul, by name christened. They decided to get together because they were the getting together type. When they were together they wondered what for after all, what for? So all of a sudden they all grew guitars and fashioned a noise. Funnily enough, no one was interested, least of all the three little men. So-o-o on discovering a fourth little even littler man called Stuart Sutcliffe running about them they said, quote 'Sonny get a bass guitar and you will be alright' and he did – but he wasn't alright because he couldn't play it. So they sat on him with comfort 'til he could play. Still, there was no beat, and a kindly old man said, quote 'Thou hast not drums!' We had no drums! they coffed. So a series of drums came and went and came.

Suddenly, in Scotland, touring with Johnny Gentle, the group (called the Beatles called) discovered they had not a very nice sound, – because they had no amplifiers. They got some. Many people ask what are the Beatles? Why Beatles? Ugh, Beatles how did the name arrive? So we will tell you. It came in a vision – a man appeared on a flaming pie and said unto them 'From this day on you are Beatles with an A'. Thank you, Mister Man, they said, thanking him.

But before we could go we had to grow a drummer, so we grew one in West Derby in a club called Some Casbah and his trouble was Pete Best. We called 'Hello Pete, come off to Germany!' 'Yes!' Zooooom. After a few months, Peter and Paul (who is called McArtrey, son of Jim McArtrey, his father) lit a Kino (cinema) and the German police said, 'Bad Beatles, you must go home and light your English cinemas.' Zooooom, half a group. But even before this, the Gestapo had taken my friend little George Harrison (of Speke) away because he was only twelve and too young to vote in Germany: but after two months in England he grew eighteen, and the Gestapoes said 'you can come.' So suddenly back in Liverpool Village were many groups playing in grey suits and Jim said 'Why have you no grey suits?' 'We don't like them, Jim' we said speaking to Jim. After playing in the clubs a bit, everyone said 'Go to Germany!' So we are. Zooooom. Stuart gone. Zoom zoom, John (of Woolton) George (of Speke) Peter and Paul zoom zoom. All of them gone.

Thank you club members, from John and George (what are friends).

Readers told Bill Harry they liked the piece, so he asked John to contribute a regular column. 'He turned up at the office with an untidy bundle of papers and I leafed through them, completely enchanted by the strange stories, drawings, short tales, and political satires.' As a fan of the *Daily Express* column Beachcomber, Bill Harry decided to call John's column Beatcomber because John's work seemed to have 'inspired lunacy'.

His first piece under the name Beatcomber, was headlined SMALL SAM, and read:

> Once upon a Tom there was a small little Stan, who was very small. 'You are very small, Stan,' they said. 'I am only little,' replied Stan answering, feeling very small. Who could blame him, for Stan was only small. 'You must be small, Stan,' people were oft heard to cry, noticing how extremely small Stan was in fact. But being small (Stan was small) had its condensations. Who else but Stan (the small) could wear all those small clothes?
>
> Stan was highly regarded by everyone (for Stan was small and little). However, one day Stan saw an adverse in the Mersey Bean for 'Club you quickly grow your boots.' So on that very day Small Stan (by name called) purchased a pair of the very same. So now when Stan passes by, folks say, 'Is that not small Stan wearing a pair of those clubs you quickly grow you boots?' And it is.

In a satire on the hit record 'The Lion Sleeps Tonight', by the Tokens, John's Beatcomber column one week had a safari theme:

On Safairy With Whide Hunter

In the jumble. . .the mighty jumble. . .Whide Hunter sleeps tonight. At the foot of the bed, Otumba kept wogs for poisonous snacks such as the deadly Cobbler and Apple Python.

Otumba awoke him with a cup of teeth, and they lit up towards the jumble.

'Ain't dat Elepoon Pill?' said Wipe Hudnose, 'wearing his new Basuti?'

'Could be the flying Docker on a case.'

'No he's walking,' said Otumba in swahily which is not arf from here as the crowbarks. All too soon they reached a cleaner in the jumble and set up cramp.' Jumble Jim, whom shall remain nameless, was slowly, but slowly asking his way through the underpants (underware he was being washed by Whide Hunter).

'Beat the bus Otumbath!' commanded Whide Hunter.

'No, but mayble next week it will be my turn to beat the bus now standing at platofrbe nine.'

Jumping Gym, who shall remain Norman, spotted Whit Monday and the Barking Doctrine shooting some rhinostrills and hipposthumous and Otumbark.

'Stop shouting those animoles!' But it hab no influence upod them. They carried on shotting, alligarters, wild boats, garriffes, lepers and Uncle Tom Cobra and all. . .Old Buncle Ron Gabble and all. . .Bold Rumple Bom Dobby and all. . .Bad Runcorn Sad Toddy and all.

Walking into the *Mersey Beat* office at 81A Renshaw Street one day, John forked out with his own cash to place these five classified advertisements in the paper, asking that they should definitely not be printed in sequence, but should be scattered among other adverts:

HOT LIPS, missed you Friday, RED NOSE
RED NOSE, missed you Friday, HOT LIPS
ACCRINGTON welcomes HOT LIPS and RED NOSE.
Whistling Jock Lennon wishes to contact HOT NOSE.
RED SCUNTHORPE wishes to jock HOT ACCRINGTON

Clearly, John's early poems, together with his famous exercise book of lampooning called the *Daily Howl* which he had invented at Quarry Bank, was an indication of the literary style for which he was to be lavishly praised only a few years later. *In His Own Write*, and *A Spaniard In The Works*, were more sophisticated continuations of these early stabs at poetry and satire. There was an Englishness to his work that ran in sharp contrast to the stream-of-consciousness poetry of the American beat poets of the day, like Allen Ginsberg. John's work was to presage the rise of Liverpool beat poets and can now be seen as an indicator of the assertiveness of Liverpool people in various arts, away from the American influence of the time.

Mersey Beat acquired another occasional contributor: Brian Epstein. Aged twenty-seven, he ran the record department of the local NEMS store in Whitechapel. Fascinated by the activity of local beat groups, he had read the newspaper from cover to cover after first stocking it at Bill Harry's request. The first issue sold out a dozen copies in Epstein's department; the second sold two hundred and forty copies. 'It was a musical wonderland on his own doorstep which he hadn't been aware of, and he asked if he could contribute a regular record review column,' says Bill Harry. 'He'd call me each week and I'd visit him in his office for chats about the local scene.' About this time, the expanding *Mersey Beat* needed new offices, and during the paper's move many of John's poems were lost. When he was told, Lennon wept on the shoulder of Bill Harry's wife, Virginia.

Theoretically, Brian Epstein was the least likely mentor of the Beatles, particularly after the rumbustious Allan Williams. He spoke articulately, or, as the Beatles would describe it, 'posh'. He dressed immaculately, in suit and tie, and carried a briefcase. He was painfully shy and would wilt at the slightest dig against his personality. And he was from a middle-class, respectable, Jewish family.

Pride and punctiliousness, rather than a love for pop music, led Brian Epstein to the Beatles. He was more interested in Sibelius than any other sounds. As a businessman, though, he wanted all his teenage customers to be satisfied. One of his biggest boasts was that if he did not have a record in stock when it was asked for, he would get it.

So when Raymond Jones, a regular NEMS record buyer, walked into the shop on 28 October 1961, and asked for 'My Bonnie', by the Beatles, Brian Epstein was flummoxed. He had heard of neither the group, whose weird name he could not spell, nor the record. Jones explained that it was a Liverpool group and the record had been made in Hamburg. Epstein promised to investigate, and wrote down on his familiar pad: 'My Bonnie, The Beatles. Check on Monday'.

A few phone calls on Monday elicited some facts. The Beatles had made the record in Hamburg as a backing group and copies of it were available on the Polydor label. And not only did the group still exist – they played regularly, unknown to Brian, a little more than two hundred yards away in a cellar club he had never heard of, called the Cavern. He suddenly clicked with the familiarity of the names from the pages of *Mersey Beat*, and he asked Bill Harry to arrange for him to go to the club.

The man who was to become the Beatles manager, was a complex character. His background, although more genteel and conservative, shared one striking characteristic with the Beatles. He had been expelled from Liverpool College at the age of ten 'for inattention and for being below standard'. The crunch that caused his expulsion came when, during a maths lesson, he designed beneath his desk a programme featuring dancing girls. 'My parents despaired many times over the years, and I don't blame them, for throughout my schooldays I was one of those out-of-sorts boys who never quite fit,' Epstein wrote later. 'I was ragged, nagged and bullied and beloved of neither boys nor masters.' By ten, he had been to three schools and settled in none of them. He was top of his class at art, poor at mathematics and the sciences, and, after failing many entrance examinations for public schools, was accepted at Wrekin College in Shropshire. He went to RADA before deciding that actors were too narcissistic, and subsequently returned to Liverpool and the family business after an apprenticeship in salesmanship at Times Furnishing in Lord Street, Liverpool.

By the time he reached the Cavern, Epstein had seen the Beatles without realizing it. They had visited his record department in the afternoons, and he had dismissed them in his mind as scruffy layabouts whom he hoped would go away. 'I had been bothered a little with the frequent visits of a group of scruffy lads in leather and jeans. . .chatting to the girls and lounging on the counters listening to records. They were pleasant enough boys, untidy and a little wild, and they needed haircuts,' said Brian.

'I mentioned to the girls in the shop that I thought the youth of Liverpool might while their afternoons away somewhere else but they assured me that the boys were well behaved and they occasionally bought records. Also, said the girls, they seemed to know good discs from bad. Though I didn't know it, the four lads were the Beatles, filling in part of the long afternoons between the lunchtime and evening shows in the beat cellars.'

Brian Epstein's visit to the Cavern embarrassed him for two reasons. First, he felt conspicuous as the well-dressed adult amid a surging crowd of schoolgirls with beehive hairstyles who spoke a language all their own between Cokes and ham rolls. Secondly, Bob Wooler, the Cavern disc jockey, marked Brian's arrival with a magisterial announcement that 'Mr Epstein of NEMS' was in the audience and would the crowd please give him a big hand. Brian blushed.

'I had never seen anything like the Beatles on any stage,' Epstein recalled later. 'They smoked as they played and they ate and talked and pretended to hit each other. They turned their backs on the audience and shouted at them and laughed at private jokes.' Epstein was both irritated and mesmerized at the unruly group that radiated raw talent. Whatever it was coming from that stage in a dungeon, he could not take his eyes from it.

Although he had several girlfriends, Brian Epstein was a homosexual. It has been said that he had a fixation for John Lennon in particular, from that first sight of him on the Cavern stage. Since both men are dead, and neither spoke on the subject during his life, it is a matter of pure conjecture. Brian had a deep fascination for John, but Lennon was an extremely active hetero-sexual with the traditional contempt of those years for the people who, in 1961, were called 'queers' and who kept their preferences secret. Homosexuality was a taboo then and to Brian it was not something he allowed to be known, even among his family. To say, as some commentators have, that Brian Epstein's ambition for the Beatles was based mostly on his initial love of Lennon, is speculative nonsense. The memories of two good men should not be contaminated by rumours that can never be corroborated.

I knew Brian Epstein well enough to know that he was in love with the Beatles as an entity. He was fiercely protective of them all, ambitious for all four of them individually, and totally committed to making them the world's best-known pop act. It was something that went way beyond any sexual preferences.

'Sitting right here today,' Epstein told me in a Liverpool restaurant one night in 1962, 'I can't think why I didn't walk out of the Cavern within a few minutes. I can still remember these four ill-presented youths and their untidy hair.' Brian had invited me, as a writer with the weekly music paper *Melody Maker*, to Liverpool; I was the first London music journalist to go to the city to hear about the Beatles. He told me of his great hopes for the group, how they would be world-beaters, and how lucky I was to be in at the birth of such an explosion. I was interested, but cynically apprehensive. The British pop scene, dominated for so long by America, was slowly developing its own identity. With it came a new breed of swaggering managers who phoned me and many other writers every day to tout the new sensation. Elvis Presley and Cliff Richard had been joined by Acker Bilk's 'Stranger on the Shore', Frank Ifield's yodelling 'I Remember You', and the Tornados' number one hit 'Telstar', to mark America's first communications satellite, launched that year. John Lennon was getting heavily influenced by a raunchy American single, 'Hey

A scruffily dressed John with Paul and drummer Pete Best prepare for a
'Riverboat Shuffle' down the Mersey on the ship *Royal Iris* in July 1962.
Top of the bill was Acker Bilk's jazz band

Baby', by Bruce Channel which was to inspire John's harmonica playing. Against the general background of gimmicks and ballads and the trickle of good records, and the omnipresent Elvis Presley, a group of Liverpool boys with the unlikely name of the Beatles sounded doubtful starters. Epstein, who exuded charm, impeccable manners, and persistence, was insistent. 'Stay and meet them in my office tomorrow,' he said to me.

Brian told me how, a few months previously, he had invited the Beatles to his shop one afternoon. Although he had no firm plan of what they should do together, 'the idea of management occurred on both sides'. They had arrived at the NEMS store in Whitechapel, taking along Bob Wooler as if to mark the seriousness of the occasion. It was Lennon who broke the ice, saying 'This is me Dad,' when introducing Wooler to Epstein.

Wooler, who had seen the group's popularity soar, had confided in Epstein earlier that the Beatles were enormously popular but lacking regular work. Brian confirmed this with the group, had a general vague talk about contracts and their future, and invited them to return a week later. This time he got to the point briskly. 'Quite simply, you need a manager. Would you like me to do it?'

No one spoke for a moment or two and then John, in a low, husky voice, blurted: 'Yes.'

The others nodded. Paul, ever wary, asked: 'Will it make much difference to us? I mean, it won't make any difference to the way we play.'

Assured that it would not and assured of Epstein's enthusiasm, the five men sat looking at each other for a few minutes, not knowing what to say next.

Lennon again broke the silence. 'Right, then, Brian, manage us, now. Where's the contract? I'll sign it.'

I did meet the Beatles the day after that dinner with Brian Epstein. It was a brief encounter in Brian's office above a magic shop. John and George bounded in and asked for cigarettes. 'Love Me Do' had just been released.   They were cheerful, optimistic, and not at all unkempt. John got in a quick dig that the *Melody Maker* 'only ever writes about jazz', but he said it with the cynical smile that was to become endearing even when he was at his most cutting. I remember thinking it was difficult, though, to reconcile the tidy men with the uncouth image which Brian had described from the Cavern.

Even in those early days, Brian Epstein's impact was considerable. Before he began the long, frustrating search for a record contract, he informally laid down certain rules for them. First, he was a stickler for punctuality. Bob Wooler had trouble getting them on stage on time, and also in getting them off it. That needed tightening up, Epstein told John. Next, Brian suggested they stop drinking Cokes and eating sandwiches on stage, and they were not to shout abuse to people in the audience. He insisted on a tighter act of a maximum of an hour, and that they built a fairly rigid repertoire. The Hamburg experience of playing everything by ear and lambasting the audience was to be dropped. Their music on stage was, under Epstein, never to be as free and easy, but it was the sure route to directing their talent into mass popularity.

With slight reluctance, John accepted Epstein's theory. In a coffee bar Lennon bumped into the nude model June Furlong, who asked him how the group was progressing. He said they had met a posh man named Brian Epstein who had definite ideas for them but it would mean a radical change. 'He seemed unsure of whether it was a good thing,' says June Furlong. I said: "Go with it, John. What have you got to lose?" And he roared with laughter.

' "Yeah, June, how true. What have we got to *lose?*" '

He went also to the Renshaw Street offices of *Mersey Beat* and demanded back some of his ruder poems from Bill Harry, lest they should be published. They would, he thought, clash with the new, cleaner image that Brian Epstein intended to project. On two visits to Mendips, Epstein secured Aunt Mimi's seal of approval. 'A charming gentle man, a restless soul just like John,' she says. 'Always so polite.'

But the next part of Epstein's master plan was to shock John to the bone. As a successful salesman, Brian believed that the great British public would never go for an act that looked scruffy, however primitive their music was to remain. He insisted that the Beatles should wear suits, shirts and ties. Brian pointed to the Shadows as an example of success. Cliff Richard's backing group were the epitome of that antiseptic pop which John loathed. But secretly, however much Lennon resented Epstein's grooming, he was prepared to give it a whirl. Brian's salesmanship law said that, once a brand name had set a pattern, if it was successful then it should be followed. The Beatles would retain control over their music, of which he knew nothing but that it was spine-tingling with earthy excitement. But when it came to packaging, he told John, he knew what he was talking about: the Shadows were successful, and they wore suits.

It was a major decision, and a successful one. But John was

going against his instincts in letting Brian mould the group in this direction. It might have been the first moment the group polarized, with John and George rebelling against the 'super packaging' idea which was propounded by Epstein and strongly supported by Paul McCartney.

Clive Epstein, Brian's brother, says John was a frequent visitor to the Epstein family home long before the first single was made. 'Brian and John had long, serious discussions about how to project the group,' says Clive. Lennon was keen on learning about Brian's marketing techniques, something utterly foreign to him. 'He had a lot to say and they became very animated. Brian told me privately he believed John was a genius, and of course he assured my parents and me that they would be bigger than Elvis Presley, even before the first single was a small hit. Brian was definitely closer to John than the others; there was a mental contact between them that was perfect and really vital for the group's future.'

Long after the euphoria of Beatlemania John said in the *Melody Maker*, 'In the beginning it was a constant fight between Brian and Paul on one side, and me and George on the other. Brian put us in neat suits and shirts and Paul was right behind him. I didn't dig that and I tried to get George to rebel with me. I'd say to George: "Look, we don't need these suits. Let's chuck them out of the window." My little rebellion was to have my tie loose with the top button of my shirt undone, but Paul'd always come up to me and put it straight.

'On the first television film we ever did, the Granada people came down to film us, and there we were in suits and everything. It just wasn't us, and watching that film I knew that that was where we started to sell out.' In most pictures of John he is seen with his tie at least a little askew and, often, with his top shirt button undone.

He said all that with the benefit of hindsight. But in 1962, even for John, the end justified the means. Epstein's logic was unarguable: the devoted fans who thronged the Cavern and the ballrooms for the Beatles would have to be augmented by much wider appeal if they were to be a successful concert, television, and recording group. And the route to real pop success in Britain in 1962 was through the hit parade charts. While Brian tidied them up and slowly improved their fees and number of engagements, he set about the major task of getting them a record contract. It was to prove a heartbreaking hurdle.

Meanwhile, the virtual emigration of his best friend to Germany had left Lennon feeling isolated. John missed Stuart. 'The only real friend John ever had', is how Aunt Mimi describes him. 'The bond was beautiful, whenever they met. You could see it immediately,' says Cynthia. Astrid, Stuart's fiancée, would work away in her photographic studio in Hamburg while Stuart worked in an attic in her Hamburg home, alternately painting or writing long letters to John in Liverpool.

Equally, Lennon wrote letters to Stuart with an open-hearted intensity he usually reserved for Cynthia. His twenty-page letters to Stuart were different. Each bemoaned the state of the world, and little was said of the Beatles' progress. What came through, from John to Stuart, and then from Stuart to John, was a restlessness about life, and from John the freedom at last to feel he could unleash his innermost emotions, perhaps about his own venomous tongue which had hurt so many people. Once he wrote to Stuart:

I can't remember anything without a sadness
So deep that it hardly becomes known to me
So deep that its tears leave me a spectator of my own stupidity.

As the Epstein plan gathered momentum, the Beatles were to fulfil, on 13 April 1962, an engagement to open Hamburg's Star-Club, their most prestigious appearance so far in a city which they had grown to adopt as their second home. With a new manager behind them, a fresh confidence surged within the group as they travelled. This time, Epstein's style insisted on the Beatles flying to Germany rather than going by train and boat. He wanted to impress them with his largesse and give them confidence that he was serious about making them gigantically successful.

John had been aware of Stuart's very bad headaches through his letters, but only Astrid and her mother knew how really serious they were becoming. 'There were days when poor Stu was convulsed with pain,' says Astrid. 'When I went back to Liverpool with him at Christmas in 1961, everybody said how ill he looked. He fainted at art college once and we all decided that as he was in such agony, and it was impossible to know when a severe headache was caused, he had better stay at my home in bed or in the attic, and at least my mother and I could be near him when he needed help.' It also gave Stuart the attention of the Kirchherr family doctor. He sent him for X-rays but nothing untoward showed itself.

On 10 April, as the plane carrying the Beatles took off from Manchester to Hamburg, Astrid received a phone call from her

March 1964. John and Brian Epstein look through some letters and sign autographs

On a visit to London from Liverpool in January 1963 the Beatles visit Austin Reed's store in Regent Street to buy the Cuban-heeled boots that would start a fashion style

January 1963. On the verge of the Beatles' big breakthrough to national fame, John is reluctantly dressed in a shiny showbiz suit made by London tailor Doug Millings under Brian Epstein's instructions. The show was at Liverpool's Grafton Rooms

mother saying that Stuart was in such pain from headaches that she could not even contemplate calling the family doctor. 'He has to go to the hospital right now,' said Frau Kirchherr. Astrid sped home and insisted on accompanying her fiancé in the ambulance. 'He died in my arms on that journey,' says Astrid. 'I cannot say it was unexpected but the suddenness was. . . .' Her voice trails off. Cause of death was given as cerebral paralysis.

Astrid went from the hospital to Hamburg airport to meet John, Paul, and Pete Best. (George did not arrive until next day.) They knew nothing of the drama of the day, still less of twenty-one-year-old Stuart's death. 'I don't know how I got through that moment, after what happened,' says Astrid. 'I can see John walking into the airport hall and he got sight of me and came over, waving his arms, "Hello, I'm *here*, how are you. . .oh, what's the matter?" He could see darkness in Astrid's doleful, expressive eyes.

'Stuart died, John. He's gone.'

Lennon's reaction was to burst into laughter. He said nothing at all to anyone. 'He never cried,' says Astrid. 'Not once. He went into this hysterical laughter, and couldn't stop. It was his way of not wanting to face the truth. John went deep into himself for just a little while after the news. But he and I didn't speak much about Stuart. I knew that he and Stuart genuinely loved each other. They told me so, when they got loose. I know Stu would have preferred to have died rather than go on in the pain he was suffering. But the loss to me was great, and to anyone who knew him, because he was a genius, with a great mind and an original talent as an artist. He would have been outstanding, if he'd lived. How John got over that period I'll never know.'

Lennon's method of recovery was the same that he had adopted when first he had that awful choice between his mother and father, then the death of Uncle George, then the death of his mother. His period of mourning was quiet, totally personal and not shared with anyone else. He believed in getting on with living immediately.

Astrid suffered a deep depression for months afterwards, and it was mostly John who pulled her out of it. 'He saved me,' she said. Paul and George particularly were sweet to her, she says, but John knew the onus was on him to look after her because of his relationship with Stu. 'In his rough way, he was so beautiful, and he imposed his own method of recovery on me without me knowing it,' says Astrid. 'Come on, make up your mind, live or die,' he would say. 'You're coming to the Star-Club with us tonight. Stop sitting at home – it won't bring Stu back.' John showed many times his demonstrativeness towards Astrid's mother, who had borne the brunt of Stuart's illness when Astrid was away in her photographic studio so often during the days. 'My mother would say: "John, you are supposed to be rough rocker." He would put his arms around her and carry on as if he lived in the house, which she loved.' Astrid says John kept her from becoming morose and she did, indeed, go to the Star-Club when the Beatles opened there on 13 April for seven weeks.

They were in a mood of despondency at Stuart's death, and optimism at their career prospects: the Star-Club was a step up and they had, after all, been chosen to open it. One of the men who helped run the club, Horst Fascher, recalls John as being the one with the most bizarre behaviour during the seven weeks they were at the Star-Club. 'On that opening night, we had the Beatles and other groups and Brian Epstein also came. There was lots to drink. The next morning we all went to a club and Brian was a bit drunk and John Lennon poured beer all over him. There was a slight argument.'

Fascher knew the Beatles from 1960 when he had worked in the Kaiserkeller, the second Hamburg club they had played. He was also the manager of Tony Sheridan, with whom the Beatles had made their first record in Hamburg, called 'My Bonnie', which had been the subject of that first request to Brian Epstein. Fascher recalls: 'They were different from the start. There was something I liked about them, and their clothes and special sound impressed me.' He was also amused by their eccentricity: 'One day,' he says, 'they all went to the fish market in Hamburg and bought a pig. They walked it, on a lead, up and down the Reeperbahn. Some people who saw it were annoyed and called the police, who took it away to be slaughtered. It was typical of their outlandish behaviour.'

As the kings of the Cavern back home, and now knowing Hamburg where their reputation was soaring, John, Paul, George, and Pete Best were in a lively mood. They stayed in a flat above the Star-Club. John's often outrageous behaviour, during that month, may have been traceable to his submerging of Stuart's death. The Star-Club owner, Manfred Weissleder, sometimes travelled to Africa and bought animal skins which he suggested the Beatles wore on stage. So on one occasion John appeared on the Star-Club stage as a monkey. When the show ended, he walked outside, up and down the Grosse Freiheit and the Reeperbahn, in the same outfit. Then he and the others went into a club and Horst Fascher had a call from the police, saying the Beatles had gone into a club

and 'scared people to death'. People had run away and not paid
their bills, so the owner insisted the Beatles should pay the bills.
'They had no money, so I had to pay.'

One Saturday night, after the Beatles had been playing at the
Star-Club until nearly dawn, thirty people attended a party at their
flat in the Grosse Freiheit. The toilet facilities were inadequate,
with just one lavatory shared among the flats, up five flights of
stairs; John urinated over the edge of the balcony. 'We were all
just normal human beings,' says Paul McCartney, confirming the
event. 'I seem to remember John had a pee over the edge. But what
happens is that all these stories grow into great legends.' McCartney says that the story that John urinated on nuns who were going
to the St Joseph's Catholic Church, next door to the flats, was
untrue. 'On a separate occasion, there were some nuns and we
shouted at them, not crazily, but like "Oy oy, sister" and generally
like young people do. The two stories got together, so we get this
really outrageous story where John's peeing on nuns. It never
really was like that. It all just grew into really crazy stories out of
what most people would agree is boyish craziness.'

A drunken John did take the stage of the club with a toilet seat
around his neck, but it was at the end of a show when most of the
audience wanted a bit of a cabaret, and he went along with it. But
during that trip in Hamburg John was certainly often wild. Says
Gerry Marsden, who was playing at the Top Ten club and who
saw the Beatles socially: 'Remember we were all kids who had
basically never been anywhere apart from Liverpool. You're
suddenly free of parents, friends, anybody who knows you, and
getting paid decent money. So John did his own thing more freely
because his Auntie wasn't there to say: "Stop it." Like all of us,
John went a little bit mad.

'As for booze, yes, we all drank too much, including John. He
started work around seven in the evening and played half a dozen
sets or so, ending at around two in the morning. Rum and Coke
was sixpence a big glass, and we couldn't afford that stuff in
England. So by the early hours of the next morning, we'd all had
quite a lot of bevvies. And you'll still be high because the adrenalin
was pumping away from performing your heart out. So then you'd
go out to eat, until four or five in the morning, maybe with the
Horst Fascher family, and of course sleep in till about three
o'clock next afternoon. Then it was down to the Seamen's Mission
on the dockside for a fry-up breakfast. That was the pattern for all
the groups in Hamburg. It was like a rehearsal every night, and
John told me many times afterwards that it was an experience he

(1.)

STAR CLUB
39 GROSSE FREIHEIT
ALTONA HAMBURG.

Dear Cyn
I love love love you and I'm missing you like mad where are you my little ^—

I wonder why all the newspapers wrote about Stu — especially the 'People' — and how the hell did they find out who could have told them as I wrote that I suddenly remembered theres a fellow at the 'Sucaranda' who's a free lance journalist it could have been him 'cause Alan Williams has been helping mrs Sutcliffe or something. I haven't seen Astrid since the day we arrived I've thought of going to see her but I would be so awkward — and probably the others would come as well and it would be even worse. I won't write any more about it 'cause its not much fun. I love you — I don't like the idea of Dot moving in permanently with you 'cause we could never be alone really — I mean when I came home — can't she have the other room or find another flat — imagine having her there all the time when we were in bed — and imagine Paul coming all the time — and especially when I wasn't there I'd hate the idea. I love you Cyn.

The club is massive and we only play 3 hrs one night and 4 the next — and we play an hour — then an hour break so it doesn't seem long at all really. The boss

Continued overleaf

John wrote this letter, parts of which have been cut out by Cynthia, from Hamburg a few days after Stuart Sutcliffe's death in April 1962. 'Dot' was Dot Rhone, Paul McCartney's first serious girlfriend

of this place is a good skin - we're off tomorrow 'cause its Good Friday and they can't have music so the boss - (Manfred) is taking us and the other group out for the day in his car and all the rest of them like Horst are coming so it will be a big mob in 4 or 5 cars. We're going somewhere healthy like the Ost Sea (Stuart again).

God I'm knackered its 6 o'clock in the morning and I want you (I've just found out that theres no post tomorrow so I will pack in good night I love you boo! hoo! I hate this place).

That was Friday night ~Thursday~ now its Sunday afternoon, I've just wakened up and theres no post today or tommorrow (Easter Monday I think) anyway happy Easter Cyn. I love you. We went out but all we did was eat and eat and eat (Good Friday) it was all free so it was ok. We drove somewhere about 30 mile away and ate.

My voice has been gone since I got here (it was gone before I came if I remember rightly). I can't seem to find it - ah well! I love you Cyn Powell and I wish I was on the way to your flat with the Sunday papers and chocies and a throbber! Oh yes! I forget to tell you We get a GEAR suede overcoat with a belt so I'll look just like you now! Pauls leaping about on my head (he's in a bunk on top of me and he's snoring!) I can hardly get in a position to write its so cramped below stairs captain, Shurrup McArtrey! quint quin

I can't wait to see your new room it will be great seeing it for the first time and having chips and all and a ciggie (don't let me come home to a regular smoker please Miss Powell) Hmm I can just see you and Dot puffing away I suppose that's the least of my worries. I love you Cyn I miss miss miss you miss powell — I keep remembering all the parts of Hamburg that we went to together In fact I can't get away from you — especially on the way, and inside the Seamans Mission boathoo! I love love love you. X

Did I tell you that we have a good bathroom with a shaver did I? did I tell you? well I've had ONE whole shave aren't I a clean little rocker? hee!hee! I love you I haven't written to thini yet but I know how to send her money so it gets there in 2 hrs. x x x

— I can't think what to write now so I will pack in and write some tomorrow seeing as how like I can't POST IT anyway So good afternoon Cyn I love you. Yum Yum. Will you send me the words to "A SHOT OF RYTHM + BLUES" pease? Heres not many.
It's Monday night and we finished playing about ¾ of hr ago (its 2 o'clock) I'm dead beat my sweet so I hope you wont mind if I

Continued overleaf

finish now and have lovely sleep (without your tent
it'll still be lovely - don't be hurt - but I'm so
so so tired). I love you Cyn - I hope you realize
why this letter took so long, but there has been no
post Fri Sat Sun Mon - and this one will go
by the early morning Tuesday post 'cause I will
nip downstairs and post it any minute (handy
isn't it?). I love you I love you please wait for
me and don't be sad and work hard and
be a clever little Cyn Powell. I love you
I love you I love you I love you I love you
I love you, write soon ooh it's a naughty
old Hamburg we're living in 2².

All my Love for Ever and ever
from
John

X X X X Y
Y X X X Y

P.S.
They're leather
PANTIES not pants!
(just in case y'know).

♡ I love You ♡
Goodnight
Y X Y Y Y

could never have got anywhere else. If you can survive Hamburg, with all its audiences giving you hell, and the demands of the nights, you can survive even Beatlemania! It trained John to have the really hard voice that became famous as part of the Beatles. It wrecked everybody's vocal cords singing for such long periods, but when you keep on singing every night like that, and shouting back the first thing that comes into your head at the crowds, your voice's power increases. John used to enjoy the hurly burly of it all.'

Gerry saw Lennon in many punch-ups in Liverpool and Hamburg. 'But I'd not describe him as a hard lad. He'd lose his temper and hit people, but more often than not he'd get a smack right back in the mouth. In Liverpool, John was lucky that he had a strong reputation and the name of the Beatles behind him, otherwise he'd have got beaten up even more than he did. He behaved like a typical Scouse teddy boy, a ruffian, but he was no harder than lots of other people of those days. But when he hit, he got smashed back. You don't walk away often, on Merseyside, when you give a mouthful of abuse to someone. I saw him get many a pasting.'

The worst scene Gerry Marsden saw involving John happened in Hamburg. Playing cards in the flat above the Star-Club, John was drunk. There was an argument. 'John got up and hit the fellow over the head with a bottle. I thought: "That's really out of order." Within seconds the fellow had got up and knocked hell out of John, pasting him all over the flat. And all of us just stood there and let him do it, because we agreed that you just don't go round hitting people over the head with bottles and expect to get away with it. I saw John bashed about many times, but never so hard. He really took it that night. But he asked for it, and he said later it was fair because he shouldn't have done what he did. Put it like this: I'd never have employed John as a bodyguard. He wasn't that hard.'

Twenty years after the Beatles were in Hamburg, there were still people closely connected with that period who warmed to the memories. Rosa, for example: two decades later, at eighty-six years old, she was still the toilet attendant in the Top Ten club in the Reeperbahn, extolling, through a translator, her love of the boys whom she cooked, laundered, and made beds for, and provided with her husband's houseboat for accommodation. 'John's reputation as the wild one was true,' says Rosa. 'He was like the devil on that stage. I remember John as the ambitious one. He said that one day they would be very famous. "Mama," he would say, "*Mutti*! We go to America, be very big, very famous, make LOTS of money." '

She says that he often drank too much and would lie on the dance floor and cry. 'He was really angry sometimes, but the public thought it was a show. What he was angry about was the group sound, when it was not as he liked. Then he would drink as a kind of consolation. I heard them quarrelling a lot. I would worry about the amount John was going to drink when they argued.'

Hamburg, with its punishing physical demands on stage, the absurd time-keeping and irregular sleep and food, and the combativeness of the audience, was John's gruelling training ground. With the sadness evoked by the city's constant reminder of his best friend's death, it provided him with a steely exterior. As the years went on, that characteristic became confused with toughness. The curious fact is that the older he became, the less tough and abrasive and the more human John Lennon emerged.

He was given to odd streaks of sentimentality. In Hamburg that bleak spring, trying to console Astrid and Stuart's heartbroken mother, Millie Sutcliffe, John Lennon asked particularly for Stuart's long, woollen college scarf, striped in navy and pale blue and yellow and cream. It was to remain his most prized souvenir of their bond. It reminded John of their days together, huddled in Gambier Terrace and the alleyways of Liverpool 8.

10
MARRIAGE

'Don't worry, Cyn. We'll get married'

John's obsession with deformities and afflictions has been mentioned before. On one of his private drawings, which he gave to a student as a gift, John captioned a particularly gruesome-looking figure 'The Wife', almost as a commentary about what he feared the role of a woman in his life could be: overbearing and domineering, hideously ugly.

But the first serious woman in his life, who was inseparable from him when they met at college in 1957 and became his wife during Beatlemania as well as the mother of his first child, was the opposite of that fearsome drawing. Cynthia scarcely realized how John's macabre sense of the absurd would manifest itself into a tender moment in their lives, a year after their marriage. On 8 April 1963 their only son, John Charles Julian Lennon, was born at Sefton General Hospital, Liverpool.

It was not an easy birth. Cynthia says, 'I was something like three days in hospital before Julian arrived and then he had jaundice, the umbilical cord was around his neck, and he had a very large mole on his head. He had to be left alone for twenty-four hours; I couldn't touch him. I was petrified about all these things. But I was scared more than anything about the birth mark, the mole. Knowing John's horror of deformities, I was absolutely panic-stricken about what John's reaction would be.' When Julian was born, John and the Beatles were busy criss-crossing Britain on a hectic schedule of ballroom appearances to consolidate their new fame. John phoned the hospital, excitedly enquiring about his wife and baby, and was triumphant at the news that it was a boy.

After three days Cynthia welcomed John to the hospital – and made sure that the baby's head was resting against a pillow so that the prominent mole could not be seen by the sensitive, eagle-eyed father. 'When John came in, I decided not to hide it. I said: "Oh he's beautiful, wonderful, John, but he has this birth mark on his head."

'John replied: "Oh, it doesn't matter. His hair will grow over that."

'I was still bothered because I wanted the perfect child for John, but he couldn't have cared less. He was just thrilled, the typical father.'

In the weeks that followed, Cynthia carefully covered the baby's head with a hat at every possible moment – so that John would not have his attention drawn to the mole. The prospect of a baby Lennon that was anything less than physically perfect haunted her.

Julian Lennon was conceived at Cynthia's £3-a-week bed-sitter at 93 Garmoyle Road, off Smithdown Road, a stone's throw from Penny Lane. It was also very close to Sefton General Hospital, where Julian was born. They had never taken birth control precautions, from their first experience together in Stuart's flat.

'There was no planning. There was no pill in those days. We considered nothing except ourselves and didn't consider the consequences. As far as I was concerned, ignorance was bliss. Neither John nor I gave pregnancy a thought. My parents didn't advise me and I didn't ask them, and I'm sure John wouldn't dream of asking Mimi. We weren't thinking about anything like prevention, just enjoying each other naturally as two kids.

'But when the reality dawned first on me, I was full of absolute shock. "My God, what am I going to tell my Mum?"

'And he had the same reaction: "What am I going to tell Mimi?"

'It was guilt. Even though we didn't have the pill, we did have respect for our elders. Aged twenty in 1962 was rather like being aged sixteen by today's standards, Cynthia observes. 'We were both kids basically.'

But John's reaction, on being told, was that if a girl became pregnant, the man must 'do the right thing' and marry her.

'I don't think we'd have been married if I had t become pregnant,' she says. 'He wasn't the sort at the age of twenty-one to say: "Will you marry me?" It was all so immedi we hardly realized the seriousness of it all: making love, getting pregnant, getting married.

'If we had carried on seeing each other without a child rriving, I had it in mind to obtain my qualification as an art te r. That would have enabled me to support John whatever happened, because his life at that time was music and I couldn't see his future in it. He was messing around at college and within music and I thought: "Well, I love him. Whatever happens, if he can't make money, I'll be there and I'll have my art teacher's diploma and I'll be able to teach." That was at the back of my mind.'

But her attention to her studies suffered when she got involved with John. Cynthia failed her art teacher's diploma exam. And John went on to do rather well with his music.

'One thing's for sure,' says Cynthia. 'I didn't marry John for his money. He didn't have any, I didn't appreciate it, and it's never done me any good. I had more money than he did in the early days of our love affair and I was funding him every day at college. So if money was important to me I'd have chosen a rich boyfriend.'

John's attitude to being a father was similar to his approach to everything else, from the launching of the Beatles to pursuing art, to getting married and divorced, and buying houses. The same principle applied throughout his life: first decide, then do it, then move on to the next situation – a new challenge. Although whatever he became involved in was done wholeheartedly, the restless spirit inside him was always powerful. Lennon had many varied and brilliant assets within his character, but stability was never among them.

'I don't think he was ready for a child any more than I was,' says Cynthia. 'He wasn't ready to settle down.' When they married he was twenty-one and she was twenty-two. 'Whatever happened with John was always a compromise. He had to get everything over with quickly. He was committed to it while it had to be done, but he'd want to be moving on to the next thing fast.'

Cynthia's cramped flat in Garmoyle Road was not far from Woolworth's in Penny Lane where she worked as a counter assistant during summer vacations from college. When Cynthia's father died – uncannily about the same time that John was hit by the death of his mother – her mother went to Canada to act as nanny to Cynthia's cousin. The family house at Hoylake was rented out, and Cynthia fancied a flat of her own.

In August 1962 John was visiting Cynthia at her flat when he found her particularly quiet.

'Is everything OK?' he asked.

Cynthia was in the kitchen, washing up. 'No, it's not OK.'

'What's the matter?'

'I'm pregnant, that's what's the matter.'

'Oh Christ, what are we going to do?' said John, moving over to put his arm around her. Panic seized him, then a quick flash of practicality: 'Look, I'll go and tell Mimi. Don't worry, Cyn. We'll get married.'

John's instinctive decision to 'do the right thing' and marry a girl who was pregnant in 1962 was very much a reflection of the times. They had been having an affair, but nobody knew and the first time John's Aunt Mimi knew that they had slept together was when he went home that night and said, 'Cyn's pregnant.'

Mimi erupted. 'John told me there had been the most tremendous scene, one of the worst things he'd ever had to go through,' Cynthia says. 'Mimi threw everything at him – 'You stupid children, getting yourselves into this situation!' The whole family will have nothing to do with you. You've got yourself into this mess, now get yourselves out of it.'' '

Lennon certainly did not *want* marriage at this stage. He told several people close to him that he had to get married to protect Cynthia and the child, and Cynthia will always doubt that he would ever have married her if she had not become pregnant. But Cynthia's closest friend throughout and after college years, Phyllis McKenzie, disagrees. 'They were totally opposite but right for each other and, although they came from different backgrounds, they were a perfect match,' she says. 'I think they would obviously have taken longer to get married, but it *would* have happened. They loved each other very much. There was no separating them.'

Once the decision was made, John panicked about the ceremony. 'Christ,' he said to Brian Epstein. 'What am I going to do? How can I fix it all up and get on with it quickly?'

If ever John needed evidence that he had the right manager, this was that moment. The smooth, organized skill of Epstein rose to the occasion. 'Don't worry, John. I'll fix it.'

An early sign of her acceptance of the situation came when Aunt Mimi gave John the money to buy the wedding ring. He went with Cynthia to a jeweller just a few doors from Epstein's NEMS store in Whitechapel. She chose a simple £10 gold wedding ring and there was no sentimentality attached to buying it.

For all his bravery when he was with Cynthia, John broke down with his Aunt Mimi the night before his wedding. 'I don't want to get married,' he said, wandering restlessly around Mendips. He was choking back the tears at the seriousness of the situation.

'I told you before, John. You're too young. But what's done's done.' She regarded Cynthia as not bright enough for her brilliant nephew. 'Now, John, I've said it. Once the ring's on the finger, I shall hold my peace.' She pointedly refused to attend the wedding.

Togetherness on the beach. A youthful-looking John and
Cynthia at the resort of Ostsee just outside Hamburg in
July 1961. The snapshot unfortunately shows the effects of
having been carried around for years in Cynthia's handbag

Brian Epstein arranged a special licence for the marriage at Mount Pleasant Register Office. He arranged for a car to collect Cynthia from her flat, where, shaking with nerves, she had dressed in a well-worn purple and black check two-piece suit. John was dressed formally, almost funereally, in black suit and tie, with a white shirt, and his friends Paul McCartney and George Harrison were dressed exactly the same. The other guests were Cynthia's brother Tony and his wife, Margery, who shared the honour of signing their names as witnesses on the marriage certificate with 'James Paul McCartney'.

The mood at the wedding was one of controlled panic. In the register office waiting-room John fidgeted nervously with his tie and his hair. During the three-minute ceremony a pneumatic drill outside started up bang on cue, just as the Registrar began his short speech. The noise virtually drowned the event: that broke the ice.

Giggling nervously, they walked out into torrential rain, down the hill past Liverpool's grand old Adelphi Hotel. At Brian's suggestion, the wedding celebration was a lunch in the unlicensed Reece's restaurant. John did not realize that the same register office and Reece's had been his parents' wedding day rendezvous. It was just noon, and the Beatles party had to queue for a table before sitting down to the set lunch of soup, chicken and trifle. They toasted the bride and groom with glasses of water. The bill came to fifteen shillings a head and Epstein paid.

'It was hysterical. We were like nervous children going to the dentist, from start to finish. We were laughing uncontrollably at anything in sight,' says Cynthia. 'People's hats, the women who go into Reece's – we were laughing all the time at anything to make sure we didn't take it seriously. I was the only one thinking about the future, I think, because I knew what I was in for.'

At Reece's Epstein told John and Cynthia of his special gift to them – free, unlimited use of his flat at 36 Falkner Street, a street almost opposite the art college. Cynthia believes that the shrewd Epstein did not relish the thought of the leader of the Beatles living in her spartan bed-sitter in Garmoyle Road – 'it might have been bad for the image.' Brian's flat was, anyway, comparatively luxurious and in what was at that time a fashionable area of the city. They even had use of a small, walled garden.

On the wedding night, John and the Beatles had a show at Chester. The new Mrs Lennon, relieved that one of the most testing days of her life was over, moved her meagre possessions from Garmoyle Road to Brian's flat, and relaxed. For John, though, the speed of events in his musical career was a perfect diversion from what had just happened. Brian Epstein's industrious efforts to obtain a recording contract had achieved success three months before John's wedding. Twelve days after his marriage to Cynthia, John was excitedly in London recording the McCartney song that was to start the most astonishing, influential event in entertainment, and rocket John and the Beatles into a prominence previously known only to film stars and statesmen.

On the van journey to London for that recording session they would all wait for the signal from John to recite the short poem which he had concocted. It was a little rhyme that in a year became even truer than he ever dared hope:

> *John:* Where are we going fellas?
> *Chorus:* To the top, Johnny to the TOP!
> *John:* And where *is* the top, fellas?
> *Chorus:* To the toppermost of the poppermost!

With the Beatles' career moving ahead decisively, Epstein was adding to John Lennon's arrogance a remarkable new factor: confidence that he had a spectacular future. Repeatedly, Eppy told anyone who would listen that 'the boys' would one day be bigger than Elvis Presley. Events proved Epstein absolutely accurate, but at that time most people were convulsed with laughter at Brian's promise that Liverpool lads could achieve anything like Presley status. Elvis was an untouchable god. Moreover he was American, and America always led in pop. British artists were consigned to plagiarism at best, weedy pap like Cliff Richard or Frankie Vaughan at worst. Four Liverpool scruffs to dominate the world? Forget it, Brian!

But the Beatles thrust happened so quickly under Brian's devotion and the prescience of George Martin that it needed John's total attention. Their roots at St Peter's church fete, Woolton, may have been a dim, distant memory, but John and Paul were able to draw on a formidable reserve of experience – particularly of live shows, and tough audiences in ballrooms and clubs – by the time they were pitchforked by Epstein into the big time. Lennon, more than the other three, loved the hoop which Brian was putting them through. When George Martin told Epstein that Pete Best needed replacing as Beatles' drummer before he would offer a record contract, John's reaction to an anguished Brian at Mendips one night was immediate: 'OK, but you tell Pete he's out and I'll get Ringo in.' John and Paul had always admired Ringo Starr's work with another local band, Rory Storm and the Hurricanes. Next night, John phoned Ringo, who was playing at Butlin's holiday camp in Skegness. 'You're in, Ringo – the sidies will have to go, though.' John's remark recognized that Ringo's cheek-length sideburns would clash with Epstein's master plan to tidy the Beatles up.

Mentally high on the Hamburg experiences, and having a faster instinct than any of the other Beatles, John knew that once they had recorded a song and marshalled their image and their fans properly, they would be unstoppable. From childhood he had never lacked confidence in his ability; the only difference was that now it was not a wayward, artistic talent. It had direction. It was blazing enthusiasm for music to the exclusion of everything else. When John got hold of something – anything – he became blinkered to the world beyond it.

The qualities John admired in Paul McCartney were exactly those that John lacked: Paul was artistic, creative, and a wonderful foil to offset John. But he had a valuable extra ingredient; determination to see a job through. He insisted on every detail being completed. His appearance reflected the inner man; he looked casual, but he was always pin-clean, like his tidy mind.

When John talked to Cynthia about Paul, it was in terms of incredulity at Paul's self-discipline. John, who had stalked his way through grammar school and college, and lurched into a rock band, was thrilled at the prospect of moving ahead in music with McCartney's methodical touches at his elbow. He would not have said so at the time.

There was another quality in the immensely heterosexual Lennon that he admired in Paul: an ability to attract a woman, and have a fling with her, and then move on very quickly. John did not master that art until later, in his mid-twenties. Adventurousness, and the appetite for moving on, applied to John in everything except his associations with women. It could not have been related to the death of his mother, for long before she died he was having an affair with a girl in Woolton named Barbara whom he had dated for two years before her parents warned her to drop him. The length of that affair, and his intense relationship with Cynthia, demonstrated that he never did things by halves.

Now, as a married twenty-two-year-old, John was pulled in two directions. His wife and baby were in Epstein's flat just as the Beatles caravan began to look as if it would roll. After the row with Aunt Mimi about Cynthia's pregnancy, and her boycott of

Before Beatlemania. John at the Abbey Road studios in London during the recording of their first E.M.I. single, 'Love Me Do', in September 1962

the wedding, John now felt he had to crack on with music to the exclusion of everything else.

In what must rank as one of the world's most bizarre honeymoons, John – after going to Chester on their wedding night – continued to travel, first to London, then to Manchester and other cities as the Beatles' success gained momentum in the north-west. After the Beatles' first entry into the hit parade, preparations for their first proper concert tour around Britain, with Helen Shapiro, took John away from Cynthia at the very time that they should have been consolidating their relationship.

'We were both sort of bowled over by the fact that we were married,' says Cynthia. 'It wasn't a question of "What's happened to us, have we done the right thing?" It was all perfectly natural that we should be together. But John didn't get a chance to be first a real husband or later a real father. He was too busy, and put himself under a lot of pressure to make sure that, once the Beatles ball was rolling, he kept pushing it.'

After three months of pregnancy, Cynthia had a threatened miscarriage. 'I was alone, John was away, and I started panicking.' Her brother, Tony, rushed over to be with her, but the doctor's orders were straightforward: stay in bed for three days. John phoned her at the flat, but she didn't tell him, in case he should be diverted from what she knew was vital to him at this time: success with the Beatles.

'When John came home I told him about it, and said I was particularly frightened while I was pregnant, because if I had lost Julian there was nobody there to help me at all. I suddenly said, "Why don't we go and see Mimi, ask her advice." ' He had often said to her, "I wonder how Mimi and Mendips is." He was nervous about seeing her after the terrible scenes that took place before the wedding. He hadn't seen her for three months – the first time in his life they had been separated since childhood.

Cynthia said, 'Come on John, she's your Auntie, I'm sure she'll be OK now.'

He said, 'Are you sure?'

Cynthia reflects now: 'I knew in my heart of hearts that she was missing John like mad, that she was upset about the whole business, and wanted peace. Knowing Mimi and John, I also knew it was always a quickfire temper, soon over with. She was obviously going to be missing her "son" and John was, I think, missing her.' He felt isolated from his family.

On a sunny day they got the bus, and with some trepidation walked down the drive at Mendips. John knocked at the door,

Mimi opened it with outstretched arms, and the three of them went in for a warmer welcome than John and Cynthia had dared hope for. Mimi made eggs and chips and tea and asked the now visibly pregnant Cynthia how she was feeling. Cynthia told her of the threatened miscarriage.

'I'm very worried about you,' said Mimi. 'You can't stay in that flat on your own. Come and live with me. I'll move upstairs and you and John can live downstairs. It will be cheaper, and better for you because you need someone with you while you're pregnant.' The garden outside would soon be essential for the pram, Mimi added.

The move to Mimi's house was speedy and practical, but disastrous for Cynthia. Cynthia felt that Mimi resented the intrusion on her home, despite her earlier invitation. There was another torment for Cynthia: at a meeting before she became pregnant, at Cynthia's home in Hoylake, Mimi and Cynthia's mother had clashed. Their temperaments were totally opposite: Mimi was artistic, bookish, and utterly possessive of John whom she regarded as very special; Lilian Powell was the archetypal protector of her daughter's virtues. At the frosty encounter, which had been suggested by John and Cynthia, the two women sought refuge in picking faults in John and Cynthia. John and Cynthia left the room in red-faced embarrassment as the two women carried on grumbling about them and poured scorn on their relationship. Eventually John took Mimi home, silently, on the bus; but he was never to forgive his future mother-in-law for hosting such a destructive meeting.

'John and I were very upset. We were both in love with each other,' says Cynthia, 'and for the two dearest people in our lives to stand in front of us saying what terrible people we were, and how they hated us for getting together, was awful. I think they did it because they didn't get on and they didn't want us to get on either. But the experience was horrible.'

As soon as Cynthia moved into Mendips John was off on the road again. Cynthia now felt terribly exposed: she felt uneasy because Mimi was ill with bronchitis and Cynthia's arrival had meant she had to move upstairs; and to increase her tension, John had told her that Brian Epstein insisted she keep her pregnancy secret because a married Beatle would be bad for the group's image.

In those years, pop stars were expected to be 'available' in the eyes of girl fans. A chief Beatle with a wife, heaven forbid a pregnant one, might have turned away the teenage girls who were now rallying round the Beatles as they travelled the country. At stage doors, in dressing-rooms, and as their van drove them away to their digs or cheap hotel for the night, sixties girls with beehive hairstyles, hopelessly high heels, and heavy mascara would queue in wait for a glimpse of their favourite Beatle. A chatting-up would be even better, and if it led to a night together – great. Paul McCartney's handsome, brown-eyed stare made him the early favourite among the girls, but John's tough guy stance and leer, plus his raw aggression on stage, made him a very close second. Cynthia was to be kept firmly and privately at home.

Epstein's rule suited Lennon perfectly. It tied in with his maxim that, whatever the job in hand, it must be concentrated upon one hundred per cent. The job was the Beatles, and the pace of events was speeding up.

During Cynthia's pregnancy John travelled all over England as the Beatles set about consolidating their record success with 'Love Me Do'. On tour with Helen Shapiro, he phoned Cynthia at Mendips regularly. He sounded tremendously excited that things were taking off for them, and relieved that she had had no recurrences of the threatened miscarriage. 'His music was coming together well, the crowds were gathering for them, and it was a terribly exciting time,' says Cynthia.

The pressure on her was considerable. Mimi took in students who knew that John Lennon of the Beatles was her nephew; the same students, or their friends, had lodged with her year after year. Mimi took pride now in the fact that the Beatles were having a little success, but Cynthia had to play out a charade. 'I said to these students, and people nearby, that I was John's girlfriend, but I was also a student and that's the reason I gave them for wearing smocks. "I'm an artist and I do some work here at home," I'd say. What they didn't realize, I hope, was that the smocks were getting bigger and bigger to hide the baby.'

John, on the phone, was sounding excited at the prospect of being a father. He never minded whether it was a boy or a girl as long as it was healthy. Mimi, however, repeatedly told Cynthia: 'It's got to be a boy, just like John.'

The choice of names came quickly and easily: John after the father, Julian because it was close to John's mother's name, and Charles in memory of Cynthia's father. One thing worried John in the maternity ward when he and Cynthia discussed it: 'Hey,' he said, 'someone said Julian sounds a bit poofy.' But they laughed it away and decided that the closeness to his mother was what really mattered.

Three factors had always made Cynthia's relationship with Mimi difficult and tense. Mimi was constantly worried that John's poor school results would mean that he would end up unemployed; she felt incredibly possessive about her surrogate son; and her dislike of Cynthia's mother was reflected in her attitude towards Cynthia.

'When John first took me home,' says Cynthia, 'I suppose Mimi looked on it as a childhood romance, nothing serious. We were about eighteen and no aunt would expect her nephew to be seriously involved at that age. The more it drifted on for months, the greater I could see Mimi worrying and looking concerned. It wasn't anything she said, just her general attitude towards me at that stage, after a few months of John and me together and me visiting Mendips. I don't think she went overboard.'

Mimi's full wrath had come one afternoon. For the very first time John had earned some money from some of their Cavern dates, and other work, in 1961. He proudly asked Cynthia what she would like as a celebration present. She asked for a brown suede coat. John went with her to C & A's store and spent £17 on the three-quarter-length coat. 'It wasn't very high quality, it was rough suede, but for me at the time it was the most wonderful gift,' says Cynthia.

They went straight from Liverpool city centre to show it off to Mimi. Cynthia said they shouldn't go empty-handed, so they took her a cooked chicken for their tea. Neither John nor Cynthia could believe the fury that greeted them.

'Do you like Cyn's new coat?' John said as they entered the hall.

Mimi flew into an immediate rage. How could John go buying things like that when he didn't have a proper job? 'But we've brought you a cooked chicken, Mimi.'

'Take your chicken and your gangster's moll and get out,' Mimi roared. 'You get a bit of money in your pocket and go and blow it on *her*.' Finally Mimi sat down in tears and Cynthia tried to calm her down.

'I'm sorry if you're upset, but we'll be all right,' said Cynthia. 'Take it easy, Mimi.'

'Go away. Don't talk to me,' sobbed Mimi, inconsolable.

And that's just what John and Cynthia did. When John returned later, after taking Cynthia home to Garmoyle Road, Mimi was silent. John crept up to bed and the next morning the row had been forgotten.

But it had been a sharp example to John and Cynthia of Mimi' touchiness. John knew she was not a woman to cross lightly. No he had proof. 'All over a bloody coat,' he mused to Cyn.

Mimi's fury at John's display of largesse was, of course, justified by the facts. With no O-levels at school, and now apparently having left art college, on to which she had pinned all her hopes, John was drifting into full-time pop music. That future was not secure enough for Mimi. The Beatles' success was a mere pipe dream to her.

One day she called his bluff and put the fear of God inside him. 'I said: "All right, so you don't want college and you don't want any more education. But what are you earning? Five shillings, which you're spending on your way out of that Cavern. You're just not earning enough at this music game, John, so I've found a proper job for you." '

'What are you talking about?' John said, shaken.

'It's no good, John,' Mimi went on. 'I can't go on like this. The worry's too much. I've got a job for you on the buses – as a conductor. They can't get staff anywhere. I've signed you on.'

'Me, me!!! I'm not a *working man*. If you think I'm going to go out at nine o'clock in the morning and come home at five, well I won't.'

Mimi retorted: 'What do you think you've been studying for if it isn't to be a working man? Think about it, John. It's either that or brushing the snow. I've had it with you.'

John's face went scarlet and he ran up to his room. Here was his privacy. Mimi was never allowed there. A picture of Brigitte Bardot was stuck to the ceiling above his bed.

Half an hour elapsed before John slowly walked downstairs. He said nothing but sidled up behind Mimi who was sitting in his favourite armchair. 'Make up your mind, John,' she said. But she could not keep it up any longer and her face cracked into a smile. 'I wasn't serious, but I was just trying to stir him up and worry him into work,' says Mimi now.

The scene ended when John said, 'I knew you were joking, Mimi.'

'Oh, no, I'm not, John.'

'Yes you are. I can't add two and two together – how can I be a bus conductor?'

11
FAME

'I battered his bloody ribs in'

Satire and comedy that leaned towards innuendo, rather than knockabout humour of the custard pie variety, had always attracted John. He grew up listening carefully, and tittering under his breath, to two radio programmes, *Up the Pole*, starring Jimmy Jewel and Ben Warris, a double act who lampooned each other, and, more significantly, *The Goon Show*. Spike Milligan and Harry Secombe's voices were clever, but John particularly loved the droll Peter Sellers, whose dry satire was captured on one of Lennon's favourite records of the period, *The Best of Sellers*. Another favourite was Stanley Unwin, who specialized in converting the English language into gibberish. He was a major influence on John's word-play in his own two books.

John's saltiness gave the Beatles their edge, on and off stage, in the recording studio and when they were travelling. It was a characteristic felt early on in the desperate attempt by Brian Epstein to secure them a recording contract.

Returning one night from London to Lime Street Station, Epstein had grim news for the Beatles: he was not getting any interest from the record companies. Their future was in jeopardy, although his hopes and determination were undimmed. He called Paul McCartney and asked the Beatles to meet him in Joe's Café in Duke Street, a haunt of night workers, lorry drivers and anyone else needing a cup of tea until 4 a.m.

'I'm afraid it's no use, I've had a flat "No",' Epstein began. Decca had turned them down, in what was to become one of the legendary rejections in the history of music. Pye had also said no.

John broke the spell and the gloom. As they all sat drinking tea and smoking, he flicked a teaspoon high into the air and said, 'Right. Try Embassy.' Embassy was then something of a joke record label, run by Woolworth's and featuring pale copies of the hits of the day.

John's remark was worthy of *The Goon Show*. He did not realize then that the Beatles' eventual recording contract was to be secured by Brian with the man who had been the Goons' recording manager, and who had been with them in the studios during the recording of phrases immortal to John's ears, such as 'Ying Tong'. It was a neat irony.

George Martin, trained as a classical pianist at the Guildhall School of Music, also played the oboe, and was artists and recording manager in charge of the Parlophone label at E.M.I. Although he got on immediately with Brian Epstein, whose refined accent he shared, the odds were that four young rock 'n' rollers from Liverpool would be at odds with his attitudes and his musical preferences. He was steeped in light orchestral music, but had a penchant for comedy. Lennon relished the prospect of making records with a man who had rubbed shoulders with such wonderful mimics.

It was during that fateful visit to Hamburg, with news of the death of Stuart so fresh in their minds, that Epstein's telegram arrived: 'E.M.I. CONTRACT SIGNED, SEALED. TREMENDOUS IMPORTANCE TO US ALL. WONDERFUL.' They returned their delight in crisp messages on postcards. Paul wrote: 'Please wire £10,000 advance royalties.' George wrote: 'Please order four new guitars.' John wrote: 'When are we going to be millionaires?'

Their recording career took off like lightning, with 'Love Me Do' as their début hit, helped by John's catchy harmonica playing. When they moved to London, and met the Rolling Stones, John was teased about that solo by the late Brian Jones, who played the harmonica on the Stones' first records.

On a visit to the Crawdaddy Club in Richmond, John was asked by Brian during the Stones' set: 'Are you playing harmonica or a blues harp on "Love Me Do"?'

Lennon replied: 'A harmonica, y'know, with a button.'

John recalled later that Brian wondered how he got such a deep bottom note during the record. John told Brian that it was 'impossible to get "Hey Baby" licks from a blues harp'. A top favourite of the Beatles at the time was Bruce Channel's harmonica-based hit, 'Hey Baby'. John did his utmost to copy that style when he played the harmonica.

One of John's most adamant statements, during the years I knew him, was that there was nothing original in rock 'n' roll, or in what he and the Beatles were doing. 'It's all rip-off,' he would say repeatedly. Reading the music papers, particularly the outlandish and pompous claims of some musicians, John would blurt out: 'This is a load of crap' at singers' or musicians' claims of originality. Rock 'n' roll to him was totally derivative. Elvis Presley, Buddy Holly, and the newer sounds of the Miracles and Tamla Motown were the *real* music, he kept saying. 'We're the receivers, we're just interpreting it as English kids. Don't let anybody ever kid you it's original. It's all a RIP OFF!' Depending on the quantity of alcohol he'd consumed, the five words would be either emphasized or screamed.

The momentum of the Beatles that began in that autumn of 1962 with 'Love Me Do' gathered with a speed that is often forgotten. Brian Epstein summed up the astounding pace of events after George Martin's offer of a recording session. 'Two years later', wrote Epstein, 'the Beatles were the greatest entertainers in the world; they had met the Queen Mother and the Duke of Edinburgh and their pictures were on the walls of the noble bedrooms of the young aristocracy. Prince Charles had all their records and San Francisco had the ticker-tape ready. They played the Hollywood Bowl, had the freedom of Liverpool. Ringo Starr was asked to be President of London University and John Lennon was the world's bestselling writer.'

In a single turbulent year for John, the Beatles had acquired an active and ambitious manager; they had an audition in the big city, London, resulting in a record contract with F.M.I.; his best friend had died in Hamburg; Pete Best had been fired as drummer, to be replaced by Ringo Starr; his girlfriend had broken the news that she was pregnant and they had hurriedly married; and the Beatles had made their television début before going to Hamburg for their fifth and final club trip.

Against that year's background, the Beatles began 1963 in a remarkable frenzy. They were booked for their first major British concert tour by package tour promoter Arthur Howes, who specialized in putting artists of the calibre of Cliff Richard and the Shadows around the cinema halls of Britain. John was particularly elated, particularly as the tour coincided with the release of 'Please

In Liverpool's dockland, waiting for their ship to come in. Ringo, Paul, John and George are watched by a gaggle of fans just as their second single 'Please Please Me', is released in January 1963

Please Me', their second single which shot to number one in the bestselling record charts. Top-of-the-bill singer on their tour was the most popular girl singer in Britain that year – Helen Shapiro, aged sixteen. A teenage prodigy, Helen had burst on the pop scene two years earlier as a schoolgirl, with her E.M.I. records 'Don't Treat Me Like A Child', 'You Don't Know' and 'Walkin' Back To Happiness'. Because of her youth, she became a national phenomenon.

Helen Shapiro was beside herself with excitement that the Beatles would be touring with her and that she would top the bill, because she had a colossal crush on John Lennon. On the coach that carried her with the Beatles across a Britain gripped by arctic weather conditions, on that one-night stand tour, she contrived to sit next to him and hoped he would not guess that her blushing hid a teenage fancy for the Beatle who was six years older than she was.

'I had a special feeling for John,' says Helen. 'He probably realized I had a crush on him. He called me "Helly" and was incredibly protective. I was mad on him, really mad. I had the biggest crush on him any sixteen-year-old could have on a guy.

'On the coach once between cities, I picked up a copy of the *Melody Maker* and opened it up to a headline: "Is Helen a has-been at sixteen?" John was sitting right behind me then, reading over my shoulder. I was really upset, but it was he who comforted me. "Don't let the swines get you down," he said to me.'

Helen had met the Beatles on stage where they were setting up their equipment. John told her that he and Paul had written a song for her, called 'Misery', but it had been rejected by her management.

In a Sheffield hotel room, Helen sat with John watching the Beatles on television. 'He was fascinated but rather put off by the way he looked, because he used to have this stance with the guitar across his chest and the legs rather bowed, going up and down. He was quite horrified. But he was excited at seeing himself on the screen. Then Gerry and the Pacemakers came on and John said: "Hey, this is our mate." We were leaning out of hotel windows, throwing photographs of ourselves at fans, and it was an incredible period, looking back.'

The protectiveness of John towards 'Helly' contrasted sharply with the 'hard man' image which built up even in the early days of the Beatles. She saw, so early in his successful career, the tender, caring side of the man. 'He would always look after me. I looked up to him not in a fatherlike way, but as a teenage girl with a wild crush. He never took advantage of me. He was always such a soft, warm, attentive fellow.

'He'd make sure I ate properly when we were travelling. He'd put his arm round me and make sure I crossed the road properly. Of all the Beatles he was by far the most polite.' At the Abbey Road recording studios the Beatles were occupying studio two, which Helen normally used, and she had to make do with studio three. 'It was John who came in with a cup of tea and kind of apologized because he'd heard I had been moved to make way for them,' says Helen. 'He came in with a cup of tea for me and a big hug.'

At Great Yarmouth in 1963, however, Helen was doing a summer season and the Beatles came in to do a Sunday concert. 'Then I realized how big they were. Everybody was all over them and I could hardly reach John. There were girls everywhere. I was incredibly jealous, for no reason, in my sweet innocence. I remember thinking: "Oh, they go with *girls*! And they drink *Scotch* and Coke." '

On the band coach, Lennon would both embarrass and amuse Helen and the rest of the cast: singers Kenny Lynch, Danny Williams, the Kestrels (featuring Roger Greenaway, later to become a major British songwriter and chairman of the Performing Right Society), and compère Dave Allen. There were jam sessions, John with guitar breaking into Beach Boys' and Shirelles' songs, and Helen joining in. A strong favourite of John's was Little Eva's hit, 'Keep Your Hands Off My Baby'. Then, suddenly, Lennon would take on the role of the court jester. He would launch into his manic impersonation of cripples and spastics. He'd pull faces out of the window. Passers by in busy High Streets would look on aghast at the absurd facial contortions of the leather-jacketed man with uncommonly long hair. 'He was very sick,' says Helen Shapiro. 'Especially if he saw a couple of nuns walking by. He'd pull the crudest faces at them.' One night in Sunderland, the practical joker in John petrified Helen when she awoke in her bedroom in the middle of the night, in virtual darkness, to see him standing there with a hat and a raincoat on.

For a cynic Lennon was acutely aware of his responsibility to fans. Autograph signing was a chore he undertook, if not enthusiastically, then fairly conscientiously. (Tragically, John's openness with fans who cared and waited was to be one reason for his ultimate murder in New York in December 1980. His assassin had lain in wait for him after getting his autograph earlier in the day and waited for him to return home to the Dakota Building the same night.) In 1963, before demands for autographs and Beatles' photographs had become so big that their road managers would forge their signatures, John was as diligent a signatory as any Beatle. 'He was portrayed, partly by himself, as the hard man of the group. But I recall him as a softie,' says Helen Shapiro. 'He certainly did care about the fans, in hotel foyers and stage doors. More than the other three, I think he valued the fans.'

Her memories of the man she fell for crystallize into quick images. 'I loved his very raw, bluesy voice, and told him so. He was surprised. He said I obviously didn't realize that it was him singing the high falsetto voice on "From Me To You". He said: "I can do the high stuff better than Paul." I do remember that.'

He moaned to Helen about his rotten teeth after seeing a picture of himself smiling. He told her to sing more songs by his favourite, Mary Wells, then Tamla Motown's undiscovered star, whom the Beatles eventually brought to their British tour when she had a huge hit with 'My Guy'. He used to mock Helen at the Ad Lib club in London's Soho, every time she went to the toilet. 'Ha, Helly, been for a secret ciggie, have we?' Helen used to smoke secretly at that time, as she was below the smoking age. 'Helly's a secret smoker,' he'd shout.

Although Beatlemania had not gripped Britain like the fever it became by autumn of that year, there were early signs as the Helen Shapiro package tour criss-crossed the country's cinemas. Despite Helen's popularity, John, Paul, George and Ringo were getting more cheers. The promoter, Arthur Howes, had to keep changing the concert running order around so the Beatles would get more than their allotted twenty minutes. Nobody wanted to go on just before the Beatles. It was a 'dead spot', with the girls in the audience getting too excited about the next act. Most of the bill resented the attention being focused on four relatively unknown lads from Liverpool. 'One day,' recalls singer Kenny Lynch, 'Arthur Howes came to me and said, "Look, you'd better go on just before the Beatles. You're the only one who doesn't care how badly you go down." ' Lynch became the man who introduced the Beatles every night. 'I'd only got to mention "the lads" and a cheer went up. I'd say: "I'm not bringing *them* on until you're quiet." There was bedlam. I knew it was a bloodless revolution the music business was experiencing. I'd say: "Ladies and gentlemen, *the lads*," and the kids would rush the stage. For a virtually unknown group, it was incredible. The game was up.'

Kenny, a warm-hearted, tough East End Londoner, struck up a strong friendship with Lennon. Both shared an abrasiveness, a dislike for humbug and convention. Lynch's first meeting with the Beatles had been at Liverpool Empire, before that tour, when Brian Epstein had presented them in concert. 'I'd been asked by Brian who I'd like backing me and I said: "Who's on the bill with me?"

'He said he had his own group, the Beatles.

'I said, "Oh, they'll do, then, but I've brought my own group."

'When I arrived, the Beatles said, "Do you want us to back you?"

'I said, "No thanks, I have my own musicians who always back me."

'They said, "Well, we'd like to back you."

'I couldn't let my people down, but John never let me forget the moment later on. He reckoned that I was one of the first guys to turn the Beatles down.'

A clear view of John's ambition during that first tour comes from Kenny Lynch's memory of a conversation, across a grand piano on the stage of the A.B.C. cinema, Carlisle.

'I said to John: "Well, what do you expect to get out of this game then?"

'He replied quickly: "All we want to do is earn a million quid each and then piss off." '

Lynch guffawed. 'Listen, you've got some chance! I've been at it for years and I haven't got two halfpennies to rub together.'

In those days, before the British motorway system expanded, the coach journeys took longer. The pop package tours forced creative people together for four or five hours at a stretch. Apart from sleeping and jam sessions, songwriting was often done on the coach, and stage acts were debated.

'I remember John and Paul saying they were thinking of running up to the microphone together and shaking their heads and singing, "Whoooooooooooo". It later became a very important, terrifically popular part of their act when they sang "She Loves You". But at the time they were planning it, even before the song was written, I remember everybody on the coach fell about laughing. I said, "You can't do that. They'll think you're a bunch of poofs." I remember John saying to me he thought it sounded great and they were having it in their act.'

But Lennon was less pleased when Kenny Lynch played him his

version of the song 'Misery', which was mostly John's own composition. The song had been intended for Helen Shapiro, but Kenny remembers her saying she disliked it because it sounded dreary. 'I'll have it,' said the eager Lynch.

But when he played his record to John and Paul, in the offices of their music publisher Dick James off Charing Cross Road, Lennon said, 'You're singing's OK, but who's that playing the telephone?'

It was John's way of blasting the guitarist.

Lynch replied: 'Don't blame me, I don't pick the musicians. Anyway, he's OK. It's Bert Weedon.'

Weedon, a solidly established player from the old school, played with great technical efficiency but little individuality. He epitomized the stylistic barrier between the Beatles' new vibrancy and the Old Guard of British musicianship. 'I said I thought Bert was OK, and that made things worse,' says Kenny Lynch. 'Lennon didn't stop bollocking me for days and weeks about Bert Weedon being on the first recording by somebody else of his song. "Bert WEEDON – he's fookin' LAST!" John kept saying.' The word became popular among the Beatles in denigrating what they mocked or regarded as unhip.

As the Beatles' popularity increased, and they made their first album in one eleven-hour recording session, John and Paul emerged as incredibly prolific songwriters, and John's aspirations to improve his writing became more and more evident. On the road, he would always be writing down phrases that occurred on the coach, in conversation. 'There was no booze and certainly no drugs on the road,' says Kenny Lynch. 'It was transport cafés, eggs and chips, Cokes and milk. John always smoked a lot but, whatever they'd done in Hamburg, they were getting the kicks from just performing and making such a quick impact on audiences all over England. They didn't need any false effects from drugs.'

Slowly, the contrasting personalities of Lennon and McCartney were becoming obvious. Although the Beatles as a group attracted girl fans by the million, Britain's fans, and later the world's, were dividing and uniting behind their own favourite within the group. 'Paul was more of the spokesman, but John had the veto,' says Kenny Lynch. 'John stood there in the dressing-room, for example, listening to Paul saying: "We're going to do this and we're going to do that," and John would suddenly stop him by saying: "Fuck it, we're NOT." And that would be it. John's word was law. It was like an offer nobody in the Beatles could refuse. There was very often this sudden interjection by John after Paul had tried to lead everything his way.' At later press conferences, Paul did most of the talking. He seemed to be taking the role of the most articulate of them. But John was the 'heavy'.

John's creativity was evident as much during that first tour as during the prolific songwriting years that were to follow. In hotels and theatre dressing-rooms and on the band coach, three Beatles went through a passion for ciné cameras. John would film horses and cattle in the fields as they travelled around; but, significantly, he was the first to drop the hobby.

What separated John from the others in the eyes of Ron King, the highly efficient coach driver who took them everywhere on that first tour, was his interest in the written word. He remembers John burying himself in the newspapers more than anyone else on the coach. 'And I remember him telling me he could get ideas for his songs from reading. He'd be watching television in his hotel, or in a dressing-room, and suddenly he'd jump for his cigarette packet on which he'd write a phrase or something he'd heard. Later, I'd hear it crop up in a song, like "I Wanna Be Your Man". I thought how clever he was. He always had books or magazines or newspapers when he was on the coach for hours on end. We'd forget he was there, or somebody would doze off, and suddenly John's voice would come up from the back: "Anyone got a ciggy?" ' In the dressing-rooms, Lennon was addicted to tea.

If 1962 had been a turbulent year for John, with Stuart's death, his own marriage and the Beatles' breakthrough, 1963 was his year of tumult. As well as the birth of his son John experienced four long, major tours of Britain including the one with Helen Shapiro. The other three found the Beatles sharing the bill with both Tommy Roe and Chris Montez, and then topping the bill over their old friends Gerry and the Pacemakers and Roy Orbison, the American singer who had influenced their work, and over Peter Jay and the Jaywalkers. They had such a close physical resemblance to the Beatles that they were used as decoys to fool the crowd into believing John, Paul, George, and Ringo had arrived at the theatre. Then, half an hour later, the real Beatles could coast in quietly after the stage door siege had dispersed.

Although Beatlemania did not properly grip Britain until the autumn, they were still making news and causing more adulation than any other British group. It was a year of sociological, political, and musical ferment. A British government minister, John

Profumo, figured in a sex scandal with names that have since passed into history: Christine Keeler and Mandy Rice-Davies. A telephone 'hot line' was established that year between the White House and the Kremlin, Pope John XXIII died, aged eighty-one. President Kennedy visited the Berlin Wall. One thousand people died in an earthquake in Yugoslavia. Back in Britain, £2 million was stolen in the legendary Great Train Robbery. The Rev. Martin Luther King made a vital speech that united Black Americans. And on 22 November, the night the Beatles played the Globe Cinema, Stockton to mounting scenes of fanmania, President Kennedy was assassinated in Dallas, Texas.

I saw a lot of the Beatles that year. The *Melody Maker*, on which I was then assistant editor, had its roots in jazz. Started in 1928, the paper had a tradition for upholding 'good musicianship'. Pop singers who 'sang in tune', like Frank Sinatra, were often allowed to cross the line into the paper, but teenage pop had been treated with contempt, as if it had nothing to do with music. It was regarded as the preserve of teenagers who were tone-deaf. The events of that year, and the infectious change in emphasis of the bestselling record charts towards new 'beat music', forced the paper to switch its policy and report the new sounds. The Beatles were front-page news every week and I went in and out of their tours, nagging Brian Epstein for exclusive access and for news stories.

One major reason the Beatles were so acceptable to the Old Guard, and even to jazz snobs, was the outspoken style of John Lennon. Quite apart from their records that were pounding up the charts, ('She Loves You' was at the top for seven weeks, and 'I Want To Hold Your Hand' for four weeks), Lennon's acrid interviews became the group's unexpected strength. The music could take care of itself, but the electricity generated by John, more than any of the Fab Four, was so alive that he quickly became the most sought-after Beatle.

Most pop stars before John had had a problem sustaining a conversation beyond the bland talk of their latest record and their narcissism. Lennon single-handedly stood that credo on its head. In his speech alone, pop music grew up. The worlds of jazz and adult music, which had grown too holy and insular, found themselves threatened not merely by great, energetic, self-made music led by the Beatles; in Lennon, above all, they faced an articulacy unheard of in popular music. He would talk about anything and everything, he would criticize himself and claim nothing whatsoever for his group, unlike the established singers

Top: John's arrogant stance – head slightly back, guitar across his chest, legs firmly astride – seen in close-up at a special reception thrown by E.M.I. Records at their offices in Manchester Square, London, to celebrate the success of 'Please Please Me' and launch the album of the same name in April 1963

Above: At the Abbey Road studios – John casts an eye towards George Martin's control room during the recording of *With The Beatles* in September 1963

who placed themselves on a pedestal. And to clinch it all, he didn't care if the Beatles were denigrated.

The rapport I built up with John Lennon in 1963 was, curiously, based partly on the musical snobbery of the old *Melody Maker*. Because the paper had a slightly older readership than other pop papers, we tended to ask more adult questions of everyone we interviewed. Glossy fan magazines pestered the Beatles for the names of their dogs and their aunts, and asked whether they preferred marmalade or honey for breakfast, as well as their height and weight. The *Melody Maker* treated the beat group players as the new musicians, and they would be invited to weigh in on any interesting subject, even old taboos like politics and religion. Lennon loved this. He hated jazz, anyway, but enjoyed talking to a paper that at least gave him credit for being intelligent – and fallible.

What made John stand apart, to me, was the interest he took in everything. He was always inquisitive, rarely pleased with a stage show, and generated intelligence as well as almost belligerent energy. It was obvious to me that, while the Beatles caravan was gaining speed, he was not satisfied merely with being rich and famous. There was always 'but. . .' in his armoury. Millionaire status and all that went with it as success came so quickly was lovely, he would imply. 'But then what?' Clearly, this was no moronic idol.

It was not a matter of self-improvement: that was not in his plan. Paul McCartney, with his keen eye on being the Beatles' diplomat and self-appointed publicist, was the social climber. He desperately needed self-improvement, and worked towards it. John once said to me: 'I've got a built-in shit detector.' He was talking specifically about music, but he might as well have been referring to his entire outlook.

Our interviews would be in dressing-rooms and hotel rooms, in the back of the Beatles' Austin Princess, on the phone, on a plane or train, or at his home in Weybridge, Surrey. There, John and Cynthia spent £19,000 on a Tudor-style mansion, Kenwood, in St George's Hill in the stockbroker belt. He told me he never liked it: he felt hemmed in, he said, by its 'bourgeois' atmosphere. Possibly, because he spent so little time there it didn't have a chance. His moods at Kenwood ranged from restless, creative, and talkative to monosyllabic and depressed.

At the height of Beatlemania I caught up with John on the road: I was with them on 1 November 1963 for the opening of their big autumn tour at Cheltenham Gaumont. Before the show, in the dressing-room, he had just washed his hair. 'I get such terrible dandruff, I think it'd be better if we cut it all off, nice and short. Think what that would do for the Beatles!' He relished the thought of rocking the boat.

He signed autographs, as he often did, while watching television or having a conversation. He rarely looked at the paper or book or programme as he signed his name on it. That night, John was at his most acerbic. In conversation with someone else, Paul McCartney had joked: 'Two things I hate in life, y'know: racial discrimination and coloured people.'

John weighed in instantly and uncomfortably at Paul: 'People who talk like that really don't like coloured people, otherwise they wouldn't think that way at all. I've heard it all before.' Adopting a broad Lancashire accent, he went on: 'Aye, theer all reet but they're so dirty and they bring down the value of property.'

Even at the age of twenty-three, John was contemplating his future from a position of pop supremacy. The Beatles were *en route* to big things, and when the Rolling Stones became friends of the Beatles he had discussed with Mick Jagger how long they would all last at the top. 'I said during a conversation with Mick Jagger that I didn't want to be fiddling round the world singing "Please Please Me" when I'm thirty. If we move into films, and they work out OK, I'll like that. People say that's where the Beatles are heading and I suppose that makes sense. But I also like A & R -ing records. Haven't done much of it but I've enjoyed watching it being done, like by Uncle George Martin. I'd like to see more of it. Recording interests me more than anything.

'I'd like to continue writing for other people and I hope we still carry on making records for a long time. I still enjoy playing live. I get slightly less kick out of things now compared with a few years ago before we had any hits. But that's natural.'

As the tours continued, and John and the others became trapped by Beatlemania, John became furious at the enormous demands made on him as a celebrity. The standing joke between them was the requests for autographs and signed photographs from mayors and mayoresses and police chiefs throughout Britain. These would usually be accompanied by the civic leaders saying: 'It's not for me, it's for my daughter.'

Lennon exploded once to me: 'I don't mind the *fans*. They've paid for a good show and they can go potty. That's OK. But I'm sick of meeting people I don't want to meet. Boring lord mayors and all that. It spoils things for me because I suppose I'm a bit intolerant. But is it any wonder I get fed up? They keep sending in autograph books and we sign them only to find they belong to officials, promoters, police and all that lot. Real fans, who'd wait for hours and days, get treated by the same cops as half-wits because they want our signatures. But the cops make sure they get theirs. I bet every bloody policeman's daughter in Britain's got an autograph. Half of them aren't our fans. It's unfair on the kids who really want them.'

Paul McCartney, sitting opposite and listening to John's anger, shouted: 'Hey, I've had enough of you blasting off, John.'

Lennon retorted: 'You say what you want to say and I'll say what I want to say, OK?'

The sharp division between John and Paul was getting easier to define. John didn't care much for coating what he said with a veneer of acceptability: he spoke as he felt. Paul not only adopted the role of diplomat, but sometimes trespassed into John's independence. The banter between them, joking but with serious undertones, continued during that evening.

Paul said, 'You're bad for my image!'

John retorted, 'You're soft. Shurrup and watch the telly like a good boy.'

John's waspish wit was at its most crushing when the adrenalin of travelling on concert tours gave him a special, edgy thrust. In October 1964 I was travelling with him in the Beatles' limousine when word came that the Duke of Edinburgh was reported as having said that the Beatles were 'on the wane'. Lennon's trenchant retort was immediate: 'The bloke's getting no money for his playing fields from me.'

Later, the Duke said he had been misreported or misheard: he had actually said the Beatles were 'away', meaning out of the country. John's dig at his playing fields referred to the Duke's involvement with the National Playing Fields Association.

John dealt savagely with journalists who asked absurd questions. In 1964 you'd have had to have been a monk, at least, not to know where the Beatles had come from.

One reporter asked him: 'Where's your home town, John?'

Lennon answered: 'Huddersfield.' That ended the interview.

A Leicester policeman, thrusting his autograph book into the limousine and into John's hand, fancied himself as a comedian. 'I see you have the same limousine that you came in last year. Money getting tight then, boys?'

John weighed in: 'Yeah, and you've got the same bloody uniform on that you wore last year. I recognize it.'

The perennial questions about the Beatles' trend-setting long

November 1963. High jinks during a British tour as John, towel around his head, and Paul play around with McCartney's two Hofner violin bass guitars

hair were met with some classic Lennon one-liners: 'Our popularity will never decline. It will *recede*. . . .No, we don't have our hair
cut, we have it *diminished* every now and then.' He often wore a
trilby hat when entering restaurants or hotels in a vain attempt to
pass unnoticed. But the stealth and intuition of Beatles fans in
seeking them out always impressed him. When a fan broke
through the security net, John was always fascinated to ask how
he or she had achieved it.

John rebelled against anything that he regarded as a compromise
with the truth. In the early 1960s, pop stars were theoretically
supposed to be unmarried. As the Beatles' fans were now being
counted in millions, Brian Epstein regarded John's marriage and
fatherhood as dangerous. When John and Cynthia moved to
London and the news trickled out, Epstein was furious. John
scarcely cared what was said about him by the Press and revelled
in being quoted and photographed, as long as he was interestingly
presented as someone other than a brainless 'moptop', as papers
called the Beatles. John's wife and child became public knowledge
early in 1964 when the couple moved into a flat found for them by
their friend, photographer Robert Freeman, at 13 Emperor's Gate,
West Kensington. Within weeks the flat became known as the
Beatles residence and the fans began to lay siege outside. Cynthia
became exhausted, too, with carrying the baby and her shopping
up five flights of stairs, so they started househunting and headed
for the suburbs.
    Lennon fought with Epstein about maintaining secrecy. 'Brian
had an obsession about not letting the marriage become public,'
says Tony Barrow, who was the Beatles' press officer at that time.
'At a very early stage of my involvement, John mentioned the fact
that he was married and Brian went berserk about it to me. He
said: "I don't know why he's told you that. Yes, of course it's true,
but he's told awfully few people and I want you to make quite sure
you don't tell anybody else." '
    Barrow believes that Epstein's determination to hold back the
truth about John was directly linked to his own homosexuality.
'He feared that some of his own private life could be made public.
He was particularly touchy about conceding any part of his artists'
private lives, simply because he had so much of a scandalous
nature to conceal in his own. Lennon regarded Eppy's edict as
wrong for two reasons: it was going to come out later, anyway, so
why not get it over with; and it would make no difference to the

Beatles' popularity. He was proved right, for when Cynthia 'went public' the Beatles' popularity continued to rise. She, meanwhile, knew nothing of John's battle with Epstein about their marriage. 'He kept so many things from me, bad and good,' says Cynthia. 'I only heard much later that Brian wanted me kept quiet.' John knew, however, when to draw the line. Shortly after they moved to London, I asked him if I could interview Cynthia to prepare an unusual profile of him. 'I'd like to ask her what it's like being married to you, and what it's like being the envy of millions of girls,' I said, when John asked me why.

He fixed me with a withering look. 'No bloody fear,' he said. 'I'm the bloody star around here.'

Fielding the Press, radio and television, became an art and a full-time job. Tony Barrow, Liverpool-born and the record reviewer of the *Liverpool Echo* under the pseudonym of Disker, had been pestered by Epstein from the early days to write about 'the boys'. When eventually he was lured to London to take on the job of press officer for Epstein's fast-growing NEMS organization, Barrow was invited by Brian to meet them for the first time in a pub, the Devonshire Arms, near E.M.I.'s Manchester Square headquarters.

'John was relatively quiet that night,' says Tony Barrow. 'Paul McCartney seemed to dominate the proceedings. He came round asking everybody what they wanted to drink and I was very impressed by this, until I realized that he relayed the whole order to Brian Epstein, who picked up the bill.'

Lennon did not speak for a while to the man who would handle his press work. When he eventually was introduced to him, John said: 'Well, Tony, if you're not queer and you're not Jewish, why are you joining NEMS?' Brian overheard the remark, but ignored it. It was among many taunts which John was to toss at Brian. When Eppy was writing his autobiography in 1964, he asked John if he had a suggestion for a title. 'Why don't you call it *Queer Jew*?' said John. The book was called *A Cellarful of Noise*. John parodied that as *A Cellarful of Boys*. The crushing remarks made by John simply increased Epstein's admiration and respect for him.

His fascination for Brian was obvious to Lennon, who interpreted it as a kind of weakness. It was John's clear masculinity, fearlessness, abrasiveness, and aggression, which Epstein could not match, that proved such a powerful attraction. Nor did Lennon shrink from cruelly putting Brian down in public. At Abbey Road recording studios one day, Epstein ventured an opinion about the sound they were making. Across the studio, with everyone listening, John said: 'You stick to your percentages,

Brian. We'll make the music.' When he put the verbal knife in like that, his voice would have a toughness that invited no reply.

John's resentment of Brian Epstein's involvement with their music went back a long way. He maintained that they had been turned down by Decca mostly because Brian had insisted that at their audition they did mostly standards like 'September In The Rain' and not 'ravers which we went down well with at the Cavern'. John never forgot or forgave Brian for inflicting his own, wrong choice of material on the Beatles which resulted in that rejection, and he decided that never again would he let Brian near a decision about their music. Epstein kept his peace – reluctantly, because he considered he had a good ear for music.

Three weeks after the birth of Julian, and between the vital British tours with Chris Montez/Tommy Roe and Roy Orbison/ Gerry and the Pacemakers, the Beatles were officially on holiday. John went to Spain for twelve days with Brian Epstein. 'I didn't think anything about it,' said Cynthia. 'John said he'd been working very hard, with the concert tours and the album. He needed a break.' She was frantically busy, anyway, with a new baby and setting up temporary home in Mendips.

Lennon knew, of course, about Brian's fixation on him, but he could not have anticipated the campaign of whispering that holiday would give rise to. As one who was close to him during the Beatles' rise to fame, I saw a solidly heterosexual man. He did not boast about his exploits, but he made it abundantly clear that he enjoyed women. John would hardly have taunted Brian so mercilessly about his sexual preferences if he felt any empathy with him as a homosexual.

When John returned, he was livid at the rumours. The girls in the NEMS office, naïve about homosexuality, which was illegal, giggled nervously and were told by John, patiently, and for the first time in their lives, what homosexuality meant. He told them in general conversation and 'from a distance'.

But his Spanish trip with Epstein erupted into a scandal. John and Cynthia, along with many Liverpool musicians, like Gerry and the Pacemakers, Billy J. Kramer, and the Shadows from London, went to Paul McCartney's twenty-first birthday party on 18 June 1963, a party held mostly in the garden, and in a marquee, at the house of Paul's Auntie Jin, in Dinas Lane, Huyton.

John had little to eat and too much to drink at the party. Bob Wooler, the old friend who had introduced the Beatles on stage at

John and Brian Epstein relaxing in Miami, Florida, where the Beatles did two television shows during their triumphant first American tour in February 1964

the Cavern nearly three hundred times, said something to John about his visit to Spain with Epstein. John laid into Wooler with a ferocity that landed the disc jockey in hospital with a black eye, bruised ribs, and torn knuckles. Brian Epstein drove Bob Wooler to hospital.

The party broke up in disarray. Cynthia, who left with John, recalls: 'John said: "He called me a queer so I battered his bloody ribs in." '

Billy J. Kramer was at that party. (John had injected the 'J' into his name during a chat in Epstein's office. 'He thought it had more flow. I said: "What's the J. for, if anyone asks me?" John said it was for Julian.') Billy J., as John called him was in the marquee at Paul's party with several show business personalities. 'I remember asking Bruce Welch of the Shadows what he thought of the Beatles, and his reply: "They've written a few catchy songs, nothing special. Once they dry up that'll be the end of them." ' Kramer recalls the conversation because John had said it was one of his greatest ambitions to 'blow the Shadows out – he couldn't stand their clean music'. Kramer recalls that after he had laid into Bob Wooler, John grabbed the body of a girl who was standing next to him. 'I said: "Lay off, John." But he lashed into her. He'd had too much booze. I was semi-professional at the time, and he was winding me up as I left before him, shouting: "You're nothing, Kramer, and we're the top." ' Lennon was at his most withering when the demon drink fuelled his insecurities.

Kramer was furious. Epstein apologized for John to him next day, but Billy said: 'I refuse to take a second-hand apology.' A few days later, Lennon met Kramer in a Liverpool street, and immediately put out his hand to shake: 'I'm really sorry about what happened that night,' said John.

News of John's fisticuffs with Bob Wooler filtered through to the northern newsdesks of Britain's national papers. Tony Barrow received several phone calls next day. 'What's your lad John Lennon been up to? Been a naughty boy, has he?' Barrow's first thoughts were that news of John's marriage to Cynthia had leaked and he would face trouble from Epstein. 'Although Julian was two months old by then,' says Barrow, 'the news that John was married, let alone a father, was still a secret. Some fans in Liverpool knew, but nationally it was still unknown.' When the Press confronted Barrow with the news of the Lennon–Wooler punch-up, Tony phoned John to find out what his reply should be. 'He was completely unrepentant. He said: "The bastard was saying I was bloody queer so I smacked him one, I punched him one, he deserved it, he went a bit too far, and I don't care what the Press make of that, sod it." '

But by the time the *Daily Mirror*, through its show business reporter Don Short, had got to Lennon, his story had become either more apologetic or more diplomatic, on Epstein's advice. In the first national newspaper recognition of the Beatles' import-ance, Don Short wrote in the *Mirror* under the headline: 'Beatle in Brawl – Sorry I Socked You':

> Guitarist John Lennon, twenty-two-year-old leader of the Bea-tles pop group, said last night: 'Why did I have to go and punch my best friend? I was so high I didn't realize what I was doing.' Then he sent off a telegram apologizing to twenty-nine-year-old [*sic*] Liverpool rock show compère and disc jockey Bob Wooler . . .who said: 'I don't know why he did it. I have been a friend of the Beatles for a long time. I have often compèred shows where they have appeared. I am terribly upset about this, physically as well as mentally.'
>
> John Lennon said: 'Bob is the last person in the world I would want to have a fight with. I can only hope he realizes that I was too far gone to know what I was doing.'

John badly damaged his forefinger. Back at Mendips, he walked around hiding his right hand from Mimi for several days in case she should see his injuries and ask him how it happened.

Years later, the homosexual leader of a rock band, Tom Robinson, maintained that the first gay rock song was written by Lennon in 1965. Millions heard the song, 'You've Got To Hide Your Love Away', as a sentimental ballad written in John's period of great influence by the songwriting style of Bob Dylan. But Robinson believes the words were a message to Brian Epstein.

A few years later, John wrote a message to an American publication called the *Gay Liberation Book*. The editors had solicited contributions from prominent people, and John's read as follows:

> Why make it sad to be gay?
> Doing your thing is okay.
> Our body's our own, so leave us alone
> And play with yourself today.

Anyone who knew John Lennon would dismiss the suggestion that he was a homosexual. On tour, he was an aggressive woman hunter, something he was to confess to Cynthia when their marriage foundered. He had a massive sexual appetite for women, and particularly for new conquests. Women who had been with him spoke of John as an enthusiastic lover but 'rough and ready, never kind and considerate'. All through his life, he was a woman chaser.

'I slept in a million hotel rooms, as we all did, with John and there was never any hint that he was gay,' says Paul McCartney. The rumour that caused Lennon to punch Bob Wooler for a suggestive remark was explained by Paul in an interview on London's Capital Radio with Roger Scott:

> When the group was formed John was a smart cookie. Brian Epstein was going on holiday to Spain and Brian was gay. He invited John along. John, not being stupid, saw his opportunity to impress upon Mr Epstein who was the boss of this group. And I think that's why John went on holiday. And good luck to him, too – he was that kind of guy, he wanted Brian to know who he should listen to in this group, and that was the relationship.
>
> John was very much the leader in that kind of sense, although it was never actually said, we were all sort of leaders. But in truth . . . John was probably the deciding vote. He was into that.
>
> So they say he went on holiday with someone who was known to be gay and therefore he is gay.

Paul recalls someone asking John once if he had ever tried homosexuality, and Lennon's crunching reply, 'No. I haven't met a fellow I fancy enough!'

And the girls at college with him echo Cynthia's statement on the subject: 'You'd have to look a long way to find a more heterosexual man. The suggestion that he was anything else is too ridiculous for words.'

For people inside the Beatles circle, John needed to be treated with kid gloves. Paul, ever charming, polite, informative, was never a media problem. Ringo assumed the air of a cuddly, amiable guy, lucky to be hoisted aboard the Beatles just before the group shot to fame. George, who hated invasions of his privacy, was not comfortable with the Press but he was tolerant and spoke intelligently. John was different. 'I was sometimes nervous of what impression he would make upon third parties, rather in the same way one sent home sensitive aunts and uncles if John Lennon was

Top: Author Ray Coleman is at John's right shoulder during a walk down the Champs-Elysées during the Beatles' three-week season at the Paris Olympia in January 1964

Above: February 1964. Stepping out in New York with Paul and Ringo, John is pictured in Central Park against a background of the home where he was to settle eight years later

due to drop in,' recalls Tony Barrow. 'I wasn't wary of asking him to do interviews. He was co-operative, although he'd grumble and curse if it wasn't convenient. But I was selective about the journalists I sent to him. It had to be someone sufficiently worldly, or sophisticated, with a decent and preferably way-out sense of humour, to accept John as he was. The journalist didn't have to be offended by the guy. John always asked for someone who shared his outrageous sense of humour, who would come back at him with something as nasty and cynical as he gave them. Otherwise he might just turn a bit nasty on an ill-informed or inexperienced journalist. Or he'd particularly turn on one who thought he knew too much or knew all about the Beatles.'

Billy J. Kramer later had good reason to appreciate their healed relationship. The first song given to him by Brian Epstein was a tape of John Lennon playing acoustic guitar and singing the demonstration of a song he'd written called 'Do You Want To Know A Secret'. 'John later apologized for the tape quality but said he'd done the demo in the toilet, as it was the quietest place he could find.' The sound of the loo flushing at the end confirmed John's story. 'God,' says Billy J. Kramer, 'if I had that tape now it would be worth a fortune.' John and Paul went on to give him several hits that boosted his career: a number one with 'Bad To Me' plus 'From A Window' and 'I'll Keep You Satisfied'.

John's intake of alcohol rose a lot during the heady Beatles years. As undisputed kings of the Swinging London decade, the Beatles held court at the Ad Lib club, above the Prince Charles cinema in Leicester Street, Soho. It vied with two other clubs as the focal point for pop and cinema stars, photographers and fashion people. The other night spots were the Scotch of St James in Masons Yard near Piccadilly, and the Bag o' Nails in Cromwell Road, West Kensington. The night began around one o'clock after a concert. Often, Lennon, getting steadily more drunk on Scotch and Coke, and smoking incessantly his favourite brand, Peter Stuyvesant, would become more and more emotional as the drink took hold.

A favourite habit when he was lubricated was to seize one person for a verbal hammering and not let go until that person was utterly exhausted by the sheer persistence of John's argument. There was a streak in John that could not bear to lose a battle. With Mick Jagger or Alan Price, both intelligent men with plenty of opinions, John would rant all night about music or a city or who was winning the popularity race between the Beatles, the Rolling Stones, the Animals, and the Hollies. He particularly hated

Manchester's Hollies. He regarded them as syrupy copyists of the Beatles' vocal style.

It could be argued that John Lennon was always worldly, even as a Quarry Bank pupil lampooning the teachers and as a perverse Liverpool Art College student. But those qualities grew within the fast-moving Beatles story. Music aside, and there were some catatonic moments in which he and Paul touched the heights, John was intuitive enough to understand that it was an unstoppable bandwagon. If it wasn't exactly out of control, it was moving too fast for him to have a lot of impact on it, so he might as well get stuck in and enjoy it, particularly the money, while Beatlemania gripped Britain, and quickly, the impossible dream happened: they conquered America.

Just before that happened, Britain had its first national glimpse of the subtle difference in personalities within the Beatles whom they had previously regarded as four lovable Liverpool lads with perhaps equal brightness. At the Royal Variety Show in London, it was John who entered the history books with the irreverent, hilarious line: 'Will the people in the cheaper seats clap your hands? All the rest of you, if you'll just rattle your jewellery. . . .' John was determined to have a dig of some kind at royalty. John learned, very early, the art of manipulating an event, a situation, and also a person. Cynical about the royal patronage, he told Epstein of the joke he planned backstage. Brian used every ounce of his persuasion in stopping John from saying: '. . .the rest of you just rattle your fucking jewellery'.

No group, before or since, could have 'closed ranks' more forcefully than the Beatles. However close to the band anyone felt, when the hotel suite, or limousine, or dressing-room door was shut, the four men insisted on privacy and group unity when they needed it. The only man who could remotely be described as the fifth Beatle was Neil Aspinall, who went to Liverpool Institute with Paul and George. He was the man who drove their Commer van for them back in the Cavern days, and who gave up a solid career in accountancy to become their utterly trusted friend, confidante, and world-travelling tour manager. 'Nell', as he was to the Beatles, is still today the managing director in London of Apple, the bizarre company left by the Beatles since they split.

Brian Epstein liked to regard himself as the fifth Beatle, yet for all their affection for his loyalty and what he achieved for them, the Beatles did not consider him a true insider. Precision, style, presentation and urbanity were his strengths. The more the media screamed that the Rolling Stones were unkempt and a danger to daughters, the more Epstein concentrated on projecting his 'boys', as he insisted on calling them, as intelligent and clean. It worked perfectly. As hair everywhere got longer and skirts were shorter, Beatlemania became the acceptable face of Swinging Britain.

Brian Epstein's admiration of John directly affected what the Beatles did. Eppy clashed with Paul about many things, from the timing of tours to the lists of people in the Beatles' entourage who should accompany them. There was an unwritten rule that the Beatles and the Rolling Stones would never have a single record out at the same time because a 'same day' release might split and confuse the fans – and one of the two supergroups would be kept from the coveted number one spot. It was Paul who did the arranging of the timing, usually with Mick Jagger. Epstein did not like Paul's intrusion, but just how adept McCartney was at managing his career became obvious when the Beatles split and he became the world's most successful popular musician and songwriter.

'Paul can be temperamental and moody and difficult to deal with,' said Epstein. 'This means that we compromise on our clash of personalities. He is a great one for not wishing to hear about things and if he doesn't want to know he switches himself off, settles down in a chair, puts one booted foot across his knee and pretends to read a newspaper, having consciously made his face an impassive mask.'

Epstein's interpretation of John was, predictably, more convoluted. Writing in his autobiography, Epstein said:

> John Lennon, his [Paul's] friend from boyhood, his co-writer of so many songs, the dominant figure in a group which is virtually without a leader, is in my opinion a most exceptional man. Had there been no Beatles and no Epstein participation, John would have emerged from the mass of the population as a man to reckon with. He may not have been a singer or a guitarist, a writer or a painter, but he would most certainly have been a Something. You cannot contain a talent like this. There is in the set of his head a controlled aggression which demands respect.

Brian went on to say how John had sometimes been abominably rude to him.

But because he loved him so much, Brian would take it. As the speed of Beatlemania demanded decisions faster than subtlety,

McCartney realized that Lennon was able to influence Epstein very strongly on any matter involving the group. So when he thought there might be a clash with Epstein, Paul would feed his demands through John, who could get his own way every time. Because he was such a smoothie, Epstein was intrigued by John's cruel tongue. Though it hurt him, he would take it.

Yet for all his foibles, and for all the warts, business and personal, attached to his discovery and management of the Beatles, Brian Epstein was a superb manager for them. His devotion was unyielding, his belief in their originality infectious, his sense of fairness a byword. When he died in 1967, the Beatles began to fall apart as a group. Brian Epstein was a man of strong principles, right for his time as the mentor of the world's greatest pop group. He succeeded in helping them become 'bigger than Elvis'. Those of us who knew him well remember his warmth, his passion, and his precision which was more important to the success story than we knew at the time. 'Paul has the glamour, John the command,' said Epstein. It was an astute observation in 1964, which will always hold true.

Listening to John on stage, it was difficult to believe he was the master of the sharp jibe. On the British and European tours, the screams were so loud that the Beatles' performance became more of a ritual than a show. The music was unimportant. 'It's like we're four freaks being wheeled out to be seen, shake our hair about, and get back in our cage afterwards,' he said to me. He became irritable about it but grew reconciled to Beatlemania. He expected the Beatles to last about five years, and in terms of live performances he was not far wrong. His stage personality was electrifying in 1963 and 1964. Legs arrogantly apart, head tilted back slightly to emphasize his prominent nose, guitar across his chest, John exuded an air of detached uninterest. By then he wore contact lenses, recommended to John by Bobby Goldsboro during the British tour by Roy Orbison and the Beatles. (Goldsboro, then Orbison's guitarist, later emerged as a successful solo singer, with records like 'Honey' and 'Summer (The First Time)'.) John told me that Goldsboro's recommendation was a great idea and a drag as well. 'I mean, I couldn't be seen in horn-rimmed specs on stage, that would never do for a Beatle, folks! But the contacts are not easy to control.' They were regularly falling out either on stage, causing him visual chaos, or in dressing-rooms or hotels where I, like many others who were with him, spent many an hour fumbling in thick pile carpet looking for a missing lens. 'Can you imagine what it's like,' he once said, 'hearing all that noise and playing, and not seeing a *thing*? It's frightening.'

John's reputation for repartee was certainly not born from his communications on stage. 'We'd like to sing a number from our new L.P.,' was typical of the inanity that he managed above the roar. But the difference between John and Paul was as easy to define in a concert as millions have found on records.

John would be at his blistering best on his cherished favourites, rockers like 'Twist and Shout' and 'Money', while Paul would woo the girls in the crowd with his romantic specialities, 'All My Loving' and 'Till There Was You', the unlikely song from the show *The Music Man* which the Beatles used on stage to break up their rock 'n' roll diet. John would roar into his own songs 'I Feel Fine', which he claimed was the first-ever record to feature the feedback technique, and would lead on the autobiographical 'Help!' Paul dominated on 'Can't Buy Me Love' and, as if to reclaim his rock 'n' roll roots, often hammered out a powerful 'Long Tall Sally'.

Lennon's lack of interest in live performing struck me forcefully one night in Exeter. He had forgotten the words to 'I Want To Hold Your Hand', and asked me to write down what I could remember of them on the back of his hand. They were ingrained into my consciousness at the time, so I did it, in biro.

'It wouldn't matter if I never sang,' he said cynically. 'Often I don't anyway. I just stand there and make mouth movements. Nobody knows. I reckon we could send out four waxwork dummies of ourselves and that would satisfy the crowds. Beatles concerts are nothing to do with music any more. They're just bloody tribal rites.'

Just as he got no thrill from performing, John took no interest whatsoever, in the sixties, in seeing other artists on stage. 'I'm a record man,' he said. 'I just like records. It always spoils it for me when I see someone whose records I like – they're never as good live.'

The squeals of Beatlemania seemed insane to John. The debasement of the music, the pandemonium, the hurling on stage of dolls and teddy bears, and jelly babies once they had said they liked to eat them, was all too juvenile for his speedy mind. He went along for the ride, but, as always in his life, there was a 'get-out' clause. he devised his own method of coping with the lunacy. 'Nice endings to songs don't work in that situation,' said John. 'The kids are all getting worked up about something that's not music.' He let

Top: A straw sunhat for John as he relaxes in Miami in February 1964
Above: November 1963. John chatting to the secretaries at the offices of NEMS Enterprises and the Beatles fan club headquarters in Monmouth Street, London

out that pent-up shriek of resentment at what he had to do to get to the top and stay there. At the end of a song, as a wave of screaming cascaded around the hall, John would screech out an obscenity to complete the song. It was his own release.

'The others didn't have John's resentment of having to do what he was doing to be a Beatle,' says Mike McCartney. 'They thought they were just bloody lucky they were getting away with it for so long. But John always had that drive, something ticking over, the need to do something else. It was: "Ah, so *this* is what we have to do to be bigger than Elvis? OK, let's go, but I'm not going to give it one hundred per cent of me." ' That individuality stayed and marked him out as the most original of the four.

'On the road, in dressing-rooms and hotels, John usually had an aggressive attitude,' says British tour promoter Arthur Howes, who presented most of their concerts right from the start of their nationwide popularity. 'But I could see it was defensive, a cover-up for the real John who was a nice, soft-hearted man. At dinner after concerts he would launch into Stanley Unwin-type double-talk. I'd never met anyone with such a fast style in one-liners. At Dublin airport once, a reporter asked the Beatles where Brian Epstein was, and, quick as a flash, John replied: "Oh, he's in America signing up a new rhythm-and-Jews group." On aggression alone, John was the leader of the Beatles.'

'When he wasn't bullying or bellowing, he could be very kind and considerate,' says Tony Barrow. 'He was very friendly and very popular with the NEMS office staff in Liverpool. And once, when Brian Epstein fired a girl typist in a fit of temper, merely for messing up a Dictaphone tape, John was there and turned the whole episode into a joke. He laughed a lot about it. And if Lennon laughed, Epstein laughed. So the girl got her job back.'

His sense of the absurd and obsession with deformity in people gave him both laughter and tears on the road. This was another escape route. He once autographed a programme: 'Sodoffy from John Leper'. And when he spoke of things he did not like, he would sometimes say: 'It was horrible – really spastic.' I challenged him about it one night over one of Cynthia's chicken dinners at Weybridge. He had made a strong little speech about success. It was in 1965.

'I want no more from being a record star. I'm not uninterested but there is more, now, than making good records and selling them. I'd like to see us making better and better films. That's very difficult. Unlike pop music, it allows you to grow up as a person. I'm not craving for any more gold discs even though they're a nice boost. That's all over. I just want to be an all-round spastic – think how awful it would be to be an old Beatle, or a grey-haired Beatle, or a spastic Beatle.'

Cynthia gave him a crushing look.

'Enjoying your dinner?' said John. 'Look, I mean nothing *nasty* about these spastics. I don't think I'd know a real spastic from a Polaroid lens. I'm not hung up about them. When I use the word "spastic" in general conversation, I don't mean it literally. I feel terrible sympathy for these people. It seems to be like the end of the world when you see deformed spastics, and we've had quite a lot of them on our travels.

'In the States, they were bringing hundreds of 'em along backstage and it was fantastic. I can't stand looking at 'em. I have to turn away. I have to laugh or I'd collapse from hate *of the situation*. Listen, in the States, they lined 'em up and you got the impression the Beatles were being treated as bloody faith healers. It was sickening.'

Tough, cantankerous, and iconoclastic John was, but there were also signs of enormous wit and compassion. That night, after dinner, we all went out to a private showing of the Michael Caine film *The Ipcress File*. On the twenty-mile journey from Surrey back into London, John's Rolls-Royce was smeared with lipstick and dented by fans as they waited at traffic lights and they spotted a Beatle in the back. Girls banged on the doors and wings and blocked the road. 'John, John,' they screamed. He carried on reading and locked himself in. The chauffeur became irritable and was about to get out and push them away. 'Leave them,' snapped John. 'They bought the car. They've got the right to smash it up.'

12
DRUGS

'But Cyn, it's fantastic, it's wonderful'

It was not a normal marriage and he could never be a normal father. When Cynthia was heavily pregnant in February and March 1963, John was touring Britain; he was also appearing with the Beatles when Julian was born on 8 April in Liverpool; and by 18 May he was off again for another three-week tour, this time with Gerry and the Pacemakers and Roy Orbison.

The Beatles did four major tours that year, and went on to become one of the busiest travelling groups in pop before they finally ended live work in 1966. John was the only Beatle who had embarked on that long and winding road with a wife and son.

The first clash in John and Cynthia's marriage occurred when Julian was nine months old. John was appearing in the Beatles' Christmas Show in London and had not been in touch for several days. Cynthia decided the time was right for the baby to be christened, and went ahead with organizing it in Hoylake Parish Church, opposite her home in Trinity Road. She had gone to Sunday School there as a child.

The christening passed off quietly one Sunday morning, except for Julian's show-stopping habit of knocking the vicar's glasses off his face. But when Cynthia carried him outside the church, there were photographers. Next day, newspapers featured pictures of a Beatle's baby being carried away from his christening.

John phoned Cynthia when he read about it in the newspaper during his tour. He was livid. 'What's all *this*? He didn't need baptizing or christening.'

Cynthia argued that he did, to give him a seal of religious belief in his life. 'It's simple, it doesn't harm anybody, and it's over and done with.'

John's anger continued: 'Well I didn't want it done, and you should have told me.'

Cynthia said she was sorry, but with John away on tour she had to get things done and she did not expect him to react so strongly.

There were, says Cynthia, four major changes in John's personality during their marriage: the student, the father, the meeting with Brian Epstein that shaped his future, and the rich, famous Beatle. But the one over which John agonized the most was his fatherhood.

'As far as our marriage was concerned,' says Cynthia, 'we got on great. It wasn't the greatest whizzo-active relationship and once he became a Beatle we didn't go out much and see the sights, as husband and wife. But we had holidays with the other Beatles and we were strong as a unit in that home.'

Apart from the christening eruption, Cynthia recalls one other major blow-up by John. Returning from another tour to family life at Weybridge, John was having breakfast with Cynthia and Julian one morning. While eating, Julian made a typical three-year-old's mess of the food and everything else on the table. 'John stood up and blew his top, screaming at this little boy who couldn't understand this man who he very rarely saw!' says Cynthia. 'Julian wasn't the tidiest of eaters as a child and needed coaxing and he was a crying baby too.

'When John screamed at Julian, I flew off the handle. I disappeared upstairs in a fit of tears. I said: "If you were here more often, you'd understand your child. You can't just come home, blow your top and take it out on a little boy who doesn't understand." John was sweet then, very apologetic and understanding. It was the only real row we ever had. He'd just come home from a tour, all hyped up and nervous and, somebody was going to get it. It was unfair that Julian and I were the people he chose.'

The stress of life with this agitated, extraordinary pop star who darted in and out of their home took a heavy toll on their marriage. 'It was very hard for him to adjust to home after two or three weeks of all the adrenalin of screams and being hyped up after concerts here or in America or Europe,' she says. 'We were on different wavelengths. The patterns of our thoughts were obviously different. I decided to offer him security. I tried to stay the same person for him. It was probably the worst thing I could have done. I should have gone out and got on with other things,

June 1965. John and Cynthia pose in the garden at Weybridge

Opposite: On a skiing holiday in St Moritz, Switzerland, in 1965

developed my own activities. But I didn't. I thought: "Well, at least if I'm here and Julian's fine and he has me, he has these roots." But there were too many people pulling on these roots in those Beatle days. I couldn't get them into the ground quickly enough.'

The magic moments for Cynthia were when they took off on holidays, at the height of Beatlemania. There was Tahiti with George and Pattie Boyd, St Vincent in the Caribbean with Ringo and Maureen Starr, St Moritz with George and Judy Martin, swimming in the sea, playing Monopoly and drinking Scotch and Coke and eating well. 'John became quite hefty and was really enjoying the pleasure of being rich. I could see he felt under pressure, but I didn't know how much. But he enjoyed the holidays, there were no drugs, and he reverted to being a Liverpool lad.' They managed to stay anonymously in hotels: the machinery of Brian Epstein's organization ensured that manager and staff did not blurt out the news of their presence to anyone.

Indulgence, in fact, was John's pleasure for a time. On buying Kenwood in Weybridge, the value of the house was quickly doubled by the building of a swimming pool. John wanted the pool bottom to be a full-sized mirror, but ended up accepting a gigantic eye painted on the bottom. The pool and its adaptations cost £20,000. John didn't blink an eye at the cost.

Despite his absence from home, Lennon enjoyed the fact that he was a father. The tears of joy that welled up in him when he first visited Cynthia in hospital and held his son for the first time stayed true during the boy's years as a toddler. 'He often said it was a shame his family had to be pushed into the background,' says Cynthia. 'He regretted it, but once the Beatles wagon was rolling, he could not get off it if he wanted to. He became exhausted and irritable when he was at home, and angry at his own absence when he wasn't there.' In 1966, by which time he was heavily into smoking marijuana and sleeping until two or three in the afternoon when he was at Weybridge, John let out his thoughts in his song 'I'm Only Sleeping':

> When I wake up early in the morning
> Lift my head, I'm still yawning
> When I'm in the middle of a dream
> Stay in bed, float upstream
> Please don't wake me, no, don't shake me
> Leave me where I am, I'm only sleeping.

Everybody seems to think I'm lazy
I don't mind, I think they're crazy
Running everywhere at such a speed
Till they find there's no such need
Please don't spoil my day, I'm miles away
And after all, I'm only sleeping.

'One big change I noticed in his habits, once the Beatles got going, was in his sleeping,' says Cynthia. 'He would collapse into a dead sleep and be immovable until afternoons unless there was an appointment to be kept earlier. We were both book fanatics and read until the early hours. I'd usually fall asleep before he did.' An avid collector as well as reader, John would stop his chauffeur and make weekly swoops on bookshops throughout London and Surrey. Tennyson, Swift, Tolstoy, Oscar Wilde, Aldous Huxley, and all the *Just William* books from his childhood ranged across the huge bookcase in the lounge. When Cynthia's mother lived at the house, John asked her, 'Lil, go and fill the bookshelves.' He could not stand the sight of empty bookshelves. He chauvinistically told Cynthia she could not have a full-time nanny for Julian; he wanted his son to have the mother he had been deprived of when he was a child.

John was keen on spending money. He would make unscheduled stops with his chauffeur and return with expensive clocks, a huge leather-bound Bible, or a compendium of toys, and one day a suit of armour which he had ordered was delivered. 'This is Sidney,' John announced: the armour occupied pride of place in the hall. Nearby reposed a more quixotic, priceless gift from George Harrison: a pair of crutches.

When they closed Harrods for the Beatles to do their Christmas shopping, John arrived home and presented Cynthia with several fur coats and 'naughty nighties'. But he always forgot birthdays. 'It wasn't important to me,' says Cynthia. 'John was soft, generous, and gave when it was least expected. He never was tight, going right back to college. If he had a cigarette he would always offer you one, and light it.' But she always gazed jealously at something Ringo did when he and Maureen joined John and Cynthia at either one of their houses. 'Ringo had this habit of lighting up two cigarettes, one for Maureen at the same time that he lit his own. I remember thinking it was a loving thing to do, and wishing John did it for me. But that would have been too obviously demonstrative, maybe, for John. . . .'

what we said about it. It's not much bother really, is it? when you think about it - 'cause I'm sure Dot and Lil' and Beanos, Tommy, Dorley etc can understand something as simple as us wanting to be alone for a day. — I don't mean Julian tho' — I mean don't pack him off to Dots or anywhere - I really miss him as a person now - do you know what I mean, - he's not so much 'The Baby' or 'my baby' anymore he's a real living part of me now — you know he's Julian and everything and I can't wait to see him, I miss him more than I've ever done before' — I think its been a slow process my feeling like a real father! I hope all this is clean and understandable, I spend hours in dressing rooms and things thinking about the times I've wasted not being with him - and playing with him - you know I keep thinking of those stupid bastard times when I keep reading bloody newspapers and other shit whilst he's in the room with me and I've decided it's ALL WRONG! He doesn't see enough of us as it is and I really want him to

Part of a letter from John to Cynthia, written in August 1965 when he was in California during a Beatles tour of America. 'Dot' was Dorothy Jarlett, the housekeeper at Weybridge, and 'Lil' was Lilian Powell, Cynthia's mother. The other names are those of occasional staff and friends

I know and love me, and miss me like
I seem to be missing both of you so much.
Still go now 'cause I'm bringing
myself down thinking what a thoughtless
bastard I seem to be — and it's only sort
of three o'clock in the afternoon and it
seems the wrong time of day to feel so
emotional — I really feel like crying - it's
stupid — and I'm choking up now as I'm
writing — I don't know what the matter with
me — & Its not the tour that's so different
from other tours — I mean I'm having lots
of laughs (you know the type he! he!) but in
between the laughs there is such a drop — I
mean there seems no in-between feelings.
Anyway I'm going now so
that this letter doesn't get to draggy.
I love you very much.

P.S. Say hello to Charles
etc. for me.

P.P.S. I think you can ring
me if you have a phone there
try — if not I'll see you in about a week.
271-6565
LOS ANGELES,
CALIFORNIA.

To Cyn
from
John X + + X X X X
X X X X
X X + X X X X

P.P.S.
It's Monday the 23rd today
and I leave this house next Monday
the 30th of August - so try to ring

Her pocket money was £50 in cash a week, and a similar amount was arranged by John to go to Aunt Mimi. 'It was quite a lot, considering I didn't have any bills to pay,' says Cynthia. 'All the food and nearly everything else was on accounts, so there was nothing to spend it on.' Like royalty, John rarely carried any cash or a cheque book. 'Send the bill in,' he would say, whenever he was in a club or restaurant or bookshop.

John, as always, was in a hurry. Once Beatlemania arrived it was great, but it left him feeling strangely unfulfilled, for all the tangible benefits it brought. What Beatlemania brought John, above all, was freedom. Or so he thought.

Drugs entered their marriage, and contributed to its eventual collapse, quite innocently. 'John was always seeking interesting ways to get rid of the mundane and close a chapter. The Beatles were so big, the pressure on him and Paul so much, that he kept looking for new things to occupy his mind. We all went to a party at Brian Epstein's flat in Williams Mews, Knightsbridge, and that was the first time John and I smoked marijuana.' Paul McCartney was the only Beatle not there.

After several puffs, John said: 'The only thing this is doing to me is giving me the giggles.' Cynthia's reaction after smoking the joint was to be violently sick. She rejected offers of more marijuana at the round of dinners to which she and John were invited; but John got steadily more engrossed in smoking during 1965.

When a dentist spiked their coffee with L.S.D. the first effects were again horrific and John thought it was potentially enlightening and worth investigation.

'I warned him against it,' says Cynthia. 'At times I felt like a mother, shouting at him for being a naughty boy but he'd say: "But Cyn, it's FANTASTIC, it's WONDERFUL. Why don't you do it?'

'I said, "No, because I know what it does, it makes me ill, sick."

' "But it's great, Cyn," John continued, "you've got to be with me, you've *got* to do it." '

Says Cynthia, 'He was so enthusiastic and so happy about the whole thing, and I just couldn't be. We couldn't meet on that level, and although I did try I didn't see what he saw. He obviously saw his escape from whatever he was running away from. I wasn't running away from it. So I didn't really need it.

'What I think John wanted was a kind of mental freedom. He was trying to shed responsibility. I don't think John was a very responsible person. He didn't want to account all the time to anybody but himself. He didn't want to account to Mimi all the time when he was living with her, and now he didn't want to account to me. He's a man who should have been unencumbered until he was about thirty. He wasn't prepared for the two big things running side by side: one or the other, marriage or the pop scene, and certainly not marriage with a growing son. It was a bit too hard to take, and he was wide open when all the pushers kept offering him more and more of what he thought were interesting drugs. He was a sitting target.'

Although she does not feel drugs themselves ended their marriage, Cynthia says, 'They had an important effect in that they separated us. We were on different mental planes. John's thoughts would always be much more expansive than mine. I'd seen the effects of drugs and I didn't want to be there. He did. He kept saying that on his trips he was seeing beautiful things.'

One heavy drug-taking weekend occurred when John went, alone, to the Ascot house of Derek Taylor, the former *Daily Express* writer who had been lured into the Beatles' coterie by Brian Epstein, to whom he became personal assistant. Taylor, an early convert to marijuana and L.S.D., had a particularly strong intellectual rapport with John.

Derek and Joan Taylor also had five children. Returning from their home, John was aglow at the L.S.D.-tripping he had enjoyed during the weekend. Derek had done wonders for John's ego, 'telling me what a good person I am', he explained to Cynthia. Normally, during drug experiences John was the more experienced one, guiding less frequent users, this time Derek had assumed the dominant role.

Derek had just returned from a lengthy stay in California, where the blossoming of flower power had made drug-taking almost mandatory. Taylor strongly advocated its use at the time, and to John he was virtually a guru. Mentally, John was going through a period of uncertainty about his marriage, his fatherhood, the Beatles, and himself. During several L.S.D. trips that weekend away from Cynthia, John had his ego massaged by Taylor: it was just the kind of pampering John needed. 'You're OK, you're clever, and you have no real problems,' Derek Taylor told John Lennon in many different ways. John returned to Kenwood smiling through the haze.

'Oh, Cyn,' he said when they reunited at Weybridge. 'It was wonderful. Why don't we have lots of children, a big, big family, and everything will be wonderful? That's what we should do. . . .'

Cynthia nodded. She knew he was tripping but felt her hands

tied behind her back. She remembered the last time John was so clearly high on dope. He had talked gibberish then, about 'buying an island in the sun, switching the sun on and off and totally controlling the weather'.

'I couldn't switch John's brain off, could I?' asks Cynthia. 'One normal person couldn't compete against that barrage of experiences. Unless they were extraordinary, dominant, and in a position of power. Which I wasn't. I was just Mum.'

Reading about the new drug culture, and the Beatles' endorsement of it, Aunt Mimi was on the phone immediately to John in Weybridge.

'By jove, I had a lot to say very quickly,' she recalls. 'John said: "Mimi, I'm *old enough* now. You don't understand the kind of lives we lead. The tension. I've had lots of tensions. And anyway, I used to see you taking aspirins."

'I said: "Yes, John, but only when I had a very bad headache. Look, the worry of it is nearly killing me. I don't approve of it any more than your Scouse accent. I still can't understand a word you're saying in all these interviews, and now there's this worry over drugs. What do you need drugs for and a Scouse accent?"

'And he answered: "Don't worry, Mimi. The accent's put on for money. They love it in Brooklyn. And I can handle the drugs." '

Mimi was equally strong with her final words: 'Well, don't have me to come over to your house while all this is happening.'

Julian Lennon has two prized possessions: one is a big brown floppy hat on which is embroidered 'Dr Winston O'Boogie', John's nickname for himself; the other is an electric guitar, a Les Paul copy, which Julian received as a Christmas present in 1974. Featuring a plaque with the inscription 'To Julian, Happy Christmas', the guitar is adorned with mirrors. Both were unique gifts from John to his son.

What John could not give Julian during his growing years was time. From his birth at the onslaught of Beatlemania through the turbulent years at Weybridge, Julian was a toddler and a growing boy with an absent Dad.

When John was at his most frenetic as a Beatle, from 1964 to 1966, Julian registered very little of his father's fame. 'All I knew was that he was away a lot. When he came home, and we were together, I recall most of all the fun like flying a kite in the garden, or the riding on the back of Dad's motorbike down to Ringo's home. The rest of my childhood with Dad is a fog.' He says he has

Top: June 1965. Domestic bliss at Weybridge with Cynthia and
two-year-old Julian
Above: Cynthia and John happy on holiday in Miami in February 1964

picked up the full story of his father's old group from news clips and films. 'More than anything, I can remember Dad's way with words, his humour and sense of fun. I know he used to say something about enjoying a good laugh.'

Julian has grown into a great admirer of his father's work – more his non-Beatle songwriting and efforts for peace than his straight Beatles hits. But he finds life today, as Lennon's first son, hazardous. He has regrets about the lack of father–son relationship which he says he desperately needed. 'But if Dad was going to be a musician, then he obviously had to be away from home a lot. Nobody's blaming him. I just missed him and wished he was around more.'

Educated at private schools, Julian went first to Heath House, Weybridge, then to Kingsmead in Hoylake, Cheshire, going to a variety of preparatory schools and finally settling at Ruthin School in North Wales. There, he followed the family tradition of John and his mother, leaning heavily towards art and hoping for an A-level in the subject. He lacked interest in most other subjects and planned a career in engineering. But he failed all his O-levels, just like his father, and set his sights firmly on music. At school in Hoylake he had a year's tuition on guitar, and with his close friend Justin Clayton played rock 'n' roll classics like 'Roll Over Beethoven', 'Rock Around The Clock' and 'Kansas City'.

As he grew up and listened to his father's work, particularly his lyrics, Julian decided to carry on his tradition. 'But in my own way, and playing mostly piano,' says Julian. 'I prefer ballads to hard driving rock 'n' roll. I don't want to face any comparison with my father for the songs I'm writing, although I'd have to agree that his work has been a big influence.' His favourite song is 'Isolation', with tracks like 'Dear Prudence', 'Sexy Sadie' and 'A Day In The Life' among the ones he particularly loves.

Growing up as John Lennon's son brought its hurdles for Julian as a schoolboy. 'The other kids thought I was a rich brat, and made jokes like: "He's got ten pound notes as wallpaper", but there were only a couple of times the kids in North Wales tried to beat me up just because of jealousy over who I am. The kids at Ruthin School really thought I had a fortune, and it was never like that.'

Julian recalls very few conversations with his father about his life as a musician, songwriter, or pop star. 'He didn't like to talk to me about it much when I was growing up,' says Julian. 'He'd had enough of talking about the Beatles by the time he got home. He just talked about normal things – like my school work, my games, my clothes. I remember asking him once if he regretted anything about the Beatles and he answered: "No, it was great fun, but I'd hate to have to go through it again." '

In 1984, as Julian prepared for his own entry into a musical career, as a songwriter, pianist and bandleader, his father's words echoed in his mind. Julian wants to keep the Lennon tradition of songwriting aflame. 'My father's name and reputation has made me even more keen to follow on. I see my work as a continuation, though I'm aware of the dangers of comparison. I'll do it my way, and don't want to be compared with him. I'm just glad I had a father with so much talent.' And what would John say to him if he saw his son launching himself into a career in music? Julian thought for a long time. 'I think my father would say: "Do it – but don't blame me." '

Living life as the son of John Lennon, despite its problems, fills him with pride. 'I know everything my Dad did, good and bad,' says Julian. 'He said I was born out of a whisky bottle on a Saturday night. Makes no difference. I love him and respect him and I'm really proud of him.'

13
MONEY

'A room and a car and a car and a room'

Fame was hemming him in, but there was one massive compensation – money. By mid-1964, with American success assured, and record sales and songwriting royalties pouring in, John was a millionaire. Only four years after leaving art college, and only two years after signing with E.M.I., the material world was at his feet. In America, merchandising of Beatle-related paraphernalia (wigs, pillows, scarves) swelled their income beyond John's wildest dreams. Only George, who nursed a grievance even bigger than John's at the craziness of Beatlemania, shared John's understanding of the mayhem that was surrounding them.

Yet for all the status and all his money, which he enjoyed, John kept his feet firmly on the ground. He told me on tour once that he still had Mimi buy his combs from Woolworth's in Penny Lane because they were the best and he'd grown up with them. He was a great experimenter with fads: he tried vegetarianism but quickly rejected it. 'Nut cutlets! Ugh! I chucked them away and asked Cyn for a fry up of bacon and eggs.' Mentally he was on a fame planet, but deep down his roots were unshaken.

George was absorbed by the money. He prodded Brian Epstein as much as he dared about how much this record had made, how much their royalties were, what concerts would yield. Quickly, Harrison was dubbed the 'money Beatle'. He fought a vain battle for recognition by John and Paul of his own songs, but was mostly held off by the sheer weight of Lennon and McCartney's output. In their sense of humour, the more time the Beatles spent together the closer John and George became. The friendship was strengthened when, cost being of little consideration, John bought his

Surrey house, Kenwood, in St George's Hill, Weybridge, while George bought Kinfauns, Claremont Estate, Esher, four miles away. His girlfriend and wife-to-be Pattie Boyd soon moved in with him. She got on well with Cynthia. Ringo was a neighbour of John's at Sunny Heights, on the same estate. Paul stayed in London, initially at Jane Asher's flat in the West End, but he eventually bought his own home at 7 Cavendish Avenue, St John's Wood.

George was a regular visitor to John's home, which was a pop star mansion, a symbol of success. It was bought hurriedly by John and Cynthia as a refuge from the fan-besieged flat in West Kensington. Within a month of buying it, John was off to America on tour. When John returned, the home and possessions began to interest him more. There was his art nouveau Rolls-Royce eventually painted in a rainbow of swirling floral patterns on a bright yellow background, with smoked one-way glass in the side and rear windows to keep the curious at bay. It had a television and drinks-packed refrigerator inside. He bought a Ferrari and a black Mini Cooper, and took driving lessons, successfully passing his test in February 1965. 'He was a terrible driver,' says Neil Aspinall. He had no sense of direction, often getting lost on the way home. The décor of the house was both spectacular and bizarre, a distinct contrast to the conformity of the sedate estate on which the house stood: purple velvet lined the dining-room walls – 'It sets off the old scrubbed table we eat off,' said John. Most rooms had a television set, which John liked to have permanently switched on with the sound off. He was a self-confessed T.V. addict: 'I get lots of ideas from it,' he explained to me. 'I think with it on.'

'Then there's the funny room upstairs. I painted that pink and green, changing from one can to another as I emptied each can of paint.' A conducted tour of the house by John gave me an insight into the Beatle insisting on his individuality when he felt it was threatened by Beatlemania. Shortly after he moved in and took me on a tour of Kenwood, I asked him for a list of prized possessions, and he came up with this list:

My first Rickenbacker guitar: it's a bit hammered now, I just keep it for kicks. I bought it in Germany on the hire purchase – whatever it cost, it was a hell of a lot of money to me at the time.

Three cars: a Rolls, Mini Cooper and Ferrari. The Mini for pottering about in, the Rolls for relaxing in and the Ferrari for zoom. I do very little driving. I'm not a good driver.

John, a powerful and
enthusiastic swimmer,
enjoying a pool in Miami,
Florida, in February 1964

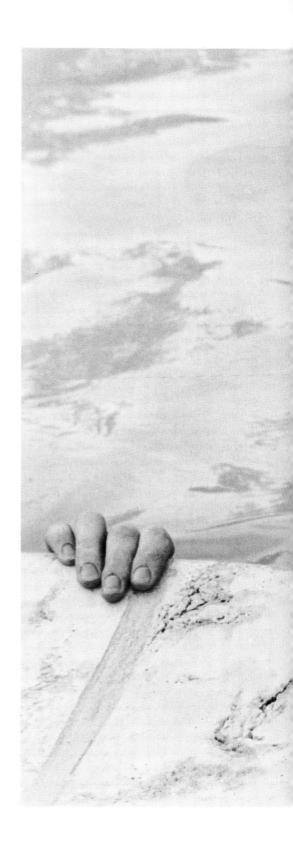

Swimming pool: I enjoy a swim at home. It's a luxury. All rich people have to have a pool.

Two pictures drawn by Stuart Sutcliffe, our old bass player. I'll always keep those, for sentimental reasons.

A lump of stone: we found it on the doorstep and somebody said it was prehistoric. I've since been enlightened and I believe it's a load of crap.

A stone frog: I like to see this in the fireplace, near the T.V. set, looking at us all.

About twenty suits; but I only wear about two, both black. I've got an evening dress but I only wear it when I have to because it's so uncomfortable. I get my clothes from Dougie Millings.

The Singing Postman's record: just part of my huge record collection, but I particularly like this 'cos it's stupid. I've got everything, electronic, Indian, classical and modern jazz.

Pin table: football game machine and fruit machine: in my 'den' here at home, just for a laugh.

Juke box: it's got forty-eight records on it, but I keep it mainly for rock 'n' roll standards like Gene Vincent's 'Be Bop A Lula', and the Big Three's 'Some Other Guy'.

A studio which has two very good tape recorders from which I can make my own records. And twelve guitars, some of which are wrecked.

Aldous Huxley books. I've just started reading him, because he's the new guvnor, it seems to me.

There were several tape recorders on which John would write his songs. He claimed to be the first British owner of the Mellotron, which occupied pride of place in the middle of the lounge. And on the mantelpiece was the winking 'nothing box' which begged the question: 'What's it do?' John enjoyed replying: 'It does nothing. It's a nothing box. It just winks all day and all night, but you can't tell where it's going to wink next.' The red flashing lights on his cherished nothing box had a hypnotic effect on all visitors. Its useless absurdity made John smile every time he looked at it.

John was always determined to move forward creatively, particularly in the Beatles' use of instruments. When he adopted the harmonica on 'Love Me Do', their début single, he hoped it would mark a breakthrough for the instrument, but he was just beaten to the bestsellers by Frank Ifield with his harmonica-accompanied number one, 'I Remember You'. In 1963, John became interested in the first 'organ-guitar' being developed in Britain by the entrepreneurial instrument manufacturer Jim Burns. John became deeply involved in all stages of the instrument's development. 'I played a Hammond organ on our second L.P.,' said John, 'and I fancy a guitar that plays like an organ as well as a guitar. It'd be gear.'

By the time the Beatles went on tour and into the recording studios as a successful group, John's pride and joy was the guitar he had hankered after during his lean, struggling years. It was a Rickenbacker model number 1996, slimline. It cost an astronomical 159 guineas at the beginning of 1964. John cherished it like a child with a new toy and asked the Beatles' road manager 'Big Mal' Evans to take great care of it. It can be heard making the particularly pretty guitar figures during one of John's most under-rated solos, 'You Can't Do That'.

John enjoyed indulging himself. 'I do get fits worrying about money,' he told me about this time. 'I worry about being one of those idiots who spend, spend, spend and do it all by the time I'm thirty. I thought I'd been a bit extravagant and bought too many cars, so I put the Mini and the Ferrari up for sale. Then one of the accountants said I was all right, so I got the cars back from the showroom.'

The problem was that he did not know how much money he had. 'I've tried to find out, but with income tax to be deducted and royalties coming in from all over the place, the sums get too complicated for me. I can't even do my times table. Every now and again the accountant clears some money of tax and puts it in my account and says: "That's yours but don't spend it all at once." But I have learned this much: to spend £10,000 I have to earn £30,000 before tax to get it.' His generosity often overtook him: on the rare occasions when he carried money he would give £5 or £10 tips to astonished waiters in restaurants.

He would leave messages on the answering machine of Wendy Hanson, Brian Epstein's personal assistant. One said: 'Wendy, send Aunt Mimi one of those maps of the world that has bottles in it.' She had several similarly enigmatic instructions from him. 'I knew he'd have seen it in Asprey's,' says Wendy Hanson. 'He was always rushing through there making mental notes. It was a globe. He was very impetuous, rather than acquisitive. Asprey's was a favourite. I once had John Asprey keep the place open late just for the Beatles to tour the shop, like they did at Harrods one Christmas. John thought it was a joke. He simply bought some jam.'

Wendy, who as Epstein's chief lieutenant was on the receiving end of John during what she feels was 'one of the most extraordinary phenomena of modern times', describes him as 'like a crab, a tough shell outside, a softie inside. . . . He wasn't tough at all. In France a fourteen-year-old girl fan hid in Lennon's bedroom to await his arrival at the Negresco Hotel, Nice. Her mother phoned Wendy to say: "A Beatle has raped my daughter."

'John was distraught for this girl,' Wendy continues. 'He said: "Wendy, call this woman up and tell her that her child hasn't been touched. She's hiding under my bed and won't come out. She's absolutely fine but worried because she says her mother's going to beat her up when she gets home." It was extraordinary. We got the girl out, but I remember how much John cared and was very gentle about it. He made sure long after the chaos of the event that we checked to make sure the girl got home safely. I remember saying to someone: "So much for the tough guy." '

The change in status, from a college student who had had to scrounge cigarettes and cinema money only four years previously, to being one of the most sought-after personalities in the world, amused John. His telephone answering machine at Weybridge reflected his frivolity. A favourite game would be to play the messages over and over again, laughing maniacally at people's accents, mimicking them, and rarely returning phone calls. It was John's Goon-like sense of humour surfacing. Guests at the house, like singer P.J. Proby, whose audacity Lennon admired, Liverpool schoolfriends like Ivan and Jean Vaughan and Pete Shotton, were bemused by the new Lennon.

As Beatlemania mounted, John became irritable at the lack of privacy. Kenwood was invaded on Saturdays and Sundays by fans who regarded the sighting of a Beatle at home as a pilgrimage to the Promised Land. 'I'm fed up with it,' he told me during one particularly exasperated night. 'Some weekends it gets so bad we go away, anywhere, to get away from the fans who come to gawp. No, stop that word, they're not *fans*! They treat my house like a bloody holiday camp, sitting in the grounds with flasks of tea and sandwiches. What do they think this is, a Beatle National Park? They're adults too, not all kids. I went out and told them all to sod off once, and they said they wouldn't buy any more of my records! I said they should find something better to do with their spare time.'

The fans collected anything as mementoes of their visits. They took photographs of the strange brass doorknocker in the shape of a naked woman. They took blades of grass from the lawn as souvenirs of a Beatle mansion. John wanted it to be a haven for himself, Cynthia and Julian, their two tabby cats, called Mimi and Babaghi, and their brown labrador dog, Nigel. But it was an uphill fight. He never knew what was going to await him when he returned home.

John's own spare time when he had not been writing songs or travelling or in the recording studio, had been spent writing and doodling. On the backs of envelopes, in cars and trains and planes and hotel rooms, John scribbled away and drew caricatures of the characters he invented. It was his private diversion from the mayhem of Beatlemania. The stories were continuations of the theme he had begun, seven years earlier, at Quarry Bank school, in the *Daily Howl* exercise book. Brian Epstein, seeing John's verse and doodles one day, offered to get them published. It had not occurred to Lennon, but the result was the début, in 1964, of John as an author.

In His Own Write, published by Jonathan Cape in 1964, was lionized by the literary establishment. 'Worth the attention of anyone who fears for the impoverishment of the English language and the British imagination,' said *The Times Literary Supplement*.

The obvious influences at work in the book were Lewis Carroll, Spike Milligan and *The Goon Show*, and the gobbledegook linguistic comedian Stanley Unwin. The 'Alice' books had exerted a strong influence on John since childhood and were later to percolate into his writing, notably 'I Am The Walrus' which derived from Carroll's 'The Walrus and the Carpenter'. The first verse of 'Lucy In The Sky With Diamonds' recalls Alice's gentle voyage with the sheep in *Alice Through the Looking Glass*. Lennon was familiar with Carroll's lengthier, surrealistic poems like 'Jabberwocky' and 'The Hunting of the Snark', and loved his verbal word-play and jumbling of images. The titles of John's hilarious essays told their own story of the satirical slants. 'On Safairy With Whide Hunter' (written, as John put it, 'in conjugal with Paul') and 'No Flies On Frank', 'The Fat Growth On Eric Hearble', and 'At The Denis', demonstrated a grasp of humour that had the critics showering praise. One Conservative M.P., Charles Curran, seemed to miss the point. He stated in Parliament that John's book highlighted the poor education in Liverpool, and claimed Lennon was illiterate.

John's first book topped the British bestseller list. It sold more than 100,000 copies in its first printing, and he was feted at a prestigious Foyle's literary luncheon at London's Dorchester Hotel. Immediately, John was recognized as the intelligent Beatle. Demand for tickets at the lunch exceeded the requests when George Bernard Shaw was the guest. The lunch itself was animated enough, with a high attendance of the literary establishment, but John was not to be drawn into making the customary speech for a guest of honour. He rose and said: 'Thank you very much, God bless you.' Many were disappointed, but he explained later that he did not feel up to it. 'Give me another fifteen years, and I may make a speech. Anyway I daren't today. I was scared stiff.'

John's speechlessness did nothing to dent his mystique among the expensively dressed debutantes, bejewelled dowagers, waiters and aristocrats who jostled outside the Dorchester Hotel like teenage fans, demanding John's autograph. 'For my daughter,' of course.

One woman clutched ten copies of his book and thrust them into his hand, saying: 'Put your name clearly here.'

John looked at her, astonished, as she said to her friend: 'I never thought I would stoop to asking for such an autograph.'

John cut her with: 'And I never thought I would be forced to sign my name for someone like *you*.'

John's second book, *A Spaniard In The Works*, was more disciplined than the first. 'It was starting from scratch,' explained John. 'The publisher said you've got so many months to write a book in. With the first book, I'd written a lot of it at odd times during my life.'

John had nearly a year to produce *A Spaniard In The Works*, during which he observed, as always, the passing scene and was able to develop his thoughts into prose and satire. There was a tilt at the *Daily Mirror* columnist Cassandra (whom John called Cassandle), which John said was because the writer had been knocking the Beatles. There was a send-up of newspaper letter columns called Readers Lettuce. There was John's glorious irreverence captured in Last Will and Testicle:

> I, Barrold Reginald Bunker-Harquart being of sound mind you, limp and bodie, do on this day the 18 of September 1924th, leave all my belongings estate and brown suits to my nice neice Elsie. The above afformentioned hereafter to be kept in a large box until she is 21 of age. . . .

'The National Health Cow', 'Snore Wife and some Several

Top: April 1964. Red wine, lots of it, was required by John to endure the formality of the Foyle's Literary Luncheon at London's Dorchester Hotel to mark the publication of his first book, *In His Own Write*. He is sitting with songwriter Lionel Bart

Above: John bought Aunt Mimi this bungalow overlooking the harbour at Poole, Dorset, in August 1965. Pleasure launches soon included the spot on guided tours of the area

Dwarts', and 'The Singularge Experience of Miss Anne Duffield' – in which John had some help in writing from George while they were on holiday in Tahiti – were more examples of John's acute sense of the ridiculous.

A keen insight into the literary Lennon came with his broadcast in July 1965 on B.B.C. radio's *World of Books* programme. Interviewed by Wilfred De'Ath, John said his books were mostly spontaneous and undisciplined productions.

'I'm selfish about what I write, or big-headed about it. Once I've written it I like it and the publishers sometimes say, "Should we leave this out or change that?" And I fight like mad because once I've done it, I like to keep it. But I always write it straight off. I might add things when I go over it, before it's published, but I seldom take anything out, so it's spontaneous.'

That desire reflected John's recording preferences. He hated songs to linger for long, to be refined in the studio. He liked to work, in records as apparently in books and all his art, rather like a daily newspaperman: write it, see it released very quickly, then move on. He wanted his records out overnight, and when his life as a Beatle was replaced by the Plastic Ono Band John did have records out within days of completion. It mirrored, also, his philosophy of life as a fast run.

On that radio interview John admitted only two influences in his literary work: Conan Doyle, who had marked his work in the Sherlock Holmes-inspired tale, 'The Singularge Experience of Miss Anne Duffield', and Lewis Carroll. 'I always admit to that because I love *Alice in Wonderland* and *Through the Looking Glass*, but I didn't even know he'd written anything else, I was that ignorant. I just had it as a birthday present as a child and liked them.'

'A lot of people say your pieces are sick. What do you say to that?' asked the interviewer.

'If it makes people sick. But I can read it and it doesn't appear sick to me,' replied John.

Denying other influences tossed around by literary reviewers, who quoted Edward Lear, James Thurber and others as his evident inspirations, John said: 'I deny it because I'm ignorant of it. Lear I'd never heard of. Well, I'd heard the name obviously somewhere but we didn't do him at school. The only classic or very highbrow anything I read at school or knew of is Chaucer. I might have read a bit of Chaucer at school because I think they do that. And so I bought all the books they said it was like. I bought one book on Edward Lear, I bought *Finnegan's Wake*, Chaucer, and I couldn't see any resemblance to any of them.'

He only read what he stumbled across, he said, not what it was 'right' or accepted to read. He had never read anything by Jonathan Swift. 'Charles Dickens I don't like too much. I've got to be in a certain mood. It's too *school*. I'm too near school to read Dickens or Shakespeare. I hate Shakespeare. I don't care whether you should like him or not. It doesn't mean anything to me.' He had just discovered Winnie the Pooh, 'which I'd never read as a child. I just discovered him about a year ago.'

By far the longest essay in *Spaniard In The Works*, 'The Singular Experience', spread over nine pages. When Wilfred De'Ath described his written works as 'mini pieces', John said: 'To you they're mini pieces, to me they're *marathons*. With Sherlock Holmes, I was seeing how far I could go. I forget which characters have come in and I just get lost and fed up and bored. That's why I usually either kill them off – well, I killed the lot off in the first book.'

On his Cassandra lampoon, he said, 'I did it mainly because he knocked us. We get a lot of knocking which we don't mind. We don't want everybody to love us, if somebody doesn't like us they're entitled to but we have no defence against people like that writing about us in newspapers, because we can't say anything back. And this is just my way of having a go back. It was just a sort of personal joke amongst ourselves. I'm definitely planning on Bernard Levin for the next one.'

Singer George Melly met John at a party to launch John's first book. Melly had written a glowing review of the book in the *Observer*. 'I approached him,' says George, 'in what I thought was a friendly manner, with perhaps an element of patronization. He was quite drunk and so was I.

'He started on me about the fact that I came from trad jazz which he hated because it blocked him and his friends from the Cavern. So he called me one of the blockers. He was quite aggressive.

'I said, "Did you like the review?"

'He said he hadn't read it.

'I said how much I enjoyed it, and referred to his James Joyce influence.

'He said: "I don't know who you're talking about. I've never heard of him. Who the hell's Joyce?" '

This was not true, because he *had* heard of James Joyce.

Finally Lennon and Melly nearly came to blows when Melly brought up the subject of black singers. George said: 'Of course, you must feel as I feel in my sphere, that one's real debt is to black singers like Muddy Waters and Chuck Berry, who invented the idiom in which we both sing.'

John became furious. He said he accepted nothing of the sort. He refuted all influences. 'I could eat 'em for breakfast. . .they don't make anything like I make,' he roared, the drink talking. The shout-up continued, with Melly insisting that Lennon's music was as derivative as his own. 'It nearly came to a fight,' says Melly. 'I'm glad it didn't because he would certainly have won.'

Yet once he had achieved success, John felt ambivalent about singing on the same concert bill as black acts. With the other Beatles, notably George Harrison, he had invited cult Tamla Motown singer Mary Wells ('My Guy') to tour with them in Britain in 1964; but when she came, superb though she was, John felt uncomfortable. 'I hate singing "Twist and Shout" when there's a coloured artist on the bill,' he told me. 'It doesn't seem right, you know. It seems to be their music and I feel sort of embarrassed. Makes me curl up. . .they can do these songs much better than us.'

He had no patience with other beat groups, who, he declared, 'are pinching our musical arrangements down to the last note'. He said to me: 'Look, we copied nobody. I am not a Negro so I can't copy a Negro singer. We've got our own style based on the music we grew up with, and it annoys me a lot to find groups getting on the wagon by copying sounds we were playing two years ago. Why can't these copyists make their own styles like we did? It happens in hairstyles as well. I see players in some groups have even the same length of hair as us. It's no good them saying they're students and they just happen to have long hair. *We* were students, as well, before we came to London, and we didn't have these hairstyles then. The difference between the Beatles and some of these others is that we didn't sit around in the 'Pool saying: "We're going to be big stars." Music was part of our lives. We played it because we loved doing it, not just for the loot. Unlike some groups, we don't go around even now saying: "Look, we're stars." I just consider myself a lucky layabout from Liverpool who has had some success. My auntie used to say (and here he would brilliantly mimic Mimi's authoritarian voice): "You're not seriously thinking of making a career in *that* line! The guitar's all right as a hobby, John, but you'll never make a living from it."

'And I'd say: "No, it's just a passing thing." '

When he was speaking fast and furiously and wanting it reported, John would urge a journalist: "Get it *down*, get it down in that book.'

Asked by a radio interviewer whether he would prefer to be

remembered as a writer or as a Beatle, John replied: 'I don't care whether I'm remembered or not. After I'm gone, I don't care what happens.'

John adapted to the lifestyle of a millionaire star with ease. He drank too much, but some kind of release from the pressures of being in what he later called a 'goldfish bowl' was essential. He had a few formal dinner guests at his Weybridge home, and those who did stay, like the pianist-singer Alan Price, would find themselves driven there nearer breakfast-time after all-night drinking at the Ad Lib club, exchanging hilarious tales of fights in their mad youth – John regaling people with stories of Hamburg, Price with ones of his Geordie childhood.

Spectators who did not participate in debates, like American singers Dionne Warwick and Mary Wells, would look on in disbelief at Lennon's Scotch-and-Coke-soaked antics. This was not the cosy Beatle whose moptop image had been pumped across the Atlantic as something clean and pure. Here was a drunk!

John's realization of just how enormous his group had become occurred when the Beatles returned home for a civic reception at Liverpool Town Hall. More than one hundred thousand people turned out for the day, and John, on a secret visit to Mendips, found his old home had become a shrine. Fans and journalists from all over the world were besieging his house, and Aunt Mimi was too exposed for comfort. She lived there alone, since John's move to London, save for Tim, the fat ginger cat.

'I kept changing the phone number,' says Mimi, 'but the fans would keep discovering the new one within a few days.' Rich and successful with the world at his feet, John's welcome was tempered by Mimi with her traditional reserve. 'He knew better than to tell me how well they were doing,' says Mimi.

'I simply said: "I'm glad it's working out well, John."'

'He said: "I told you it would."'

'And that was that.'

A year later, John persuaded Mimi to stay with him at Weybridge. 'I'm going to buy you a new house, Mimi,' he said to her over his usual breakfast of two or three bowls of cornflakes topped with bananas. 'Where's it to be?'

Mimi, stumped for a reply, said the first seaside place that came into her head: 'Bournemouth.' That morning, John and Mimi set off in his Rolls-Royce, chauffeured by the faithful Les Anthony, armed with maps of Hampshire. John never just sat in his Rolls.

He lay down in it. He operated the electrically controlled windows with his feet, playing ups and downs with them all the time. He smoked a lot, often passing a cigarette to his chauffeur. At traffic lights, people glanced inside in disbelief at sighting a Beatle. He gave them the world's most freezing stare.

The estate agents in Bournemouth provided them with some suitable houses for sale, and Mimi took a fancy to a white-painted bungalow overlooking Poole Harbour. She particularly loved the view, with its lounge window facing the terrace which led down to the water. Mimi pictured herself here, watching the pleasure launches and seeing the seagulls. 'Like it, Mimi?' said John. Within hours of starting the search, he was on the phone to his accountant and had bought the house in Panorama Road, Sandbanks.

Mimi sold Mendips, finally persuading John, who wanted the backdrop to his childhood years preserved, that there could be no turning back the clock. For the next eight years, John rang her phone several times a week on his world travels as he developed increasing love and respect for the daunting woman who had brought him up. He visited her regularly too, slumping in the armchair with its sea view and over cups of tea confiding his innermost thoughts about the Beatles, his marriage, and his restlessness. 'The older he got, the better we got to know each other,' reflects his aunt.

When the time came for Mimi to leave Liverpool, John asked her to take special care of his childhood books and the huge grandfather clock on which Uncle George had taught him to tell the time. 'I'll need it some day,' said John.

During an interview I had in 1964 with Bob Dylan, he referred to a song whose title he could not remember: the Beatles' 'I Want To Hold Your Hand'. It held the number one position for seven weeks in America. 'You know,' he said, 'that song about dope?' I must have looked even more baffled than I felt.

It transpired that Bob believed the real words, 'I can hide, I can hide', at the end of one chorus, were 'I get high, I get high'. Dylan was astonished that it was not a drugs song, and by his discovery, on meeting them in America, that they were not into marijuana. British pop stars were several years behind their American counterparts in adopting drugs as part of their lifestyle.

Dylan is popularly regarded as having switched the Beatles on to marijuana during their visit to America. But his significance to John, during the mid-1960s, was his spectacular command of words and ability to combine intelligent imagery with electric folk music. Lennon was quickly hypnotized by Dylan's album *Bringing It All Back Home*, a brave adventure by a former folk singer–guitarist into the world of rock. John played the album a lot at home, but would not be drawn much on it. It was as if he felt the presence of a genuine literary rival.

His inquisitiveness, though, triumphed over his apprehension. There followed a distinct 'Dylan period' as John called it, when he wrote songs in Bob's style and even invited the singer to his home. But there was an edginess, a nervousness of each other, in the air, and the Weybridge meeting did not form the basis of a long and lasting friendship. Spiritually, as totally original artists, Lennon and Dylan were too alike to become close. Recognition of each other was enough, and John, who before Dylan turned him on to marijuana had only got high on booze or 'Prellys' in Hamburg, acknowledged the maestro with songs like 'I'm A Loser' and 'Norwegian Wood', both introspective. One of his favourite 1965 singles was Dylan's 'Subterranean Homesick Blues', which John described as 'very Chuck Berry-ish'. He and I spent a lot of time at his Weybridge home trying to work out the words.

Dylan, and Lennon's fresh songwriting phase of looking in-wards, had arrived at an important juncture in John's life. It was natural, thought Brian Epstein, for the boys' personalities to be captured in films. Their first tentative move was in *A Hard Day's Night*, followed the next year, by *Help!* and subsequently by John's solo role in *How I Won The War*, alongside Michael Crawford. The director of all three films was Richard Lester. John struck up an immediate rapport with the laconic American, partly because, like George Martin, Lester had been involved with John's cherished Goons, having filmed Spike Milligan and Peter Sellers, in *The Running, Jumping and Standing Still Film*. Zany comedy was still John's favourite brand and he envisaged a desperately needed switch from the rigours of Beatlemania. The scriptwriter was Alun Owen, a Liverpudlian who went with Lester to meet the Beatles during their Paris trip in January 1964.

A Hard Day's Night was devised, simply, as a black and white fictionalized documentary of the Beatles' crazy life as pop stars, covering their experiences as musicians, in the recording studios, their television appearances, their pressures in concerts. 'The film was based on their life living in small boxes, as prisoners of their own success,' says Richard Lester. 'The concept came from John's reply to a question I asked him about a trip they'd made to Sweden.

April 1964. John pays rapt attention to Walter Shenson, producer of the film *A Hard Day's Night*, during lunch on the train from London to Taunton, Somerset. The train was part of the location work

Waiting for the action during the filming of *A Hard Day's Night* on a platform covered with broken glass

February 1965. A pensive John pictured during the filming of *Help!*

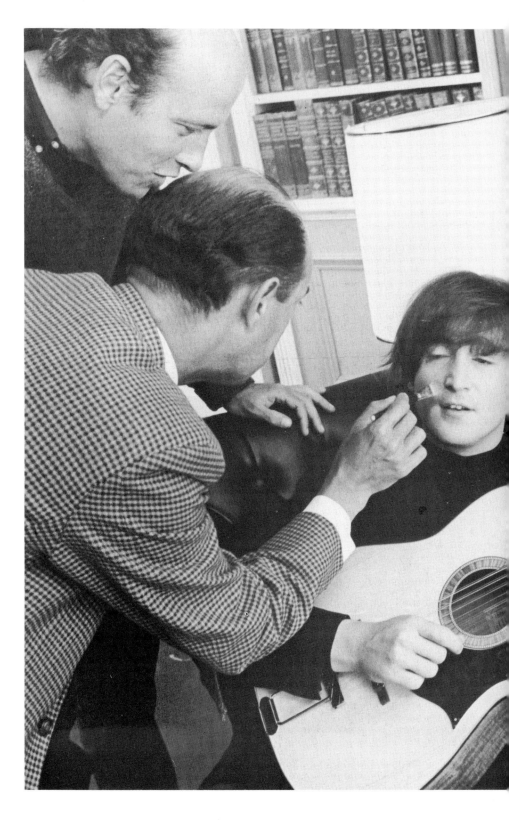

Filming *Help!* at
Twickenham Film Studios.
Director Richard Lester
watches a make-up artist
apply the paintbrush to a
wary John's face

' "How did you like it?" I said.

'John said: "Oh, it was a room and a car and a car and a room and a room and a car."'

'That became our signal of how to do *A Hard Day's Night*.' The film was shot on location at Marylebone Station in London and on trains.

'We tried very hard to make sure that nobody had more than one sentence to learn at any given time,' says Richard Lester, 'and John fell into line with the rest of them. It was eight o'clock every morning make-up and eight-thirty on the set, no arguments. I think that came as a great shock to them, but their road managers, Neil Aspinall and Mal Evans, made sure that they were all there on time.'

Wherever the Beatles went in the public eye in the mid-sixties, fans gathered in their hundreds or thousands very quickly. 'The biggest problem in making *A Hard Day's Night* on location was that we could, at best, get two takes on anything when we were on a street,' says Richard Lester. 'The streets would get so blocked with fans we'd have to change locations and start again. We had to get the Beatles on and off the set very quickly! This meant the Beatles tearing quickly into a shop, doing their scene, and making a rapid exit at the other side of the shop to fool the crowds. All this had to be done in minutes, and led to one of the most expensive days in John Lennon's life.

Darting in and out of Asprey's, the exclusive and ultra-expensive store in Bond Street, John managed to spend about £80,000 within minutes. 'God knows how he managed it. I think even John was amazed at how much he ordered from the place,' says Richard Lester. He ordered furniture, jewellery, and bric-à-brac.

The song title became the title for the film after Ringo had come up with the phrase to recall a heavy night. John's composition, and his searing vocal, make it one of the most enduring Beatles songs.

Help! was a more adventurous enterprise. Filmed over a nine-week period, it had a weak story similar to the James Bond themes. A crazy scientist joined a search for a valuable ring that ended up on Ringo's hand. The movie began life as *Eight Arms To Hold You*, but when John wrote the title track it was such a powerful song that it was adopted as the film's title.

Shooting began over two weeks in the Bahamas, where John quickly showed that, even as a multi-millionaire pop and film star, he was not likely to be conned into high society. 'One didn't want to have a tongue lashing from John, but it did come out in

Nassau,' recalls Richard Lester. 'We were all guests at dinner of the Governor, and we had been filming in a mental hospital where conditions were outrageous.'

Actor Victor Spinetti, who was there and who developed a strong friendship with John, says, 'We all went looking around what appeared to be an army barracks. We thought it was deserted. In fact there were a lot of spastics and cripples and old people in there and John was shocked that they had been shoved away under this terrible corrugated-iron army hut.'

'It was a black tie affair,' says Richard Lester, 'with the equivalent of all the hoorays of the Bahamas. John let loose. It was a perfectly justifiable sense of outrage for anyone with a sense of social conscience.'

Victor Spinetti says Lennon was especially appalled by the contrast between the champagne and caviare they were offered at dinner, and the living conditions of the afflicted. John said to the Minister of Finance: 'I saw this place today which was meant to be a hospital. People were in there under the most terrible conditions.'

'The Minister replied: "I do my best, you know. I'm not being paid for being the Minister of Finance."'

'To which John answered: "Oh, in that case you're doing better than I thought you were doing." '

The press turned on the Beatles because of John's sharpness, but he was unrepentant and told everyone he loathed the Bahamas.

'He made the very strong point,' says Richard Lester, 'that these people were hypocrites and condescending to the Beatles because they *were* the Beatles, and that he couldn't stand. He was very, very tough on the authorities after that. The power of John's attack on that government figure makes me remember him very strongly from the weeks in the Bahamas, much more than the others at that time.'

After the Bahamas, the location work moved to the ski slopes of Austria, in a small town called Obertauren, two hours' drive from Salzburg. By now John and the others were smoking marijuana heavily, but not so much that they could not work. They would hardly have been able to work so vigorously, or write the songs, or drink until the early hours in the hotel, if they had been heavily stoned. But John's euphoria after going to his room for a smoke, and his enlarged pupils, made it obvious when he was high.

Perhaps it was a release from the Bahamas, but John was in a particularly buoyant mood when I visited Austria for a week during location work. He was agile at skiing, which he enjoyed.

He thought the film story was ludicrous but was able to laugh at the fact that it was unstoppable, expensive, and a waste of such a lot of time and money; he struck up a warm friendship with actress Eleanor Bron and was often to be heard in conversation with her, talking politics and philosophy, over drinks in the hotel bar. In political beliefs John thought like a socialist but said he would have to vote Conservative because they knew how to manage the country. Money came into it quite strongly, he used to tell me. 'Deep down,' he said, 'I'm Labour. Politics is a state of mind but you've got to protect your money, haven't you?'

It was in Austria that John and Paul and I concocted an amusing, childish, but absorbing word-game one night in the hotel bar. The game was called Winners and Losers, and appealed immensely to John. One person called out the name of a person, country, drink or anything tangible, and the others would pronounce it a winner or a loser. There were no hard rules for this daft, arbitrary game. It relied purely on intuition rather than definition. Thus, John pronounced E.M.I. a winner, Decca a loser; France (where the Beatles had just appeared,with only moderate success) a loser country, America a winner; Coca-Cola was a winner, Pepsi-Cola a loser; New York was a winner, Los Angeles a loser; tea a winner, coffee a loser; the whole of Fleet Street a loser because the journalists were so very late realizing the Beatles were a force. And so it went on, becoming highly personalized, argumentative, often cruel and great fun.

In a chance remark to a British musician he greatly admired, Tony Sheridan, John said, as the Beatles' success grew: 'I've sold my soul to the devil.' Sheridan, who had recorded with the Beatles in Hamburg, had been particularly friendly with John and knew immediately what John meant, for fame of this kind was never what Lennon expected.

The *Help!* film coincided with what John later called his 'fat Elvis' period. It was difficult to realize it until later, but John was slightly overweight, eating and drinking too much, materialistically collecting possessions, but too much of an artist to be swept along by show business. He was more dissatisfied even than he realized: he thought he had lost his art. Cynthia, however, maintains that 1965 was his finest songwriting year.

When he wrote 'Help!' something from deep within him gave vent to his insecurity, his feeling that all was not well, despite the millions of record sales, the adoration, the frustrating mansion in Weybridge which he described as 'like a bus stop, you wait until something comes along. . .'.

John's *cri de cœur* emerged with painful honesty, although nobody was listening carefully to his title song as the autobiography it was. . .

When I was younger, so much younger than today,
I never needed anybody's help in any way.
But now these days are gone, I'm not so self-assured
Now I find I've changed my mind, I've opened up the doors.

Help me if you can, I'm feeling down
And I do appreciate you being 'round
Help me get my feet back on the ground, won't you please,
  please help me?

And now my life has changed in oh so many ways
My independence seems to vanish in the haze,
But every now and then I feel so insecure
I know that I just need you like I've never done before. . .
Help, I need somebody, help, not just anybody, help. . .help!

Characteristically, John was the first Beatle to debunk the Beatles. He could not stand the inflated descriptions of what the Beatles were, or being constantly paraded, or the dukes and lords who regarded it as a social cachet to be photographed with a Beatle. To John what had begun as rock 'n' roll had become an industry. He did not see himself as a profound performer, and while he admired Paul McCartney's musical strengths, the two men were not reacting in the same way to fame. Paul loved it.

One rainy afternoon in 1965, in an interview with me at Weybridge, John was in a morose mood. His restlessness was evident as he took me up to the music room where, amid countless tapes, recorders, and amplifiers, and a mess of paper, he was strumming his guitar and writing a song which turned out later as 'Nowhere Man'. With hindsight, it was a prophetic title: a moment, a day, when the change in John Winston Lennon was more evident than at any time since they first scored a hit record.

He was both defensive and confused about fame as he ate his afternoon breakfast of cornflakes, a dish he was likely to eat at any time of the day. He smoked incessantly and started talking about how he felt old at the age of twenty-five. 'According to the rules of the pop world, we're old,' he said. 'But we don't look any older than the Stones, do we? We certainly don't act any older. I've seen Jagger looking a hundred and The Who looking at least thirty some nights. Christ, we felt old when we started, when Brian Epstein found us. We thought we'd left it too late to make it. Years don't affect your mind. They can give your face wrinkles, but it's your attitude and outlook that counts. I've met people of thirty who aren't thirty in their mentality. The calendar alone says they've lived thirty years, and although age can give you experience, some people aren't capable of using that experience. I'm twenty-six next year. The rules say that I'm a fully grown man, settled down and all that. I'm not – I've still got a young outlook!'

What nagged away at him was the fear that the Beatles were no longer a rock 'n' roll group but were generally appealing to mothers and fathers and adults. 'There was a time back there when we seemed to be doing everything at once – getting older people interested in what we're doing as well as the young. But I don't like that.' He said he had not enjoyed their Christmas concerts in London for that reason. 'It doesn't seem natural to see old people out there looking at us. They should be at home doing the knitting.'

Asked if he regretted the size of the Beatles' popularity, John said, 'No, I'm glad things got as big as they did. Because when we got *nearly* big, people started saying to us: "You're the biggest thing since. . . ." And I hated that. I wanted the Beatles to be just *the* biggest thing. It's like gold. The more you get the more you want.'

John said British fan mail for the Beatles was declining from the peak it had reached a year or so earlier. 'I'm talking about the stuff I get myself now. Paul gets a lot every day. Mine fluctuates – goes up when we've got a new record out. Since our European tour we've been getting plenty of mail from Yugoslavia, Italy, and for some reason, Japan.'

The attitude of the fans still bothered him, he told me. 'It's annoying when people turn round and say: "But we MADE you, you ungrateful swines." They did, in a way, but there's a limit to what we're bound to do, as if it's a duty. When I had black windows put in my Rolls-Royce, a fan wrote to me: "You're hiding, turning your back and running away from the people who made you."

'Rubbish! If I go to a shop down the road and buy a bunch of roses I don't expect the bloke to be so grateful that he spends his life bowing and scraping. I like the roses, so I buy them, and that's that.

'I don't want to sound as if we don't like being liked. We appreciate it,' said John, his Aunt Mimi's training conspicuously keeping him balanced. 'But we can't spend our lives being dictated to.

'Think about these Kellogg's cornflakes. If you buy cornflakes, do you expect Mr Kellogg to spend his life being told how to do everything, how to behave? No. And if you buy a loaf of bread and it's lousy, you just don't buy it again.

'It's not all that different with us. We make a record and if you like it you buy it. If you don't, don't buy it. It's up to the public to decide.

'The Beatles can't win at the moment. if we try to please everybody, right across the age groups, it's impossible. We'd end up in the middle with nobody liking us. People think of us as a machine. They pay six shillings and eight pence for a record and we have to do what they say, like Jack-in-the-box. I don't like that side of being a pop star.'

Cynthia came into the room, with Julian and John's cup of tea. Julian stayed a while, and I casually asked John how old the boy was. 'He's two, I think,' said John. And then, in a rare flash of correction. 'That's awful. I'm away so much I've forgotten how old he is. Yeah, two it must be.'

When Cynthia left the room, John said how glad he was that his, and Ringo's, marriage had been accepted by fans. 'I don't think the two of us being married has had any bad effects on our popularity. Remember, when it got out that both Ringo and I were married, there hadn't been anybody in such a position as we were in, who had got married. It was Silver Disc, as opposed to Gold Disc, people, who'd got married before us! People who relied on the fact that they wiggled, sexily, in their stage acts. We didn't rely on wiggling, we still don't, and we won't. We were never dependent on fans being in love with us so much as others are. Not like Jagger. He's the Charlie Chaplin of rock 'n' roll. Now *he* can't afford to get married! The Stones would be all over.'

Although John and Mick got on well superficially, there was a distinct impression that Lennon thought Jagger was trying, through the Stones, to overtake the Beatles, and John regarded that as pathetic. Later, John slammed the Stones' *Satanic Majesties Request* album as an imitation of *Sgt Pepper*, and loathed the Stones' record 'We Love You' which John said was 'She Loves You' backwards. Coincidentally, both John and Paul had sung on the record which Lennon blasted so forcefully. John had very little artistic respect for the Rolling Stones. When he was drinking, he tore into them for merely copying black music.

The trappings and status of fame seemed strangely, suddenly

Arriving at Kennedy
Airport for the Beatles'
triumphant first visit to
America in February 1964

shallow. The fine wines in the cellar at Weybridge were ordered by John or Cynthia or the housekeeper, Dorothy Jarlett, at random. Expensive restaurant dinners were nice but were making him mentally, as well as physically, bloated. He and Cynthia dined with good friends, like Victor Spinetti, who introduced him to light escapism in the theatre and shows like *The Student Prince* and *The Desert Song*. Afterwards, they would adjourn to La Cappannina, an Italian restaurant in Romilly Street, Soho, and talk the night away. John enjoyed visiting the home of Peter Cook, whose sense of humour was endearing, and he was a regular, often alone, at the trendy discotheque called the Scotch of St James, where he traded stories with visiting American musicians. 'Before going out for a night on the booze,' he said, 'I drink a pint of milk and take two Aspro. Stops you getting a hangover.' John was funny when inebriated, but could be aggressive if he didn't win an argument. And in that period, he was subconsciously seeking new routes. He would vent his tension in odd ways.

In Paris, at the posh Hôtel Georges V, John stubbed a cigarette out in the middle of a giant, extravagant cake which reposed in the Beatles' suite. It was John's way of commenting on the sickliness of the cake and the stupidity of its appearance and extravagance. Next to the Queen, nothing in Britain was a better-known institution than the Beatles, and privately that was precisely what bothered John. At Kenwood, he had spent nearly £50,000 on decorating and furnishing a house which had cost only £19,000 to buy. Now, nourished by his success as the author of two books, he started looking around outside the Beatles for activities.

Touring was a drag. The film *Help!* had been a disaster to John, whatever anyone else said. 'I was only an extra in my own film,' he told Richard Lester. He was encouraged to make another film, away from the Beatles, the following year, but by then John had a built-in distrust of acting. 'Of the four, he would have been the best actor, an unexpected actor,' says Lester.

'I told him: "You're obviously a good actor if you want to be."
'He replied: "Acting's silly and daft." '

Concert tours were a wider issue. Live work was what the Beatles had been born from, yet now, mounting a tour was more like a military operation than ever. The 'car and a room and a room and a car' syndrome had gone beyond anyone's comprehension and was no longer a joke. On the road, particularly in America, the compensations were the women and the speedy American way of life. But to the Beatles on stage the shows were charades. They could hear only deafening screams, and the music counted for nothing. They were like a circus act. 'Just dummies,' John said. 'They can't even see us from that distance. We're specks on the horizon. Why they pay money to come and see us, like fifty-five thousand at Shea Stadium in New York, I'll never know.'

And then there was flying. John had always hated it. Next to George, who had a pathological fear of getting on a plane, John was the worst flier. He joked his way nervously through most flights, and shored himself up with alcohol. Yet the jokes flowed when he was aboard. Flying Lufthansa from London to Munich, he said to me in a voice that thankfully none of the German crew heard as we climbed the steps: 'It's good to fly Lufthansa to London – all the pilots know the way.'

John's tongue was at once his most endearing characteristic and his worst enemy. On stage in Hamburg during the Beatles' emotional return there in 1966 for a triumphant German concert tour, John told the crowd, 'Don't listen to our music. We're terrible these days.' He meant that their stage work had lost its bite. It was the truth, but he hurt a lot of people with the remark. And he could not understand why all those millions of screams came from people who simply wanted to attend an *event*.

Lennon had a macabre sense of humour about dying in a plane crash. 'We'll either go in a plane crash or we'll be popped off by some loony,' he said to me on a plane in America. The remark was to echo with devastating, appalling irony in New York fourteen years later.

Once, as the Beatles' plane was coming in to land at Portland, Oregon, the group were joking with the *Daily Mirror*'s Don Short that they were so famous, there could be no more big stories. They had cracked America wide open, and they would soon no longer be newsworthy. John and Don sat together drawing up a list of what could be concocted to spin out the Beatles' news value.

John said, 'I know. I'll run off with Ringo's wife on Howard Hughes' plane.' Just then, one of the plane's engines caught fire and the plane started billowing black smoke.

Short said: 'Well, John, this is one story we haven't accounted for yet.'

And John answered: 'Oh Christ, how are we going to tell this?'

John then wrote his own obituary, got a film spool from a travelling photographer, wound the paper round the spool and sealed it down, so that when the plane crashed his own 'black box' would be there to tell the story of his death in his own words.

The plane landed safely, amid ambulances and fire engines and general pandemonium. John roared above the madness: 'Beatles and children off first!' In Paris, before that tour, John had studied a list of American cities they might visit. They had escaped from the Hôtel Georges V at four in the morning for a stroll and wandered into one of the cafés on the Champs-Elysées, just like they used to on the Reeperbahn in Hamburg after their club work. Someone reflected on that forthcoming American tour, and pondered how Beatlemania, which was so enormous, could possibly end. 'It will all end in an air crash,' John said, throatily through his Gauloise. 'It's got to be Cincinnati. Just as the plane is landing. Cincinnati sounds a great place to die.'

Meeting Elvis Presley was something that John Lennon could never have comprehended when he was a devoted fan as an art student five years earlier. But in the summer of 1965 he was to come face to face with the idol who had changed his life. It happened during the Beatles' stay in Los Angeles when they rented a house on Mulholland Drive, and the meeting was arranged by journalist Chris Hutchins of London's *New Musical Express*. He persuaded Colonel Tom Parker, Presley's manager, and Brian Epstein, to get them all together. Hutchins had no trouble persuading the Beatles, but for days there was tension over who should be the host: the Beatles were undoubtedly hotter than Elvis, but Presley was the more senior act and it was his town. 'In the end,' says Hutchins, 'the Colonel's wisdom and experience won over Brian Epstein's lack of determination and basic politeness.' An evening was set for the Beatles to glide in their limousines to Elvis's gigantic mansion in Bel Air.

John was full of genuine anticipation as Elvis entered the room dressed casually in red shirt and grey trousers. But the first few minutes seemed like hours: both Elvis and the four Beatles were struck dumb at the size of the occasion. Finally, John and Paul wandered off to corner Elvis and talk about songwriting.

Presley asked how many hits they had written and it was Lennon who confronted the King with the question all self-respecting rock 'n' roll fans throughout the world were asking: 'Why don't you go back to making rock 'n' roll records?' Presley had been pummelled by all his old fans, like John, for slumping into a tiring routine of making trashy Hollywood movies and his records were soundtracks.

'It's my movie schedule,' Elvis said. 'It's so tight! I might just do one soon, though.'

John retorted: 'Then we'll buy that!'

John, in Paris during the Beatles' three-week season at the Olympia in January 1964, prepares to go for a stroll down the Champs-Elysées

They jammed a while on Elvis's guitars, only riffs and no complete song tunes, and adjourned to the games room to play the pinball machines. But the atmosphere was stilted and, although he enjoyed the occasion, John was disillusioned by his idol. 'It was like meeting Engelbert Humperdinck,' he later said scathingly. The Beatles' mementoes of the uneventful meeting, handed to them by Colonel Parker, were a complete set of Presley albums each, a table lamp shaped like a wagon, and holsters with gold leather belts. 'It was obvious Elvis was high and the Beatles knew very little about dope then,' says Chris Hutchins. 'Neither side desired the meeting that much and the politics of it made it so heavy.'

14
MUSIC

'DO something with my voice'

The combination of John Lennon and Paul McCartney, as friends as well as songwriters, must rank as one of the great examples of opposites being drawn to each other like magnets. McCartney's background, with a father as a jazz pianist and a mother determined that her academic son stayed on course to a 'proper job' in one of the professions, was traditional and musically conventional.

John carried the scars of a lost father and a mother killed in a road accident, at the time he and Paul set off on their musical collaboration. Lennon had been a teddy boy who had virtually roared through Liverpool, leaving broken hearts and many scars among the hundreds who knew that he would either end up a catastrophic loser, or that his streak of artistic genius and prescience might carry him through to the heights. McCartney was simply an orthodox teenager.

By the time they reached London and became immersed in recording, the general opinion was that it was easy – despite the songwriting credit line of Lennon–McCartney which appeared everywhere – to detect who wrote what.

Whoever sang the lead vocal had usually written the song. If it haunted you, it was a McCartney. If it baffled you, made you think, it was a Lennon. If it grabbed you by the heart ('Yesterday', 'All My Loving'), it was one of Paul's. If it was autobiographical, and made a pungent personal statement, ('In My Life', 'Norwegian Wood') it was John's.

It was certainly music, rather than their contrasting personalities, that drew John and Paul together. Although John had established that he, as a Libran, was theoretically supposed to get on well with Paul, a Gemini, they were poles apart in personality and temperament. That difference extended deeply into their musical collaboration, with great mutual benefits.

Or so it seemed. In reality, both men were utter contradictions. Lennon's apparent toughness was always a complete cover-up. Inside that fierce exterior beat a softie's heart. He was a complex man who seemed afraid to let his inner self be seen. The hard front was without a shred of doubt a screen for the real, tender man of which there were hundreds of examples, particularly when the Beatles split.

McCartney, conversely, came across during the Beatles years as the Beatle who melted most girls' hearts, with his big brown eyes and his songs of unashamed love. On the surface, he was the suave, smooth, debonair romantic. This misconception paralleled the inaccurate theory that John was a tough nut. In fact, McCartney was always the tougher of the two. He totally outstripped John when it came to business acumen, planning his life with a fine eye for detail that later made him popular music's richest man.

From the moment the Beatles went to London and marshalled their raw talent as musicians and songwriters into tunes the world could whistle, one man stood beside them in what at first seemed an incongruous partnership. John, in particular, had always made blistering remarks about 'the men in suits'. Yet when it came to associating the Beatles with them, he would always say that the end would justify the means. John always said he wanted to be rich and famous – particularly rich. Brian Epstein was attractive because his respectability seemed a good bet to get them a record contract, John and Paul's most cherished ambition.

The man who eventually came to be linked with the Beatles as their record producer, and forge a unique bond with them at a critically formative peak in their lives, was George Martin. He wore a suit and a tie. He was a staff producer at the giant E.M.I. Records and recorded classical music, jazz, pop and particularly comedy by such artists as Peter Sellers, Bernard Cribbins, Spike Milligan, and Flanders and Swann.

Heard today, 'Love Me Do' is simple, catchy, earthy – a natural début sound from the Beatles as we grew to love and understand their music. But at the time George Martin was unimpressed. 'To begin with, they gave me very few songs,' says Martin. 'Love Me Do' had been written by Paul when he was sixteen, with John contributing to the middle. 'That was the best of the stuff they had, and I thought it pretty poor,' says Martin. 'I offered them

"How Do You Do It" as their first song (later this became a number one hit for Gerry and the Pacemakers) although this was not written by them. They didn't fancy it and we pressed on with "Love Me Do". But they learned very quickly after that and when they got the success of "Please Please Me" under their belt they were fired by it, and from then on everything they brought me was pure gold.' 'Please Please Me' was written totally by John; he later told the author that he was imitating the falsetto sound of American singer Roy Orbison. The haunting harmonica sound by John on 'Love Me Do' was inspired by another hit – 'Hey Baby', by American singer Bruce Channel. The harmonica player on the disc whose style Lennon admired was Delbert McClinton.

Success came so rapidly to John and Paul, and their creativity flowered so speedily as a result, that George Martin's role as a catalyst became a joy to him. George believes that rivalry, rather than competitiveness, was the key to their mutual respect. A spark of tension, each songwriter wondering what the other would do or say next, gave them both a thrusting edge. 'It was like a tug of war,' says Martin.

'In the studio, their rivalry was based purely on friendship. They had a very close relationship because in many ways they were incredibly similar. Some people accentuated the differences between them – John being the acrid, bitter one and Paul the soft one. That was basically an image built up by the Press.

'The truth is that deep down they were very, very similar indeed. Each had a soft underbelly, each was very much hurt by certain things. John had a very soft side to him. But you see, each had a bitter turn of phrase and could be quite nasty to the other, which each one expected at certain times.

'They did love each other very much throughout the time I knew them in the studio. But the tension was there mostly because they never really collaborated. They were never Rodgers and Hart. They were always songwriters who helped each other out with little bits and pieces. One would have most of a song finished, play it to the other, and he'd say: "Well, why don't you do this?" That was just about the way their collaboration worked.' Gradually, as they were always individual songwriters, they became positively solo operators as success led them on.

'Imagine two people pulling on a rope, smiling at each other and pulling all the time with all their might. The tension between the two of them made for the bond.

'John was such a creative thinker, one notch higher than most,' says Dick James, the man whom Brian Epstein turned to on his

December 1963. After twelve months of smash-hit records
('Please Please Me', 'From Me To You', 'She Loves You', 'I
Want To Hold Your Hand' and two albums), the euphoria in
John and Paul's expressions is evident as they scan a summary
of their year

arrival in London, and who became the publisher of the Beatles' songs. 'He had more sensitivity. John *had* to be cynical, because he was very vulnerable and could hurt very easily, and so he surrounded himself with this cynical crust. He was very difficult, particularly later in his career.'

Dick James had the unique position of hearing all the Beatles' early work before it went on record. 'To this day,' he says, 'my office receives tapes from groups who are trying to sound uncannily like Paul or John, as lead singer, with the same kind of appeal. But the original model was so special. I could hardly believe my ears when Brian Epstein would come into my office and play me the next song.

' "What do you think, Jamesy?" John would say.

'And right after "Please Please Me", I'd have to say: "Dare I say it, John and Paul? Another number one." '

In 1963 James borrowed £10,000 and handed it to Brian Epstein as an 'advance' on their royalties. 'It's usually six to eight months before the initial income comes in from world sales. The boys were in debt to Brian, who had given them eating money. They couldn't believe the figures we were talking about. They'd been in poverty street. I hadn't known them then, but I did know the song publishing world and knew they would be earning a lot of money. I had to borrow the money for them against that first number one, "Please Please Me". I had no trouble getting the cash. I knew it was a winning investment.'

As a veteran of the old school of songwriters, Dick James looked on the new school of beat musicians led by the Beatles with a critical ear. 'If the songs came around today, brand new, they'd still be world-wide smashes. The quality was amazing. I could not believe what I was hearing. It was the perfect entertainment machine: John, Paul, marvellous songwriters, George a splendid musician, Ringo a wonderful drummer for them, and a foil.'

His outstanding memory of John was of 'a great stubbornness which was essential to them in their early days. His contribution to the Beatles' success was definitely equal to Paul's, not one iota less.' Lennon looked on James as an amiable benevolent uncle. It was a view that was to change in 1969 when a business clash divided John and Dick. 'But when we went public with Northern Songs in 1965, I said to John: "The songs will go on earning money well into the next century."

'He smiled. "Good on yer, Jamesy." '

Visitors to London's Abbey Road number two studio during Beatles recording sessions could not be aware that pop music history was being made. A Liverpool group, bucking the trends of the time (Cliff Richard, traditional jazz, and Chubby Checker's big Twist craze) did not represent an overnight phenomenon at the recording studios. Martin, tall, angular, punctilious, was an easy target for the Beatles' quicksilver, raw sense of humour. And so because of that they would rarely tease him. They respected him and enjoyed his straightforwardness and particularly his expertise.

As the lynchpins for the group, writing hit after hit, John and Paul had a special relationship with George Martin. It began as record producer and young pop stars and then developed into that of a wise uncle, and eventually to friendship. But when their popularity began moving swiftly upwards, a marked difference became apparent in John and Paul's make-up.

Typically John would want to move from song to song in a hurry. He would be involved in a song for only as long as it took to get it recorded satisfactorily. Then he was on to the next. McCartney took a different, more thorough attitude. Later, Paul's persistence in worrying a session to death, until one of his songs had been drained dry of every possibility and permutation, irritated John.

John nursed an inner grievance that McCartney's songs got more studio attention and finishing touches than his. 'That's probably true,' Martin reflects, 'but that's because Paul was more interested. John's irritation was a little unfair. John's songs got a great deal of attention, but possibly what he meant was that they never got the attention to detail that he thought they needed. So they didn't quite work out the way he wanted them. But they worked out the way I wanted them.

'Maybe I thought my communication was pretty good in getting inside his brain and finding out what he wanted. He would always say: "Yes great, lovely, OK, fine," at the playbacks. But only later did he tell people he'd never been really happy with anything he'd written.

'Some of John's works we recorded in the Beatles days were some of the best stuff I've ever heard, so it's a matter of opinion.' As he outgrew the early Beatles, John asserted that George was 'always more like a Paul McCartney producer than for my music'.

John's reputation as the most intelligent Beatle with literary aspirations was firmly established by 1964. Each one of the four was quick-witted, but none of the other three matched Lennon's perception and lucidity. Only in the recording studios, with Paul's melodic strengths and eagerness to discover every twitch of every switch, was there any contest. That was because John's restlessness to move on to the next song differed from Paul's need to get the current work meticulously right. That year, George Martin released his own orchestral album of Beatles hits. Despite Martin's natural affinity with McCartney, his album featured a commercially powerful sleeve note written by John which allowed Lennon to hark back in dry literary style to his satirical *Mersey Beat* newspaper ramblings. He wrote:

George Martin is a tall man. He is also a musician with short hair. In spite of this he records rock groups such as (Beatles, Billy J. Kramer, Gerry and the Pacemakers) to name four, and has earned the respect of everyone in the business (what business you might well ask). We all owe a great deal of our success to George, especially for his patient guidance of our enthusiasm in the right directions (it was a patient George Martin who, on one of our early sessions, explained to a puzzled Ringo that it was a bit much playing a full drum kit, tambourine and maracas at the same time).

Us Beatles are genuinely flattered that a 'real musician' as we call him should turn his talents to arranging an L.P. of our songs, considering that he has previously worked with such great artists as Peter Sellers, Shirley Bassey, Jimmy Shand and a machine that sings 'Daisy Daisy'. Some of the sounds on the album may be new to you (and me), that's 'cause George has a great habit of matching unlikely instruments together (like a Jew's harp and a twelve-stringed finger) but the results are great and I think he should get a raise. So plug yourselves in and listen.

P.S. Please tell all your friends to buy it too, so George can be rich and famous − after all why not?

Good George Martin is our friend
Buddy Pal and Mate
Buy this record and he'll send
A dog for your front gate
Chorus: With an arf arf here
And an arf arf there, etc.

Sung to the tune of Old Macdonald Had An Arm by the Beatles a band.

Martin felt the sharp end of Lennon's tongue when John went to New York and publicly attacked old friends like Derek Taylor and George Martin, for, as he implied, having too big an idea of their own importance. Lennon snapped his frequent jibe that nobody made the Beatles, the Beatles made themselves. It was always true . . . but this time he chose old pals like Martin and Taylor as his targets. They were deeply hurt.

When the Beatles split, John adopted a fiercely defensive stance on behalf of his old group. It seemed that only he, or the other three, were allowed to damn the achievements, particularly, of the Beatles. John's comment about George was: 'Who does he think he is, anyway? What songs has he ever written?' But Martin remembers going for dinner with John in Los Angeles in 1973 and, typically, John apologized for his outburst which had embarrassed Martin. 'I'm sorry George,' John said. 'I didn't really mean those things about you and all the others. I was smashed out of my mind when I was speaking.'

The difference inside the studios between John and Paul was obvious to George from the start. 'Paul would sit down and ask what I planned to do with his songs, every note virtually. "What do you think the cellos should be doing here, George?" and I'd have to describe to him on the piano what it would be. He'd say: "Yeah, OK, but what about changing that note?" Lots of the arrangements to his songs were very much his ideas which I would have to implement.

'John would be more vague in what he wanted. He would talk in metaphors about his ideas. I'd have to get inside his brain to find out what he wanted. It would be more of a psychological approach. He'd say – for example, on "Being For The Benefit Of Mr Kite!" – "This song's about a fairground. A little bit mystified. I want to get the feeling of the sawdust and the feel of the ring. Can you do something about it?" I'd then have to think how that imagery could be transformed into sound. The difference between John and Paul, fundamentally, was that Paul would want to know *how* I was going to go about achieving what he wanted. John couldn't care less. He just wanted the result.

'On "Strawberry Fields Forever", we did one track and he said: "Well, I like it but it's worked out much harder than I thought it would be. I'd like you to do a score and maybe use a few cellos and a bit of brass." That was it.'

Another odd clash of opinion between Lennon and Martin occurred from the start of the Beatles' success. John's singing voice – leathery, raw, lung-bursting on their anthems like 'Twist And

Shout' and 'Money' – was a stark contrast with Paul's melodic qualities. But John had that distinctive, lived-in, untrained hardness in his voice. It made him stand out; it was the voice of a new breed of rock 'n' roll guitarist who couldn't give a damn. There was nothing crude about it, but it was the voice of someone who had lived, for all his youth. John was genuinely bashful about his voice. I remember telling him how much I liked it on one particular track, 'You Can't Do That', and he was astonished that anyone should single out his vocal work for any praise. 'You really mean it?' he asked incredulously. 'I can't say I ever liked hearing myself.'

The nagging self-doubts about his vocal abilities were to manifest themselves into a considerable issue with George Martin. 'John was a great admirer of Elvis Presley's early records, particularly the "Heartbreak Hotel" kind of sound. He also had an inborn dislike of his own voice which I could never understand, as it was one of the best voices I've heard,' recalls Martin.

'He was always saying to me: "*Do* something with my voice! You know, put something on it. Smother it with tomato ketchup or something. Make it *different*." And he was obsessed with tape delay. In technical terms, it's only a delay of about thirty milliseconds which gives you that kind of effect John sought, a sort of very near-echo which he used a lot when he made his own records. I used to do other things to him, and as long as it wasn't his natural voice coming through, he was reasonably happy. But he'd always want his vocals to get special treatment.

'On "Tomorrow Never Knows", he wanted to sound like a Dalai Lama singing on a hilltop. He actually said to me: "That's the kind of sound I need." So I put his voice through a loudspeaker and rotated it. It actually did come out as that strangled sort of cry from the hillside.

'He simply always wanted to distort his voice. But I wanted to hear it in its own natural quality. So after he left me, he did all his own distortion to his heart's content. And I didn't like that – after all, the raw material was so good.'

Martin looks on John's work since the Beatles split with mixed feelings: 'There were lots of things I didn't like about them and that I would have done differently. My favourite song of all was "Imagine" and that was a great album – I loved that. Some of the stuff he did on that was pure magic. I'd like to have produced that.'

Conversely, Martin was disappointed with John's final album, *Double Fantasy*. 'He hadn't been in the studios for a long time,

February 1964. Tie askew and a shirt button undone, John is watched by
73 million viewers on America's *Ed Sullivan Show*

and it shows. It's not vintage Lennon, not the greatest stuff he ever did.'

And to the question that concerns Beatles students throughout the world: who was the more important to the group, Lennon or McCartney, Martin reflects: 'I'm a melody man rather than a lyric man, being a musician and not a lyric writer. My brain accommodates music much more easily than it does words. Paul's melodies and his harmonic structures appealed to me more than John's because John's melodies and his music were tailor-made to fit his words rather than the other way round. The lyrics would lead and develop John's songs. He would write one verse and the music was already there once the words told him the way the line would go.

'As for comparing their value to the Beatles, it's impossible. It's like asking what's the most important constituent in a sauce vinaigrette, the oil or the vinegar. Both were fundamentally important: one without the other would have been unthinkable in terms of the Beatles' success.

'It's quite likely that, in terms of success, Paul's songs will last longer than John's because they get more to the average man, to the heart strings, than John's did. That's being really commercial about it. But I couldn't put a cigarette paper between them.'

On a British concert tour in 1964, I interviewed John specifically about his attitude to his guitar. Asked if he ever practised, he laughed and took another drag on his cigarette, 'I never *did* practise! I only ever wanted to learn to play to back myself. In the early days, we all used to sing. Originally, I'd do one, then Paul'd do one, then George and so on. So you didn't need to be a genius of a guitarist to back yourself.'

Did he find it a handicap, not being able to read music? 'It's not essential for what I'm doing. No, I've never found it a handicap. These dance bands that play pop on the B.B.C. radio programmes — they sound all right at *that* because they can read it off music sheets. But have you heard some of them trying to play rock? It's rotten!'

'If I wanted to read music I'd have to pack all this in and start from scratch. Sometimes I think I'd like to, but I'm a cheat. I can't play finger style. I just manage to do something that makes it sound like I can. I started with a banjo when I was fifteen, when my mother taught me some banjo chords. She could play it pretty good. When I was young, I played the guitar like a banjo, with the sixth string hanging loose! I always thought Lonnie and Elvis were the greatest and all I ever wanted to do was vamp. I got some banjo things off OK, then George and Paul came along and taught me other things.'

Asked why he took to the guitar, he told me: 'Oh, the usual kid's desire to get up on stage, I suppose. And my mother was a big encouragement. She said she could play any stringed instrument and was able to give me the first ideas.'

Of his musical role within the Beatles, John, who was officially described as rhythm guitarist, said: 'The job of the normal group rhythm guitarist is to back the solo guitarist like the left hand does on a piano. Unless the lead guitarist is very good and can back himself like the finger-style guitarists can, he needs someone else to help fill out. Most of our stuff in the early days was twelve-bar stuff. I'd play boogie and George would play lead. I'd vamp like Bruce Welch [of the Shadows] does, in that style of rhythm.

'We always have someone playing rhythm in the set style all the time, although it's too thin for records so we just both go full-out.

'I'd find it a drag to play rhythm all the time so I always work myself out something interesting to play. The best example I can think of is like I did on "You Can't Do That". There wasn't really a lead guitarist and a rhythm guitarist on that because I feel that the rhythm guitarist role sounds too thin for records. Anyway, it'd drive me potty to play chunk-chunk rhythm all the time. I never play anything as lead guitarist that George couldn't do better. But I like playing lead sometimes, so I do it.'

Of his songwriting tactics, he said: 'When Paul and I started writing stuff, we did it in the key of A because we thought that was the key Buddy Holly did all his songs in. Holly was a big thing then, an inspiration, sort of. Anyway, later on I found out he played in C and other keys but it was too late and it didn't worry us anyway. It all sounded OK in A so that's the way we played our stuff. Oh yeah, we keep up with all the keys – C, D, G, F (joking) but we keep out of B flat and that. It doesn't give you an artistic sound. Heh Heh!'

John Lennon was an addicted rock 'n' roll *fan*, just like the teenage Paul Simon or Bruce Springsteen and thousands of other musicians for whom it was a force as tribal as it was musical. All were mesmerized by Elvis Presley, who brought colour and meaning into their lives. Rock 'n' roll was the foundation for John Lennon. The ensuing years may have seen him stray into strange unconnected territories; may have seen him put his head on the chopping block of public scorn and ridicule, but right to the end Lennon stayed true to the *idea* of rock 'n' roll. On record and in print, Lennon was moved to the core, and that music still had ability and power throughout his life, even when it was obvious that the music he was making far transcended in impact and quality the music which inspired him. 'There is nothing conceptually better than rock 'n' roll,' he said. 'No group, Beatles, Dylan, or Stones, have ever improved on "Whole Lotta Shakin' "for my money, or maybe I'm like our parents: that's my period and I dig it, and I'll never leave it.'

When 'Heartbreak Hotel' floated across the Radio Luxembourg airwaves into Mendips, John Lennon succumbed and was forever lost. 'When I heard it, I dropped everything!' Elvis across the ether was followed by dozens more, each as glamorous, raucous and liberating – Buddy Holly, Jerry Lee Lewis, Gene Vincent, Little Richard, Lloyd Price, Chuck Berry, Eddie Cochran, Larry Williams. That music, those performances, made real the world which had been glimpsed in the movies. Part of the appeal of rock 'n' roll was its remoteness, which helped create a code amongst the young English audience. The terms used were alien, but the emotions were direct. In a whole generation of English teenagers, those raw emotions touched a chord.

Lennon's first group, the Quarry Men, was formed with school mates and everybody mucking in for fun. The gigs were standard for the time – working men's clubs, club dates, ballrooms, and fortuitously, village fetes. Rock 'n' roll was for (and by) the young. Rock 'n' roll was for NOW! Lennon remembered the time: 'As kids we were all opposed to folk songs, because they were so middle-class. It was all college students with big scarves and a pint of beer in their hands, singing folk songs in what we called la-di-da voices. When I started, rock 'n' roll was the basic revolution to people of my age and situation.' That revolutionary aspect obviously appealed to the rebellious Lennon. Before – so the cliché ran – the only way out was through crime or boxing. Now there was a third, more glamorous, alternative – music. It meant you could get girls, get drunk, and get somewhere. That early, classic rock 'n' roll was raw and primitive, it could be learned, if you practised, which was boring, or if someone taught you. That was the sound that John Lennon wanted George Martin to record.

Years later, Lennon could remember with great accuracy and affection the music which so moved him as a restless teenager: ' "Long Tall Sally" – when I first heard it, it was so great, I couldn't speak! "Bony Maronie" – I remember singing it the only time my mother saw me perform before she died. "Ain't That A

Shame" – the first rock 'n' roll song I ever learned. My mother taught it to me on the banjo before I learned the guitar. "Whole Lotta Shakin' " – I like the take he did in 1956, on the record. I'm not interested in the variation of a theme . . . I'm a record fan . . . Those are the records I dug then, I dig them now, and I'm still trying to reproduce "Some Other Guy" or "Be-Bop-A-Lula". '

Thrown together in Liverpool and Hamburg, Lennon and McCartney collaborated, bolstering each other, goading each other to reach new heights. Such was their diversity, they could assimilate virtually any style into their songwriting; the lyrical dexterity of Leiber and Stoller, the touching teen pains of Goffin and King, the hiccuping sensitivity of Buddy Holly. The evidence of the earliest Beatles recordings demonstrates Lennon tearing into such rock classics as 'Ain't She Sweet', 'Memphis', 'Money', and 'Sweet Little Sixteen'. Even early on in their career, the Beatles were typecast – Paul was cute and John was hard. Like all clichés, there was an element of truth in it, but Paul was also capable of whipping up a storm on rock standards, and John proved he could be a sensitive performer handling ballads.

For fans tired of the saccharine sweetness of British and American pop, tired of the manufactured idols, they found something raw and refreshing in the Beatles performances. There was a healthy irreverence in Lennon's crashing about the stage, cajoling and insulting the audiences. They poured their hearts into the music, sweating it out night after night, playing from dawn to dusk, with an astonishing turnover of music. The music came from diverse sources – show tunes like 'Besame Mucho', 'Falling In Love Again', 'Till There Was You', the first tentative performances of their own songs, 'I Saw Her Standing There', and 'Ask Me Why', classic rockers like 'Twist and Shout', 'Honey Don't', and contemporary hits like Joe Brown's 'A Picture Of You'. These marathon sessions proved invaluable in shaping the Beatles' music. It gave them an edge and a variety their contemporaries never matched. While the pop world sank in the quicksand of mediocrity, and Elvis went missing in trashy Hollywood films like *Blue Hawaii*, the Beatles kept a flame burning for the music which had so moved them as teenagers.

The earliest known live recordings of the Beatles available on disc were recorded by Ted 'Kingsize' Taylor, at the Star-Club in Hamburg at the end of 1962. Despite the dreadful sound quality they make great listening and provide a fascinating insight into the roots of the Beatles' music. Recorded during one of those marathon sessions, the group are ragged and committed, tearing into their songs, young and full of fervour, determined to rattle the walls. It was that musical baptism, forged in Hamburg and honed in Liverpool, that gave the Beatles their musical edge. But, tellingly, one of the reasons the Beatles came out ahead of Faron's Flamingoes, Rory Storm, and Gerry and the Pacemakers – all of whom paid their musical dues in Hamburg – was that they had their own two songwriters, and didn't have to go on endlessly pillaging the familiar pool of material which all the Mersey beat groups dipped into.

The evidence contained on the album of the Beatles' Decca audition displays just how Brian Epstein had cleaned the group up (and how he was thinking of 'the end of the pier show' as the ultimate ambition). The Beatles sound stilted and uncomfortable as they meander through 'The Sheik of Araby' and 'To Know Her Is To Love Her'. Their collective studio knowledge was minimal. Aside from some late fifties' Quarry Men demonstration recordings, the Beatles' inauguration in recording took place in Hamburg. John, Paul and George cut 'Fever', 'September Song', and 'Summertime', in a Record-Your-Voice booth at the back of Hamburg Railway Station in 1960. They were backing a singer called Wally – Lou Walters – from Rory Storm's group, the Hurricanes. Rory's drummer Ringo Starr also sat in on the impromptu session, two years before he joined the Beatles.

The best-known pre-Parlophone recordings were with the Hamburg-based singer Tony Sheridan in May 1961. The subsequent album (issued long after their initial success) is of historic interest, featuring a raucous Lennon vocal on 'Ain't She Sweet', and the only known Harrison–Lennon collaboration on the instrumental 'Cry For A Shadow'. But it took those sessions to bring the Beatles to Brian Epstein's attention. The Sheridan/Beatles version of 'My Bonnie' was a moderate chart success in Germany.

By the time the Beatles arrived at Parlophone in 1962, they were pretty near the bottom of the pile. Decca turned them down in favour of Brian Poole and the Tremeloes, because they were more accessibly based in Dagenham. It took the intuitive sympathy and knowledge of house producer George Martin to realize the Beatles' sound fully and coalesce it on record.

Those early Parlophone sessions harnessed the Beatles' enthusiasm and Martin's studio mastery – a combination which was to prove unbeatable over the next seven years. Parlophone was always regarded as a joke by E.M.I., its parent company. But by working closely together, Martin and the Beatles came together. They respected his innate musical pedigree, and he saw their

At the height of the twist dance craze, in February 1964, John and Cynthia went to the club that was its birthplace, New York's Peppermint Lounge – fake 'Beetles' were already installed there

strengths as lying in their harmonies, and the fact that they wrote their own material – with strong views on how it should be recorded – rather than accepting their manager's hand-me-downs. The fruits of that collaboration were first seen on 5 October 1962, when the Beatles' first single, 'Love Me Do', was released.

It eventually reached a healthy number seventeen on the British charts (in competition with the perennial Cliff Richard and 'Bachelor Boy' and Little Eva's 'The Loco-Motion').

It was the release of the second single, 'Please Please Me' in early 1963, that really established the group. It's hard to imagine the effect it had on the record-buying public. Initially Lennon's harmonica was the novelty that drew the casual listener in. Lennon remembered hearing it on Bruce Channel's 'Hey Baby', and decided to pinch it. The prominent guitars and driving rhythm were emphasized by the rudimentary harmonies. Hearing it again now, what still strikes the listener is the Englishness of the vocals. Until then, English pop stars adopted mid-Atlantic accents, or went for stage Cockney like Anthony Newley. The Beatles made no effort to disguise their Liverpudlian origins, even if the vocal mannerisms were American. 'Please Please Me' was a Lennon original: 'I remember the pink eyelet down over the bed, sitting in one of the bedrooms in my aunt's house on Menlove Avenue. I heard Roy Orbison doing "Only The Lonely" on the radio. I was intrigued by the double use of the word "please" in a Bing Crosby song. So it was a combination of Bing Crosby and Roy Orbison.'

As a writer, Lennon was a great one for plucking individual lines or phrases from other songs, and expanding them into his own material. 'Run For Your Life' came from Elvis's 'Baby Let's Play House'; 'Do You Want To Know A Secret?' was a line from 'Snow White And The Seven Dwarfs'; 'I'll Be Back' was based on a chord variation from a Del Shannon song.

The infectious 'From Me To You' repeated the Beatles' hit formula, and went to number one in May 1963. But by then the Beatles had proved their merit on album. 'Please Please Me' was released in March, and proved remarkable in a number of ways – there were eight Lennon–McCartney originals, a remarkable achievement in those days of manufactured product. Hit songs either came from established shows, or writers were chosen by a manager or, more likely, British pop songs were innocuous covers of American hits. To write and perform your own material was revolutionary, and threatened the Tin Pan Alley stranglehold.

The bulk of material on the Beatles' début album encapsulated their influences to date. Much of the original material was jointly written while touring Britain, on the long coach journeys up and down the newly opened motorways. 'I Saw Her Standing There', though, was a composition John and Paul knocked off in Paul's front room, playing truant from school. Of equal interest, though, were the cover versions. Instead of going for the obvious versions of Elvis or Pat Boone hits, the Beatles chose obscure songs which they admired – the Shirelles and the Cookies were not names English audiences were too familiar with. 'Twist And Shout' had been a hit in America for the Isley Brothers and was written by Bert Russell and Phil Medley.

It is to George Martin's credit that, in an eleven-hour spurt, he managed to capture the verve and enthusiasm of the Beatles on record. But the vigour sprang from *them*. As writers and performers, the Beatles obviously had something fresh to offer a jaded public. Lennon is seen and heard as a sensitive interpreter on that first album, notably on 'Ask Me Why', and 'Anna' (written by Arthur Alexander, who also wrote the Stones' 'You Better Move On' and Ry Cooder's 'Go Home Girl'). Lennon also sounds plaintive on 'There's A Place', a place where he can go, when he feels low. Conversely, his manic version of 'Twist And Shout', which closes the album, recalls the ardent rocker from the Cavern. Nothing that demented had been heard on record since 'Hound Dog'.

It was that hard side which the world saw in Lennon – the hard rocker, embittered by his mother's early death and his father's desertion, his own belief in himself, his inability to display a softer side. Lennon was painted the hard man of the Beatles.

Despite the typecasting – the 'hard' Lennon and the 'soft' McCartney – it helped give their partnership a balance which was crucial. Their individual writing efforts were born out of a desire to prove themselves, out of individual insecurity. Once they gained confidence in themselves, they grew apart, but there was still that question of balance. They sparked each other off, and even if it was only altering a word, suggesting a title, Lennon and McCartney could, and did, inspire each other. That balance saw them through the hysteria. They couldn't go out, so they stayed in, and – among other things – wrote songs. That partnership lasted a long time and only grew irrevocably apart when they found other partners.

With their second album, Lennon and McCartney were already being called 'the outstanding English composers of 1963' and William Mann of *The Times* singled out 'the Aeolian cadence at the end of "Not A Second Time" ' (the chord progression which ends Mahler's *Song Of The Earth*). Lennon said he thought 'Aeolian cadences were some sort of exotic birds!' William Mann's eulogy, which finally set the seal on the Beatles as being more than 'just another pop group', is of interest for his comments on the group's early impact. Leaving aside the 'pandiatonic clusters' and 'melismas with altered vowels', he does make a number of interesting points: 'For several decades in fact, since the decline of the music hall, England has taken her popular songs from the United States, either directly, or by mimicry. But the songs of Lennon and McCartney are distinctly indigenous in character. . . .' Mann went on to cite 'the exhilarating and often quasi-instrumental duetting' and the 'discreet, and sometimes subtle, varieties of instrumentation', which led him to conclude: 'These are some of the qualities that make one wonder with interest what the Beatles and particularly Lennon and McCartney, will do next, and if America will spoil them or hold on to them, and if their next record will wear as well as the others.' If only he had known; if only *they* had known.

With the Beatles had been preceded by the fourth Beatles single, 'She Loves You', which established them as *the* British showbiz phenomenon. The song became an anthem, which helped a nation Yeah, yeah, yeah its way into 'the swinging sixties'. Lennon remembered that crucial song thus: ' "She Loves You" was written by the two of us together. I remember it was Paul's idea. Instead of singing I love you, again, Paul decided we would have a third party passing by and latch on to something else . . . the woo-woo was taken from the Isley Brothers' "Twist And Shout". We stuck it in everything – thinking when Elvis did "All Shook Up", that was the first time I heard "uh huh", "oh yeah" and "yeah yeah" all in the same song.'

By the end of 1963 it was apparent to everyone in Britain that the Beatles were more than just a pop group about to be usurped by the Dave Clark Five. There were invitations to perform before royalty, eulogies in the press, and hysteria at their every appearance. But they were still judged by their music. *With The Beatles* (released on the day of President Kennedy's assassination) again dipped back to the Hamburg days ('Roll Over Beethoven'; 'Till There Was You') and, despite the prolific Lennon–McCartney partnership, the album contained six cover versions. But this time, drawing heavily on the contemporary music sound of black America – 'Please Mister Postman', 'Money', and 'You Really Got A Hold On Me', all emanated from the burgeoning Tamla Motown. Here was the 'hard side' of Lennon, screaming 'Money', and 'It Won't Be Long', while Paul opted for the softer 'All My Loving' and 'Till There Was You'. With George Martin drafted in as ancillary pianist, the Beatles made their first tentative steps to expanding their group sound in the studio.

From *With The Beatles* on, things started getting crazy: 'I Want To Hold Your Hand' sold 12 million copies. There was the first American tour, their first film, endless concerts. Brian Epstein still saw touring as the logical step to ensure that the cash came in, and that the Beatles' name was kept in the public eye. Who could blame him? There had never been any precedent on how to handle a phenomenon such as the Beatles. Touring kept John and Paul together, and in the interminable gaps between shows and venues they stared out of their cocooned existence and wrote. Fragments, images and catch-phrases cropped up in their songs. Hermetically sealed, they poured their energies into their songs. Creatively, those rigorous years of touring paid off.

A Hard Day's Night was the first album consisting solely of Lennon–McCartney originals. Composed during their visits to France and America, and when filming in England, the finished album reflected a remarkable variety and assurance. Remarkable too was the prolificacy of the partnership. Consider the pressure they were under from the moment Beatlemania broke at the end of 1963, and indeed the pressures which lasted until the end of touring in 1966 – the Beatles were expected to undertake at least two major tours every year, and come up with three original singles, two albums of original material, plus T.V. and film work. It is an itinerary which would make many of today's pampered groups blink with disbelief. What makes the Beatles' achievements so astounding is not only the quantity, but more importantly the *quality*, of their music those years inside the bubble.

Once the hysteria began, the Beatles' performances became little more than a charade. They *were* a fine live band, as evidenced by *The Beatles Live At The Hollywood Bowl*. The album of those 1964–5 concerts was only released, finally, in 1977, at the height of the punk explosion. What comes across from those recordings is how good they still sounded. Given that there were no feedback monitors, so they couldn't hear themselves play, nothing could beat the persistent, cacophonous screaming. The Beatles still sounded hungry, angry! It is a testament to their musical inventiveness and ability. The studio recordings are the ultimate proof, but contained on *The Beatles Live At The Hollywood Bowl* is the proof that there was a certain chemistry, or *magic*, which sustained them.

Concerts by then offered fans little more than an opportunity to see the gods made mortal. There were the constant problems of security, isolation, and safety. Then there was the music. Within a year, the Beatles had found themselves elevated from a 'beat group phenomenon' to an international showbiz institution. It was a double-edged sword, and one which Lennon particularly resented. He told *Rolling Stone* magazine editor Jann Wenner, in 1970: 'Brian put us in suits and all that, and we made it very, very big. But we sold out, you know, the music was dead before we even went to the first theatre tour of Britain. We were feeling shit already, because we had to reduce an hour or two hours' playing, which we were glad about in one way, to twenty minutes, and we would go on and repeat the same twenty minutes every night. The Beatles died then as musicians ... because in spite of all the things, the Beatles could really play music together.' The Beatles had, after all, only set out to make it 'bigger than Elvis'. Within months, they had already achieved that. And after that, where else was there to go?

Lennon found the whole thing developing into a macabre charade, which was, inevitably, reflected in his music, the only place where he could relax, create, and be himself. Listening to the album of *A Hard Day's Night*, one is struck by the aching cries for help and the feelings of isolation. Here he was, the idol of millions, one of the world's most eligible men, an acclaimed author and composer; but in his songs you find introverted sentiments, and feelings of great sadness and lost innocence. That innate sadness was, of course, buried beneath the ebullient high quality of the Beatles' music. By the time of *A Hard Day's Night*, Beatle fans, like Lennon himself, only listened to the *sound* of the record. The lyrics, if they made any impact at all, were simply the choruses the fans could memorize and sing along with.

'Tell Me Why' is full of tears, lies, moans, apologies, pleas: 'I'll Cry Instead' has tears and loss, 'a chip on my shoulder that's bigger than my feet'; 'Any Time At All' cries for a response, begs a friendly response. 'I've got no time for trivialities,' sang Lennon on 'When I Get Home'. The public and the private Lennon merged on *A Hard Day's Night*.

Lennon's musical experiments were encouraged by George Martin and the other three Beatles, notably the first recorded use of feedback on 1964's 'I Feel Fine'. Lennon had a small studio at Kenwood, where he tinkered with tape recorders and fragments of songs, the results of which would manifest themselves the following year. But the greatest impact on Lennon's music during those

Dear Ted,
    Having a
wonderful. The weather
is quite. Wish you
were. The food is.
So are we. See you
when we get.
    Ours truly
    Them Beatles.

RAY COLEMAN.
MELODY MAKER.
FLEET STREET.
LONDON, EC.4.
ENGLAND.

This 'postcard', made by tearing an autographed publicity photograph in
half, was sent to the author from Genoa in Italy, during a European tour in
June 1965. The message is typical of John's laconic sense of humour

crazy 'Beatlemania' years was made from the only man who could be said to have rivalled the group in terms of influence – Bob Dylan.

During the early and mid-1960s, Bob Dylan gave pop music a voice. His songs had lyrics of personal and political relevance – even his early love songs were bitter and aching, hardly the fodder for unthinking pop fans. But Dylan swiftly found an audience and articulated their dissatisfaction and compassion in striking, vivid images. Dylan was now tiring of his typecasting as 'spokesman for a generation'. From adolescence he'd been a fervent rock 'n' roller. His high school ambition, he said, had been 'to join Little Richard'. When Dylan heard the Animals' electric re-working of the traditional 'House Of The Rising Sun', and the Beatles' 'I Want To Hold Your Hand' in 1964, it helped him decide which direction his music was to take. The British invasion was a prime force in making Dylan switch to 'folk-rock', with his devastating *Bringing It All Back Home* and *Highway 61 Revisited* albums of 1965.

Dylan first met the Beatles on their first American tour in 1964 and turned them on to marijuana, but made a more permanent impact in shaping their musical direction. Latterly, Lennon denied Dylan's influence on the group, saying he never listened to anything after the seminal 1965 albums, and was quoted as saying: 'I remember the early meetings with Dylan, he was always saying "Listen to the words, man" and I said "I can't be bothered. I listen to the sound of it, the overall sound." ' Lennon did admit, though, that, like so many others, Dylan's music helped him think for himself and inject more honesty into his own lyrics. The two did enjoy a sporadic friendship. Lennon appears in the rarely seen *Eat the Document*, a surreal account of Dylan's controversial 1966 British tour.

Dylan's achievements then became Lennon's goal, an attempt to marry the power of rock 'n' roll to lyrics of some substantiality. The Dylan influence first manifested itself on the Beatles' fourth album, *Beatles For Sale*. Derek Taylor's sleeve notes announced that the album was 'straightforward 1964 disc-making. . .there is little or nothing on the album which cannot be reproduced on stage!' Such jolliness disguised the intensity with which Lennon approached the album. *Beatles For Sale* displayed the bleaker side of the Lennon persona. 'No Reply', 'I'm A Loser', and 'Baby's In Black' formed a pretty bleak trilogy to open an album by the Fabs at the height of their power.

'No Reply' opens with the jaundiced 'This happened once

John fingers his beloved Rickenbacker guitar during the recording, with producer George Martin, of *A Hard Day's Night* in June 1964

before', a song which bitterly sifts through the embers of a dying relationship, symbolized by the failure to communicate. The song is conveyed by a particularly lugubrious Lennon vocal, a dispirited opening to an album which was meant to celebrate *triumph*. On 'I'm A Loser', the title says it all, and Lennon's singing is suitably atmospheric as the song traces the disintegration of a love affair. It may not match Dylan's searing sense of loneliness or loss evoked by his contemporary 'Boots Of Spanish Leather' or 'Ballad in Plain D', but it was an attempt to inject some honesty and genuine emotion into the fairytale world of the Beatles.

Similarly, while never reaching Dylan's heights of absurdity or depths of despair, Lennon's couplet 'Although I laugh and act like a clown/Beneath this mask I am wearing a frown' seemed an ironic comment coming from a man with the world at his feet. 'Baby's In Black' continues in the Dylan vein, another splint to help bolster up a shattered soul: 'Baby's in black and I'm feeling blue.' He was juggling with dark colours, but questioning, probing, pleading rather than celebrating.

Hindsight reveals the internal friction in the group by then, which subsequently led to open antipathy. Lennon's character was always the rebel, the cynic, and he was the one to express his dissatisfaction most forcefully. As he admitted in a *Playboy* magazine interview: 'I was always like that, you know. I was like that before the Beatles. I always asked why people did things and why society was like it was. I didn't just accept it for what it was apparently doing. I always looked below the surface.' The overt politicizing didn't come till much later, but Lennon was keen to avoid the showbiz stereotypes: 'We don't want to learn to tap dance or take elocution lessons,' he told Michael Braun in his 1964 book, *Love Me Do*.

Critics have pointed out that *Beatles For Sale* was cut at the height of Beatlemania, which accounted for the number of cover versions. In many ways, though, the Beatles' fourth album is perhaps their most revealing in terms of musical influences. The six covers take them right back to those manic all-night rave-ups in Hamburg – Carl Perkins' 'Everybody's Trying To Be My Baby'; and 'Honey, Don't', Buddy Holly's 'Words Of Love'; Leiber and Stoller's classic 'Kansas City', sung by Little Richard; and Chuck Berry's anthemic 'Rock and Roll Music'. Such was the Beatles' enthusiasm that they disinterred 'Mr Moonlight' from the B-side of a single by the original Dr Feelgood, Willie Perryman (Piano Red). It took the Beatles' championing for these (by now) forgotten rockers to re-acquaint American audiences with their own rock 'n' roll history. It was only by studying the songwriting credits that thousands of American fans realized that 'Words Of Love' wasn't a Lennon–McCartney original, and the dedicated pursued it back to its source, thereby discovering the joys of Buddy Holly. The Beatles' pioneering work in helping Americans trace their rock heritage did not go unrecognized by musicians. Bob Dylan's 'Bringing It All Back Home', his first wholesale rock 'n' roll work, was a title which acknowledged the group's efforts.

The Beatles' fifth album, *Help!*, was also the soundtrack of their second film. Although removed from the documentary pressures of *A Hard Day's Night*, the Beatles were, by their own admission, constantly high on marijuana during filming. Lennon was also obsessed about his obesity, concerned about the state of his marriage, and worried that his role as 'pop singer' was too insubstantial for someone of his abilities ('If there is such a thing as genius, I am one! If there isn't, I don't care.') On the surface 'Help!' was another catchy Beatles single which went automatically to number one. It contained all their hallmarks – an unforgettable chorus, infectious harmonies, and quaintly memorable lyrics. But, as Lennon admitted, it really *was* a cry for help.

The finished album is riddled with insecurities, lack of assurance, and self-doubt. Lennon gratefully accepted the instant obliteration offered by drugs, barely disguising his distaste for the parody he felt the Beatles had become. That distaste is nowhere more evident than in 'You've Got To Hide Your Love Away'. The Dylan influence is particularly strong, vocally, musically and lyrically. ('That's me in my Dylan period. I am like a chameleon, influenced by whatever is going on. If Elvis can do it, I can do it. If the Everly Brothers can do it, me and Paul can. Same with Dylan.') The song finds Lennon as the poet alone, head buried deep in hands, surrounded by clowns. The paranoia is obvious; twitchy at what people will think, he is told to hide his love away, fearful that any open display of emotion will be ridiculed.

The growing distance between Lennon and McCartney musically was demonstrated by the sequence of two of their tracks on the finished album – Paul's rather smug 'Another Girl' ('She's sweeter than all the girls, and I've met quite a few'), and John's jaundiced 'You're Going To Lose That Girl'.

Help! is probably remembered for the haunting McCartney ballad, 'Yesterday'. Lennon was predictably scathing about McCartney's best-known song, and, as if emphasizing his rocker credibility, finished the album with a blistering version of Larry Williams' 'Dizzy Miss Lizzy'. Williams was one of Lennon's early

September 1964. A subdued John considers the Beatles' life on the road from the back of their Austin Princess limousine

musical heroes. The Beatles recorded his 'Bad Boy' in 1965; 'Slow Down' appeared on their 1964 'Long Tall Sally' E.P. and Lennon included Williams' classic 'Bony Moronie' on his 1975 *Rock 'n' Roll* album. 'It's Only Love' displayed Lennon's softer side on *Help!* but even that is tainted by druggy imagery and a reliance on Dylanesque word-play.

The use of a string quartet on 'Yesterday' and the flutes on 'You've Got To Hide Your Love Away' marked the first inclusion of musicians outside the Beatles' immediate orbit on their material. With such an intuitive and astute interpreter as George Martin, the group could experiment in the studio and feel genuinely creative. Live, it was impossible – the screams obliterated everything. Even with the intolerable pressure of touring and filming, the Beatles could relax in the studio and were receptive to Martin's ideas and suggestions on how to expand their sound. Lennon and McCartney's compelling musical codes found swift acceptance with George Martin's classically trained musical mind. By the middle of 1965 they were setting themselves dauntingly high standards. Creatively, George Martin was certainly 'the fifth Beatle', but he could only work with what was presented to him *by* them. In a 1983 interview, Martin said: 'I've always held that the role of the producer is the person who can look back on the picture, and not just at the detail. When you have your picture taken in a school form, the first thing you look for is "Where am I?" You don't look at the picture, you look at yourself. And this is true of most instrumentalists, of most people who make records, they tend to listen to the bit they were doing.

'I also believe that the producer's role is a minor one compared to the performer's. There's been a tendency in recent years for that to be a reversal. I think that the fellow who creates it is the important thing, and the producer is the guy who helps him shape it. I don't see the producer as a Svengali mastermind. The role of the producer has become slightly inflated, and it's strange for me to say that, because maybe I've had something to do with that. But it's something I haven't been comfortable with.'

The high standards the Beatles had attained can be seen simply by looking at their two film soundtracks. The normal thing for soundtracks (particularly 'pop' film soundtracks) was to stretch one theme song over an album, patched up with 'mood' instrumentals. The Beatles changed all that – *A Hard Day's Night* and *Help!* were crammed full of potential hit singles, and there wasn't an ounce of surplus flesh on either. By *Help!*, the sound of the Beatles on record was a lot deeper, deferring to Martin's orthodox musical knowledge; the group were keen to enrich the standard two guitars, bass and drums sound. The percussive effects on 'Tell Me What You See', John's harmonium on 'We Can Work It Out', and the pianos and organs, strings and woodwinds dotted around their records of the period all point towards a flexing of the Beatles' musical muscles, which would culminate with the majestic *Sgt Pepper* only two years later.

Running parallel to the album, of course, were the astonishingly assured and varied singles. Again, the Beatles set new standards, even down to the packaging of their material. Prior to them, L.P.s were simply regarded as vehicles for collected singles, B-sides and cover versions, which the record company duly issued to extract the final penny from diehard fans of these short-lived phenomena – pop groups! The Beatles changed all that.

By the middle of 1965, Beatles' songs like 'She Loves You', 'I Want To Hold Your Hand' and 'Can't Buy Me Love', had entered the public consciousness. The experimentation started with 'I Feel Fine' (with its use of feedback and jagged rhythms); the Motown feel of 'Day Tripper' and the fairground atmosphere of 'We Can Work It Out', the fluid 'Ticket To Ride'. The quality of those singles is reflected by the variety of artists who covered them, an astonishing cross-section – Ella Fitzgerald, Otis Redding, The Carpenters, Dollar, and Stevie Wonder.

From early on, the Beatles were determined that their albums should be regarded as separate entities. It helped, of course, having what press agent Tony Barrow called 'their own built-in tunesmith team of Lennon and McCartney'. Even at the time it was apparent that the compositions were no way split fifty–fifty. If John sang a 'Lennon and McCartney' song, you could bet that the majority of the work had been his, and vice versa. There were arguments in the studio about whose songs should get priority as A-sides.

Even as they grew apart as writers, there was still that balance to the Lennon and McCartney partnership. The individual contributions to joint compositions may have been minimal, but they mattered, and helped shape the songs. Such was their intuitive reading of each other that they played off against each other, goading each other into making the song perfect. It may only have been a change of tense, a switch in direction, but this joint honing strengthened the song.

Lennon defined the partnership around this time when he told *Playboy*: 'In "We Can Work It Out", Paul did the first half, I did the middle eight. But you've got Paul writing "We can work it out", real optimistic, y'know, and me, impatient: "Life is very

short and there's no time for fussing and fighting, my friend. . . ." '
The full flowering of that creativity was to come with the Beatles'
sixth album, the punningly titled *Rubber Soul*. Newly honoured
by Queen and Country, despite the unremitting pressures (the
album was recorded in under a fortnight) the Beatles, M.B.E.,
showed they were well ahead of the field. In these days of
high-technology recording, where months and sometimes years
are spent preparing an album, it is remarkable to look back on the
pressure under which the Beatles recorded, and see how confident
and progressive, in the best possible sense, their music sounded. By
the end of 1965, rock 'n' roll had grown up. Dylan's electric
experiments had spawned a clutch of imitators who gradually
grew into their own style (Simon and Garfunkel, The Byrds) and
the Beatles were under pressure from their contemporaries (Who,
Stones, Animals, Yardbirds) to stay one step ahead. They were no
longer the cocky rockers of only three years earlier but they hadn't
forgotten their roots. And they proved they could still whip up a
storm on a song like 'Dizzy Miss Lizzy'. But with their growing
confidence as writers, and their growing understanding of the
studio, the Beatles' material grew in stature.

Lyrically, at the end of 1965, they found themselves commenting on the craziness of their situation, occasionally distorted by
drugs. 'Norwegian Wood' was John's veiled admission of an
affair; 'Nowhere Man', his observations on the unreality of it all;
there was also the wistful nostalgia of 'In My Life'. Paul's 'You
Won't See Me', and 'I'm Looking Through You', were remarkably
bitter comments on the price of fame and the superficiality of the
Beatles' status.

Musically, too, *Rubber Soul* was a progression. The public
noticed the introduction to pop of the sitar on 'Norwegian Wood'.
But there was also a greater reliance on keyboards than before.
Rubber Soul catches them between the hysteria of Beatlemania
and the acid excesses of *Sgt Pepper*. They finally sound comfortable in the studio, willing to experiment, but never straying too far
away from the three-minute pop song, a form they had perfected.
Rubber Soul will always stand superbly on its own merits.

For Lennon, particularly, the album marked a personal progression in his craft. Personal honesty and confession, which were to
characterize his later work, were inherent. His songs are marked
by a more poetic approach, and he was beginning to find his own
voice, rather than copy Dylan's. 'Girl' opens with the plaintive 'Is
there anybody going to listen to my story . . .? ' before moving on to
what would become a familiar Lennon preoccupation. Was she

told when she was young that pain would lead to pleasure? He later remarked that the song was a personal favourite, a move away from the Tin Pan Alley style of songwriting.

'Nowhere Man' is a curiously nihilistic 'pop' song, casting Lennon as a monarch of nothingness, without opinion, power or desire. The Nowhere Man is an impotent, hollow symbol of the swinging sixties – 'Nowhere Man, don't worry/Take your time, don't hurry/Leave it all till somebody else/Lends you a hand.' It was his view of life from the emptiness of the mansion he called a 'bus stop, awaiting action'. 'Norwegian Wood' is the vacuous swinging sixties again. Druggy, floating, random ('She told me she worked in the morning, and started to laugh'). Lennon's vocal is weary, dispassionate, that of an outsider viewing something intensely personal. The song is a thinly veiled message to his wife, Cynthia, that he has had an affair outside their marriage.

'In My Life' is the curtain-raiser for a trip down to Strawberry Fields. Although nothing is mentioned by name, there is that overriding impression of nostalgia and yearning for home. Lennon said: 'It was the first song I wrote that was consciously about my life. . . . "In My Life" started out as a bus journey from my house at 251 Menlove Avenue to town, mentioning all the places I could recall. I wrote it all down, and it was so *boring*. So I forgot about it and laid back, and these lyrics started coming to me about friends and lovers of the past. . . .' It was an extraordinary position to be in. Only five years before he had been 'Lennon', a scruffy Liverpudlian rocker, with prospects as bleak as the view across the Mersey. Half a decade later, he was J.W. Lennon M.B.E., millionaire, surveying his world from the stockbroker security of Weybridge. 'In My Life' echoes the theory that 'you can never go home again', 'Though I know I'll never lose affection/For people and things that went before/I know I'll often stop and think about them. . . .' The song marked a rare moment of retrospection and sentimentality for Lennon; the lyrics are tinged with a resignation that all is gone, that the only security lies ahead.

As 1965 drew to a close the Beatles stood untouched, at the height of their influence and powers. The extent of the Beatles' popularity at that time is hard to imagine today, when every group that manages two consecutive number ones, is cited as 'the new Beatles'. No cracks had appeared in their façade; they could still be *seen*, screamed at, touched. But the drive to the 'toppermost of the poppermost' had ended. They had reached their summit. Like kings, they viewed the world at their feet.

By the Beatles' gruelling standards, 1966 was a relatively quiet year which saw them pour their creative energies into recording, rather than squeezing in sessions between tours. The earliest fruit of those labours came with the 'Paperback Writer' single in June: a bubbly, clever Beatles single, just like the old days. But the B-side, 'Rain', was of particular interest. 'Rain' was written at John's home studio, where he was experimenting with tape loops, which explains the weird, distorted atmosphere on the song. The dreamy feel was accentuated by the druggy lyrics ('I can show you, when it starts to rain/Everything's the same'). There are echoes in the song of future Lennon classics: 'Can you hear me that when it rains and shines/It's just a state of mind.' It precedes 'Strawberry Fields Forever' and 'Lucy In The Sky With Diamonds' with its remote and ethereal feel. Spiked on acid, Lennon was seeing the world through hazy shades. The drugs added a translucent element to his music, and aided and abetted the desire to drift into the dream world of Lewis Carroll, where nothing was real, and 'the slithy toves/Did gyre and gimble in the wabe'. To be a Beatle meant that reality was distorted anyway. Their cocooned existence saw them grow more and more remote. By mid-1966 touring had become a physical and mental strain, particularly after the American reaction to Lennon's 'We're bigger than Jesus' quote and their hostile reception in Manila.

The spring of that year was spent in the studio, recording what turned out to be the *Revolver* album. The first track they recorded was the last to appear on the album – Lennon's mysterious 'Tomorrow Never Knows'. It marked the zenith of the Beatles and George Martin's studio ingenuity at the time – backward tapes, loops, chanting choirs, oddball lyrics, all underpinned by some relentless Ringo drumming.

Still ahead of its time, 'Tomorrow Never Knows' has John hurling himself into the psychedelic maelstrom, with lyrics drawn from the Tibetan Book of the Dead, although the actual title was a Ringoism Lennon used to diffuse the lyrical obtuseness. It was one of the earliest attempts by Lennon actually to make music that, until then, had been confined to his mind. For the first time, it let us 'see the meaning of within'. It had been a long, crazy journey from 'Be-Bop-A-Lula'!

All sorts of other wondrous potions can be found inside the jar which is the *Revolver* album – 'I'm Only Sleeping' carried on the theme of floating, of dreaming of being at the centre of something, and letting others glimpse in through layers of sound and mystery, of being a reluctant idol, at the centre of attention, but needing to look inward, and find out exactly what makes him/them tick

('Please don't spoil my day, I'm only sleeping').

'She Said, She Said' evoked images of his druggy dreams in Laurel Canyon, California, where the song was written. It played out John's private agony in public: 'I know what it's like to be dead! Who also knows what it's like to never have been born/sad/mad.' It was a trippy odyssey from birth to death, with Lennon returning to the precious world of his childhood, to the home he never had: 'I said no, no, you're wrong, when I was a boy/Everything was right.' It never had been, but by then, he could convince himself that it was.

In 'And Your Bird Can Sing' John issued his early message of independence from the Beatles' cocoon: 'Tell them that you've got everything you want . . . But you won't get me!' For they had seen the Seven Wonders, they had heard 'every sound there is', and it still wasn't enough.

Isolated and immunized, John called, more and more, on 'Dr Robert', a euphemism for drugs, and took 'a drink from his special cup'. He had all the answers. The more the Beatles dipped into that special cup, the more reliant they became. With distorted perspective and lost time, they knew that there was always one constant: 'Day or night, he'll be there, anytime at all'. Any time at all grew into the void of 'Tomorrow Never Knows', and they were gone! They disappeared on 29 August 1966. It was actually in Candlestick Park, San Francisco. It could have been anywhere. To all intents and purposes, outside of the comfortable insularity of the recording studio, the Beatles ceased to exist.

After leaving the stage at Candlestick Park, the Beatles became their own bosses. For the first time in three years, Parlophone didn't have the obligatory Beatles album for Christmas. Without that, for many people Christmas was not complete. *A Collection of Beatles' Oldies* did appear, with its cover that epitomized the Swinging London which the Beatles had helped so much to shape. There they were, all their best songs. Created in the fiery furnace of a three-year burst, here was the vinyl proof of rock's maturing. With touring definitely vetoed, with no film projects to occupy them seriously, for the first time in a decade, the Beatles were suddenly no longer a group. From now on there would be no more 'songs', no more product manufactured to meet a particular schedule. The balloon had come down to earth. They tasted freedom. It was the end of 1966. Ahead lay the unknown.

15
PRESSURES

'We're more popular than Jesus now'

A fantastic scenario awaited John one day in 1965 on his return to Weybridge from London in his chauffeured Rolls. Sitting in his lounge, drinking a cup of tea, was his father, whom he had not seen since he was five years old in Blackpool.

Dishevelled, with long greasy grey hair and a shabby suit, totally unkempt, fifty-two-year-old Fred Lennon was working as a kitchen hand, washing up dishes in the Greyhound Hotel, Hampton Court, a few miles from John's home. Drinking in a pub one day, he had got chatting to a man who drove the Beatles occasionally for a car hire firm.

'If you're Fred Lennon,' said the man, 'I drive your son.'

Fred said: 'Oh, well give me a lift to his house. I haven't seen him for years and I'd like to see him.'

When Fred arrived, Cynthia answered the knock on the door. 'Hello, Cyn, I'm John's Dad and you haven't seen me before.' He had his foot in the hall before she could react.

'He was a charmer in his own way,' says Cynthia. 'There was no way I could have shut the door on him. He looked like a tramp but he was John's Dad. I had no alternative but to ask him to wait for John to return.'

John was staggered. After the initial shock of seeing his father sitting there, and Cynthia's obvious discomfort, John said, in the scathing voice that people feared: 'Where have *you* been for the last twenty years?' John was dumbfounded not only at his father's appearance, but at his demeanour. As a child, he had built up a totally different image of his Dad as a swashbuckling, seafaring Errol Flynn-type character romantically sailing around the world.

January 1966. John's father, Freddy Lennon, launched forth with his one and only single, 'That's My Life (My Love And My Home)', much to John's embarrassment

'Discovering him to be a pretty foul-mouthed washer-up of dishes, with a real Scouse accent which John, with his upbringing, never had, was not a pretty sight,' says Cynthia.

Freddy Lennon, an inveterate beer drinker, made good money as a ship's steward, and when he worked as a hotel porter. But he was always broke, and scrounging cash from friends and relatives.

The atmosphere grew steadily worse. 'He kept on about what a hard life he'd had, how he was having to work as a skivvy to earn a few bob, and John and I never had it so good,' recalls Cynthia. 'Within an hour or so of coming in the door, he was saying how he didn't want to take anything from his son. But it was obvious he was coming for a handout.'

John felt uncomfortable for his father almost as much as he felt irritable with himself. He remembered how his relatives, his aunts and cousins, older than him, felt suddenly different in *his* company now that he was a famous Beatle. But try though he did, he could not take the arrival of his lost father with a hard luck story.

'He was so embarrassed,' says Cynthia. 'He was in and out of the room like a cat on a hot tin roof. He was nervous and said he suddenly felt ill at ease in his own home.' John's feelings were not helped by the obvious fact that his father had come primarily for money. 'I suppose Fred was proud of what John had achieved,' says Cynthia, 'but his main object was to rip off some cash from John.'

Out of sympathy and to relieve the tension, Cynthia asked Fred if he would like to stay at Kenwood for the night, hoping that it would help the atmosphere. John fixed Cynthia with a stare that asked: 'Do you realize what you're doing?' Fred stayed for three nights and the pressures on John mounted so much that he was out more often than he was at home, leaving Cynthia with the unpleasant job of talking to his father.

When he was with his father, John's insatiable quest for the truth about his childhood and his father's reported desertion of his mother forced several confrontations. 'Why did you leave Julia — she would have had you back, y'know,' said John.

'How could I, John? Julia left *me*. I didn't leave Julia, she decided she would leave me.'

And so the conversation went on, with John insisting that his mother would have welcomed Fred back to rebuild their marriage, and giving him a happy parental background, while Fred argued that Julia had found another man while he was at sea, and didn't want him back.

It was a fruitless discussion which only confused John even

more about his childhood and reminded him of his mother's death.

To Mimi, who had a low opinion of Fred, John said on the phone: 'Oh Mimi, how could my mother marry a man like that? Why didn't you tell me what kind of father I had?'

Mimi answered: 'Dear boy, how would I know what kind of father you had? I didn't know him well myself. Did you want me to bring you up telling you he was a bad man who left you? Would that have made you any happier? You've been happy, haven't you?'

Mimi says John replied: 'Yes, I'm the happiest person in the whole family.'

Three years later Fred presented John and Cynthia with a further problem. He had met a girl and wanted to marry her, but she was only nineteen and had been made a ward of court.

John groaned to his father: 'Oh, no, isn't one failed marriage enough?'

'Fred said he was madly in love with her but didn't have enough money to set himself and her up in a home,' says Cynthia.

The girl was Pauline Jones, a former Exeter University student. Fred persuaded John and Cynthia that his life with her would be easier if she had some work to do, and as she would make a great secretary, she could help John and Cynthia typing their letters.

'John and I talked about it for a while and although he didn't like the idea much, he said he'd like to help his Dad if he could,' says Cynthia.

'I said: "Let's give it a try." '

John dealt brusquely with his father, saying, 'I think it's time for you to leave,' when it became obvious that he would have stayed there for ever, given half a chance. Pauline worked as a live-in secretary for about five months, but her sobbing and wailing kept John and Cynthia up at nights. She was tearful about her difficult relationship with Fred.

And there was not enough work for her. 'She was at as much of a loss about knowing what to do as we were,' says Cynthia. 'We'd never had a permanent secretary and she was going through a bad emotional patch in her life.' Eventually Pauline was asked to leave, but John eased the way for Fred by paying for his court cases and eventually for Fred and Pauline's wedding in Scotland.

'I want you to be happy,' he told his father, finally. He bought him a £15,000 house near Kew Gardens, Surrey, and gave him *carte blanche* to order furniture. He arranged for him to receive £30 a week from the Beatles' company, and established a reasonable, if distant, relationship with him.

Fred and Pauline had two children – John, then, had two half-brothers, David Henry Lennon, born in Brighton in 1969, and Robin Francis Lennon, born in Brighton in 1973. So when John was murdered in 1980, at the age of forty, he had a seven-year-old half-brother living in England whom he had never met.

Fred Lennon became an embarrassment to John. When Fred arrived one day after that first meeting John was under particular Beatles' pressure. He could not face another conversation with the father who had ingratiated himself into his life. John simply slammed the door in his face. Later Fred delivered his ultimate insult to his brilliant son by condemning the decorations at his Weybridge house, criticizing Beatles music as unlike the ballads he sang, and 'not as good as the old stuff, say "Begin the Beguine" ', and by hawking himself to national newspapers and magazines as the father of a Beatle. He arrived at the *Melody Maker* office to promote his unspeakable record, 'That's My Life (My Love And My Home)' and told me his record company wanted him to make more. They were even paying for him to get his teeth capped, he said. John Lennon kept up a remarkably dignified silence throughout all this. But not for nothing did he christen his father 'The Ignoble Alf'.

John had proved his generosity, and in spite of provocation had done the right thing for his father. There were other examples of his big heart. He did a special drawing for charity Christmas cards to help famine relief. He was an easy touch for many worthwhile causes like orphans. And to divert his own interest a little from the Beatles and songwriting he became, with George Harrison, a founding director of Hayling Supermarkets Ltd on the Hampshire coast. The other director, and active in running the supermarket towards which John gave £20,000, was his old Quarry Bank school mate and Quarry Men washboard player, Pete Shotton. John and George resigned their directorships in September 1969, leaving Pete in control of the supermarket.

It was impossible to compute John's fortune by 1965. Albums and singles were selling by the million all around the world. Concerts, films, and assorted tie-ins with Beatles merchandise made all four of them millionaires as well as Brian Epstein, who received a percentage of their income on a sliding scale of up to twenty-five per cent. The key to John and Paul's equal money lay in that handshake at the McCartney home at Forthlin Road,

Allerton, only eight years earlier; they would write as Lennon–McCartney, whether one wrote a song alone or not. The link resulted in Lenmac, their own company within Northern Songs, the company that raised eyebrows when it went public in February 1965. There were raised eyebrows in the city at pop stars, even the Beatles, considering themselves mighty enough to go public on the London Stock Exchange, but shares were snapped up quickly. John and Paul's income from songwriting alone made them millionaires, and the royalties soared as hundreds of artists around the world clamoured to 'cover' their work, notably Paul's romantic ballads like 'Yesterday' and 'And I Love Her'.

It was said during that year that, at any single moment in any twenty-four hours around the world, a Beatles song was being played on the radio somewhere, just as their records were selling as fast as E.M.I. in London and Capitol in America could press them. America's *Time* magazine said the 'most conservative estimate' put the net worth of George Harrison and Ringo Starr at 3 million dollars each, with John and Paul at 4 million dollars each because of their extra earnings as songwriters. 'The figures could easily be twice as high,' said *Time*. They were out of date before the magazine was published.

The Beatles were not merely bigger than Elvis, as Brian Epstein had vowed they would be. In three bewildering years they had become kings of pop, virtually a royal family of youth. The world hung on their every word, particularly John's, and he retained the title of the Most Outspoken Beatle.

Ever since the Beatles had triumphed at the Royal Variety Show in 1963, they had been courted by the Establishment. It was this very fact that got under John's skin. Rock 'n' roll, he said, was the antithesis of comfortable upper-class values. He had parodied Sir Alec Douglas-Home, the British Prime Minister, as Sir Alec Doubtless Whom, and had a generally healthy disregard for the aristocracy.

One day at Weybridge, among his usual batch of letters from Brian Epstein's office and American fans who simply addressed their envelopes: 'John Lennon, England', there was an official letter saying that he had been selected as a potential recipient of the M.B.E. He was asked if he would accept it publicly. Offering the Beatles the medal of Member of the British Empire, an award bestowed by the Queen, was staggering for pop musicians. It had been building up, surely, but the reality of it was front-page news in all Britain's newspapers that June in 1965.

John's first reaction was to say no. He had already had quite enough of the canonization of the Beatles. The knowledge that lords and ladies and debutantes were fawning over them, and the colossal distance they had travelled from enjoying the beer and sweat of Hamburg and the Cavern, was all too much. 'The money's nice,' he said to me, 'but *this*', pointing to the sweeping lawns of his Weybridge mansion, 'is not necessary. It's all too much. What I'd have liked would have been the money and the hit records without the fame.'

John threw the letter from Buckingham Palace into a pile of fan mail. 'I thought when I saw a brown envelope saying "On Her Majesty's Service" that I was being called up,' said John. A few days later, Brian Epstein asked him on the phone if he had received it. John said yes, but his instinct was to turn it down. What were the others doing? Epstein pointed out that they would all have to accept the honour, and that was that. John reluctantly agreed that to refuse an award from the Queen would do colossal damage to the Beatles. Paul, George, and Ringo felt honoured. So John grunted and agreed. He was always a terrible compromiser. 'Taking the M.B.E. was a sell-out for me,' John said later. 'We did manage to refuse all sorts of things that people don't know about. For instance, we did the Royal Variety Show [in 1963] and we were asked discreetly to do it every year after that, but we always said: "Stuff it." So every year there was always a story in the newspapers saying, "Why no Beatles for the Queen?" Which was pretty funny, because they didn't know we refused it. That show's a bad gig anyway. Everybody's very nervous and uptight and nobody performs well. The time we did do it, I cracked a joke on stage. I was fantastically nervous but I wanted to say something, just to rebel a bit, and that was the best I could do.'

John's witticisms, usually laced with a slice of irony or invective, were aroused when the Beatles' M.B.E. award became known. He said: 'I thought people got these things for driving tanks, winning wars.' Retired colonels erupted in fury at a pop group like the long-haired Beatles receiving such an award. And some people returned their awards to Buckingham Palace in protest. John rounded on them with blistering attacks. Army officers received their medals for killing people, he said. 'We got ours for entertaining. On balance, I'd say we deserve ours more.' In any case, he pointed out, the Beatles had received their medals for exports, bringing into Britain millions of pounds' worth of trade.

October 1965. Tie loose and top shirt button undone, John looks suitably bored at a press conference ('All those damned stupid questions,' he used to say). This one was at Brian Epstein's Savile Theatre after the Beatles had been invested with the M.B.E. Four years later John sent back the medal he never really wanted, incurring the full fury of his Aunt Mimi

'Beatles M.B.E.' stayed as national news in Britain for weeks, confirming John's private theory that they should never have accepted it.

Lord Wilson, then Harold Wilson, British Prime Minister, had recommended the award of the M.B.E. by the Queen. He was criticized by many for jumping on the bandwagon of youth, but Lord Wilson defends his decision: 'Some of the heavyweights in the Press had probably never heard of the Beatles, and if they had, they wouldn't have understood the role the Beatles had come to play in young people's lives. I saw the Beatles as having a transforming effect on the minds of youth, mostly for the good. It kept a lot of kids off the streets. They introduced many, many young people to music, which in itself was a good thing. A lot of old stagers might have regarded it as idiosyncratic music, but the Mersey sound was a new, important thing. That's why they deserved such recognition,' Lord Wilson told me in 1982.

Lord Wilson recalls a chat with John Lennon at the Variety Club luncheon in 1964, when the Beatles were named Show Business Personalities of the Year. As a Merseyside Member of Parliament, Lord Wilson talked to him about his background. 'John recalled they had started their learning as a group in the Labour clubs and trade union clubs near his home in Woolton. I recall that Penny Lane is a mile or so outside my constituency, so a lot of young people from my constituency would do their courting there. I thought John Lennon had an irrepressible sense of humour.'

John's wit struck Lord Wilson at the Variety Club lunch. The Beatle had risen to accept the award for the group. He was sitting between the then Leader of the Opposition and Prince Philip. Addressing the Variety Club chief, John said: 'Mr Chief Barker . . . and [turning to the Opposition Leader] . . . Mr Dobson.' The confectionery firm of Barker and Dobson was known mostly to Merseysiders: it was a beautifully timed line. Says Lord Wilson: 'It got very few laughs because they were all ignorant southerners on our table. But *we* enjoyed it.'

There was a typically Lennonesque twist to the M.B.E. affair. On the day of the investiture at Buckingham Palace, with thousands of fans crowding the gates outside, the Beatles' limousine drew up and the immaculately suited moptops stepped out. John's secret was that inside one of his black boots were several marijuana joints. Just as the investiture was about to start the Beatles adjourned together to a small toilet inside Buckingham Palace where they passed around one joint between them.

March 1964. Seen here with Harold Wilson, John gives the V for victory
sign made famous by the man who inspired his name, Winston Churchill.
The occasion was the Variety Club of Great Britain lunch in London at
which the Beatles were named Show Business Personalities of 1963. John
used to call the Labour Party Leader 'Harassed Wilsod'

The M.B.E. presentation passed uneventfully through their good cheer. That Christmas, John took his medal down to Aunt Mimi's new seaside bungalow. 'Keep it, Mimi,' he said. It occupied pride of place on the sideboard, underneath Mimi's favourite picture of John, a huge print taken by Astrid.

John very rarely, if ever, apologized. He believed it to be a sign of weakness, and that to refuse to capitulate was an example of strength. Only Aunt Mimi could elicit a 'sorry' from him, and that was when he knew that, if he didn't say it, the after-effects would last for months.

Still less had John been known to cry. The 'tough guy' bravado approach, a complete veneer for the soft, humanitarian inside, meant that he could never be seen to shed a tear. 'I never once saw John cry', says Cynthia, 'in the ten years we were together.'

The spring of 1966 became a débâcle for John Lennon. In London's *Evening Standard* he had been profiled, as always, as an iconoclastic, deep-thinking, restless man, way ahead of Beatledom and the perimeters of pop stardom. The writer, Maureen Cleave, was a friend and confidante of John's. He admired her intellect, trusted her, and was always at his frankest when journalists of her calibre treated him as a person with thoughts, outside the confines of pop music. Most sixties' stars projected themselves as vacuous. John set out to impress informed writers like Maureen Cleave that he had a sharp mind and wanted to learn. Talking to her was, for John, cathartic. As always, Maureen Cleave portrayed Lennon as a thinker; she coolly reported him as saying: 'Christianity will go. It will vanish and shrink. I needn't argue with that; I'm right and I will be proved right. We're more popular than Jesus now; I don't know which will go first – rock 'n' roll or Christianity. Jesus was all right but his disciples were thick and ordinary. It's them twisting it that ruins it for me.' He was, she reported, reading extensively about religion. And that was the end of the sermon.

Britain, numbed by four years of some pretty outrageous Lennonisms, did not react to the remarks. The comments had appeared, unsensationally, midway through an erudite article. The Beatles family applauded their leader for again projecting himself intelligently.

Four whole months after Maureen Cleave's article appeared, and had been forgotten, it reappeared under a syndication arrangement with an American magazine, *Datebook*. This time it was not submerged within the context of a general article, but was front-paged: Lennon was claiming that the Beatles were bigger than Jesus Christ!

American reaction, two weeks before the Beatles were due to begin a long concert tour, was instantaneous and devastating. The Beatles, and particularly John, were denounced as sacrilegious, and a wave of anti-Beatle demonstrations fanned out across the American South, the Bible Belt. The Ku Klux Klan marched, there were bonfires of Beatles records, and an estimated thirty-five radio stations across America banned Beatles records. The country that had adopted the Beatles as the 1960s' biggest single social phenomenon was rejecting them. Love and hate, those two closely related emotions, had met. The Beatles were bad news, and Lennon's tongue had caused it.

Promoters who had planned the Beatles' concerts of America were worried about guaranteeing the safety of the group on stage. The Vatican commented that 'some subjects must not be dealt with profanely, even in the world of beatniks'. One minister threatened to excommunicate any member of his congregation who attended a Beatles concert.

Responding to alarming phone calls from America, Brian Epstein immediately flew to New York. His first instinct was to cancel the tour, to protect the Beatles' safety. But he was told that if John made an apology at a press conference in the United States, then things might cool down sufficiently for the tour to proceed. Brian telephoned John at his home in Weybridge. John's immediate reaction was: 'Tell them to get stuffed. I've got nothing to apologize for.' He asked Brian to cancel the tour. 'I'd rather that than have to get up and lie. What I said stands.'

The seriousness of the anti-Beatles campaign was more evident to Brian, in America, than to John in the seclusion of his home in Surrey. There were hundreds of letters arriving daily, addressed simply: 'John Lennon, England', or, searingly, 'Jesus Lennon'. John took a dispassionate interest in reading some. 'How many for and against today?' he would ask Cynthia. Epstein cajoled and pleaded with John, insisting that, unless he made an exception of his golden rule never to apologize, the Beatles' future in America looked bleak, not just for the forthcoming tour but for ever. Next day, South African radio banned all records composed or played by the Beatles. Faced with mounting pressure, John had little choice; he called Epstein and said he would deal with the matter at the Beatles' press conference in Chicago three days later.

Brian, meanwhile, had tried his best to damp down the flames. He said at his own press conference in New York: 'The quote which John Lennon made to a London columnist nearly three months ago [*sic*] has been quoted and misrepresented entirely out of the context of the article, which was in fact highly complimentary to Lennon as a person and was understood by him to be exclusive to the *Evening Standard*. It was not anticipated that it would be displayed out of context and in such a manner as it was in an American teenage magazine.'

In London, Maureen Cleave did her utmost to place John's remarks in their true perspective. 'John was certainly not comparing the Beatles with Christ,' she said. 'He was simply observing that so weak was the state of Christianity that the Beatles were, to many people, better known. He was deploring, rather than approving, this.' The irony of the American uproar was, to many British clergymen, the uncomfortable truth that John was right – witness the number of people who attended the Beatles' concerts and bought their records, compared with church attendance figures.

When John arrived, distraught, in Chicago, he was met by Brian Epstein and Tony Barrow. They took him to a hotel room to brief him on what to expect from the hostile journalists and disc jockeys who were waiting to eat him at the press conference.

'We discussed very, very seriously what should be said by John,' says Tony Barrow. 'It was most unusual for John because for the first and only time in his life that I knew him, he was very willing and ready to apologize.' But under pressure, John broke down and cried: Epstein was explaining what was involved in cancelling the whole Beatle American tour, and Barrow was telling John what the line of questioning would be from the baying journalists. 'I said to John he should try to *explain*.' Brian feared the Beatles might be assassinated during the tour.

John was immediately worried for the safety of the others. He threw his head down into his lap and sobbed loudly, holding his head in his hands. 'I'll do anything,' he said. 'Anything, whatever you say I should do, I'll have to say. How on earth am I going to face the others if this whole tour is called off? Just because of me, just because of something I've said. I didn't mean to cause all of this.'

Epstein's mention of death threats made no impact on John personally. This was odd, because to be 'level' with a Beatle on such major problems and fears when there was an element of potential trouble was most unusual. All four of them were always protected from grim truths and left alone with the job of being Beatles. For Epstein to tell Lennon of his real worries was a big break with tradition. For John not to react puzzled Brian. He asked John if he realized the seriousness of what he'd said. But it was more what Paul, George and Ringo would think of him, if a remark by him had caused the danger of cancellation, that bothered John. Here was John's conscience, exposed for perhaps the first time in his life. He was definitely ready to do whatever was necessary to quell the pandemonium that was gripping America on the subject of the Beatles.

When John took the microphone at the press conference in Chicago that night he looked shaken and apprehensive as he faced a crowd of newsmen on the scent of a cowering Beatle. 'If I had said television is more popular than Jesus, I might have got away with it,' he began, 'but I just happened to be talking to a friend and I used the words "Beatles" as a remote thing, not as what I think – as Beatles, as those other Beatles like other people see us. I just said "they" are having more influence on kids and things than anything else, including Jesus. But I said it in that way which is the wrong way.'

Some journalists were dissatisfied. They thought John had made a stumbling apology, and was virtually restating his original folly.

Said one reporter to him: 'Some teenagers have repeated your statements – "I like the Beatles more than Jesus Christ." What do you think about that?'

John replied: 'Well, originally I pointed out that fact in reference to England. That we meant more to kids than Jesus did, or religion at that time. I wasn't knocking it or putting it down. I was just saying it as a fact and it is true more for England than here. I'm not saying that we're better or greater, or comparing us with Jesus Christ as a person or God as a thing or whatever it is. I just said what I said and it was wrong. Or it was taken wrong. And now it's all this.'

The apology that John had conceded would be forthcoming when he had spoken earlier to Brian Epstein and Tony Barrow was not coming out clearly. A radio interviewer brought the matter to a head: 'But are you prepared to apologize?'

John thought he had done so. His face reddened with anguish and his voice became firmer. 'I'm not anti-God, anti-Christ, or anti-religion. I was not saying we're greater or better. I believe in God but not as an old man in the sky. I believe what people call God is something in all of us. I wasn't saying the Beatles are better than God or Jesus. I used "Beatles" because it was easy for me to talk about the Beatles.'

But would he apologize?

'I wasn't saying whatever they're saying I was saying. I'm sorry I said it really. I never meant it to be a lousy anti-religious thing. I apologize if that will make you happy. I still don't know quite what I've done. I've tried to tell you what I did do but if you want me to apologize, if that will make you happy, then OK, I'm sorry.'

The press conference broke up amid the usual clatter of microphones and newspapermen fighting for the telephones. In the more traditional line of questioning that followed, few people took much notice of the resurfacing of the old Lennon venom. He condemned American involvement in the Vietnam war. Two months before that day, American planes had bombed Hanoi. John said he thought American action was unnecessarily warlike. It was his way of reasserting the real John Lennon. Public opinion on the Beatles being what it was in America at that time, he was lucky that his remark on the Vietnam controversy was not picked up and exploited. Fortunately, the general news line was that Lennon had apologized. Behind all that furore America wanted its Beatles back, cuddly, tuneful, joyful. The apology did not reach Alabama, deep in the Bible Belt, in time to prevent two thousand screaming teenagers tossing records and pictures of the Unfab Four on to a bonfire in a ceremony organized by a radio station, WAAX. But across the street, a smaller group of fans chanted: 'Yeah Beatles, Boo WAAX.' And a disc jockey, announcing the cancellation of another bonfire arranged for later that week, said he accepted the Lennon apology in the same spirit in which it had been made. The Beatles, he suggested, were now aware that they must use 'some degree of judgement and wisdom'.

Against that uncomfortable backdrop, the Beatles' 1966 tour of America could hardly lack tension. They were off the hook, but psychologically weakened and defensive. The 'Jesus' eruption had followed some riotous scenes in the Philippines. After a concert in Manila, the Beatles were alleged to have snubbed the President's wife by not attending a party. Paul said they were never invited, but the word got out that they had been rude, and they were jeered by many and jostled at the airport by thirty thugs, some with guns.

As always, the party invitation was simply a matter of confusion. But on their way out to the airport, thousands cheered while a few booed. 'All along the route there were people waving,' said John back at Heathrow, 'but I could see a few old men booing us. When they started on us at the airport, I was petrified.

'I thought I was going to get hurt so I headed for three nuns and two monks, thinking that if I was close to these people that might stop them. I was just pushed around. But that's the Philippines finished for me. No plane's going through the Philippines with me on it. I wouldn't even fly over it.'

America, in the aftermath of the 'Jesus' affair, threatened worse. With the real danger of assassination by the 'loony' John had so often joked about, it had little chance of being a coast-to-coast celebration. Fifteen concerts, two in the 55,000-capacity Shea Stadium in New York, one before a similar crowd at the Los Angeles Dodger Stadium, testified to the power of America's love of the Beatles. But something had happened deep inside; as far as John was concerned, a chapter had closed. It was turning sour and a drag. The Beatles road show was over. It had been a bore for long enough. Now it was also dangerous.

That tour was the finale of the Beatles' live work. Their last appearance, at Candlestick Park, San Francisco, on 29 August 1966, was a firm decision they made early on during that tour. When they told Brian Epstein, he was dejected. He realized his paternal role with the Beatles whom he loved would be virtually over, except for business relationships. For in the recording studio, as he had found to his cost, he was only welcome if he played no artistic role.

George Harrison had been instrumental in forcing an end to touring. Fed up with the poor sound and never enthralled by Beatlemania, he wanted to spend more time in the studios perfecting their finished recordings. There, there could be no duff notes going unchecked, unlike at the concerts where nobody cared. Now they'd proved they were enormous they didn't need the hassle, he argued. He was able to win over John because Lennon disliked the discomfort of touring. He was shouting more obscenities at the screaming crowds who knew nothing of this curious 'release' when he was on stage. He was second only to George in his nervousness of flying. The restrictions and lack of freedom, and scarcely knowing which town they were in, had finally become too much. The nail in the coffin was the bitter taste in the mouth from the Philippines and America from things that had happened *off* stage.

Paul McCartney enjoyed touring. He strongly resisted the Harrison–Lennon partnership and argued that that was what a rock 'n' roll band was all about. A showman in the grand tradition, Paul needed an audience's approval and applause. He said that was a vital part of the act. But while George laid out the unarguable facts about the quality of their music in the huge stadiums, John weighed in with: 'It's got too far from the Cavern.' Even though Ringo enjoyed touring, there could be no road show with John and George so reluctant. The only bright aspects of tours were the women and drugs and parties which customarily marked the end of the American tours: the camaraderie between the Beatles and other musicians which became a ritual in the rented house high in the Hollywood Hills. But now, that too, had lost its appeal.

Britain was hopeless, anyway. The halls were too small to contain their millions of fans. A tour would disappoint more people than it would please. So on the road, at least, it was all over. On the plane back from San Francisco, George breathed a sigh of relief: 'Now I don't have to pretend to be a Beatle any more.' Brian Epstein, who had not been able to bring himself to attend the final concert, just got drunk on champagne. In London, weeks later, when Brian told John of the concern of promoter Arthur Howes that they would never tour Britain again, Lennon snorted down the phone: 'Tell him to send out four wax dummies of the Beatles that shake their heads at the right time. The kids won't know the difference.'

Returning from the tumult of touring to Weybridge proved very hard for John. Cynthia was there to welcome him, with Julian and a big batch of post from religious zealots, particularly from America, seeking to educate John about Jesus. For a few days John enjoyed domesticity, putting Julian to bed, reading him a story, making his tea occasionally. There was, though, a fear inside him: though the Beatles had not disbanded, 'What the hell am I going to do?' All his working life the Beatles had been a travelling band. Now they were not. Of all the Beatles he was the most individualistic, and the least reliant on the group. But he felt suddenly alone. The rungs on the ladder from the Cavern had been quickly climbed until he had reached the very pinnacle: hit songs, no money worries, films, wife, child, fame, power of a frightening nature, and two bestselling books.

The restlessness that had driven him since childhood now gnawed away at him. 'Doing more of the same was never my solution to a problem,' he said. The Beatles, although they still had years of good music to make, was no longer a challenge. John was now an insatiable newspaper reader, particularly of the *Daily Mirror* and *Daily Mail*.

Cynthia noticed a softening in John in the aftermath of the

American débâcle. The tongue was not so quick. The battle for the Beatles had been won and an era closed, and John seemed more like his old self than the cocky Beatle-on-the-road. He told her that he was pleased touring was all over.

His ego remained strong. Offers for him to build up his literary and artistic career poured in. Would he design another charity Christmas card? Would he open this, give his blessing to that, donate some money here, there, and everywhere? John sought refuge by accepting his first solo acting role in the film *How I Won The War*. John would take the role of Private Gripweed in a story that tilted against war, a favourite theme for John, and, importantly, the producer and director was Richard Lester. 'I was flattered at being asked,' said John. 'The ego needed feeding, with the Beatles at a kind of crossroads.'

It was the first move by a Beatle outside the Beatles. And for John it involved not merely an acting role, but a significant change in his looks. First he was symbolically shorn of all his long Beatles hair, and next he needed to look like a soldier, so he adopted wire-framed National Health spectacles – 'granny glasses' as they became known. The specs, a bizarre flashback to the ones he had rejected when Aunt Mimi took him to an optician in Liverpool as a schoolboy, started a craze as surely as the Beatles' haircuts had seen to it that any self-respecting man of 1966 in the Western world had a hairstyle resembling that of the moptops.

Shooting for *How I Won The War* was in Germany, where John's locks were cut, and Almeria, Spain. Ringo and Maureen went out to socialize with John, who broke with his own tradition and invited Cynthia to visit him in Spain. Conditions were primitive in the rented house, but there was glorious solitude. After four years of relying to some degree on Paul, George, and Ringo, John was now alone in a creative situation. He played cricket with Richard Lester, enjoyed the company of actor Michael Crawford, and practised music making for much of the time. 'The harmonica was with him throughout the filming,' says Richard Lester.

Lennon identified completely with what the film projected: 'It represented a genuine, heartfelt emotional attitude in response to its time,' says Richard Lester. 'It will live on because it doesn't lead, it doesn't change society, but it does reflect a desperately sincere attitude towards the glorification of war by show business that was prevalent in the mid-sixties.'

In the wake of the Vietnam conflict John was vocal about war, even though he felt like a novice as the actor. 'I was an apprentice in the middle of professionals,' he said of his colleagues in the picture. When the film was completed, he took to wearing a badge with the initials C.N.D., supporting the Campaign for Nuclear Disarmament.

What had attracted Lennon to the film was Richard Lester's theory at the time: 'One of the gross obscenities about war is the war film itself. War on the screen is treated like a great big adventure with extras being killed in the way of a Western.'

John said: 'I hate war. The Vietnam war and all that is being done there made me feel like that. If there is another war I won't fight – and although the youngsters may be asked to fight I'll stand up there and try to tell them not to. I hate all the sham about war.'

John liked the experience of that solo film, but it was not enough to propel him into a serious acting career. He loathed the endless waiting in the desert, or on film sets in Germany and Spain, and learning lines, however short, drained his patience. No matter how often Richard Lester told him sincerely that he had the ability to develop a role as a fine actor, John would have none of it. He reverted to his lifelong theory about the stage and the cinema: '. . .people up there trying to pretend they're somewhere else.'

On his return home, it was obvious to Lennon that he had already lived at a pace, and absorbed enough, that matched three times his age. Doors had opened and closed during his twenty-six years with fantastic speed: art, music, books, dramatic acting, recording, concerts, success on a scale undreamed of. Yet they all left him feeling empty, and without much sense of achievement. His scepticism about politics remained: in a British General Election year, he said to me during an interview on his political beliefs: 'The motto seems to be: "Keep the people happy with a few fags and beer and they won't ask any questions." I'm not an anarchist, but it would be good if people started realizing the difference between political propaganda and truth.'

His own search for the truth manifested itself that autumn in two diversions that were dramatically and tangibly to affect the next two years of his life, and his years beyond them. Those diversions were drugs and his desire to get back in some way to the world of art from which he sprang. Combined, drugs and artistic visions would produce the psychedelic sounds, the next year, of *Sgt Pepper's Lonely Hearts Club Band*. But in 1966, desperate for a new route that nourished his own psyche, John Lennon believed

September 1966. In Almeria, Spain, John had his locks shorn and adopted 'granny' glasses for the first time during the filming of *How I Won The War*

he had found spiritual and physical uplift in the drug L.S.D. (lysergic acid) and a constant round of London art galleries.

Lysergic acid was slipped quietly into John and Cynthia's drinks one night when they were out with George and his wife Pattie, the model whom he had met on the set of *A Hard Day's Night*. For John, the mind expansion, the discovery of oneself within, the check on one's ego, the release, the heightening of his perceptions, were not just the perfect backdrop for the new vibrancy of Swinging London. The drug's ability to detach him from the mundane and transport his mind into a kind of nirvana was, he told me, an answer to his prayer. Attending a round of parties in London connected with the art world, John found out how to get what he described to me as 'the best stuff it's possible to get in the world'. He took large amounts of L.S.D. in the autumn of 1966, mixing up potions at home. He became a vegetarian, ate infrequently, and looked dangerously wasted within a few short months.

John tried unsuccessfully to lure Cynthia into his never-ending use of marijuana or L.S.D. 'It seemed to be all right for him, although I was totally against it,' she recalls. 'It opened the floodgates of his mind and he seemed to escape from the imprisonment of fame. Tensions, and bad tempers, were replaced by understanding and love as his message.' Pressured by John's constant pleading, Cynthia did relent and tried an L.S.D. trip, during which John carefully guided her. But she was not mentally receptive.

When she 'came back' from her horrifying experience of a bad trip, she decided categorically that she would never dabble again. 'This upset John, but I could not handle it,' she says. 'Suddenly there was this new mental barrier between us.' Her rejection erected an even bigger wall between them than already existed. For weeks she had become increasingly worried about the retinue of drug pushers and the undesirable caravan of hangers-on who were arriving back home with John, pouring out of his Rolls-Royce at dawn, after a night of clubbing and hard drinking in London. A drunken John was something Cynthia had learned to cope with for years, but a combination of drink and drugs and a coterie of odd unknown people who dossed down in the sumptuous lounge of their home drove her to despair. She told John she was worried about the environment in which Julian was having to grow up and go to school from, each morning. But John was deep within himself, and when he did not want to reply he would pretend not to have heard. 'I knew then that our marriage was in trouble,' says Cynthia. 'We had lost communication. John was on another planet.'

John was looking for something way beyond the Beatles, and even he did not know what it was. Slowly, his songwriting as well as his life was infiltrated by the hallucinatory effects of soft and hard drugs, though the world did not know it. He hid his marijuana and L.S.D. in the garden at Kenwood, fearing a police raid. The evidence was there in two songs in particular: 'Day Tripper' alluded to anyone who was not properly into drugs, but was what John called a weekend hippie; and in 'We Can Work It Out', written mostly by Paul, John composed the middle part. McCartney was still optimistically looking at life with the sunny outlook that inspired the title, while the suspicious John interjected the words in the middle: 'Life is very short and there's no time. . .for fussing and fighting, my friend.' Love and peace, man, was now his chief passion. The man who had told me at Weybridge at the height of Beatlemania that he was 'waiting for something to happen' set about *making* it happen.

As the seeds of flower power and psychedelia were planted in Swinging London, two of the most thriving industries were boutiques and art galleries, which opened by the score. The Chelsea set, and the tourists, gravitated to the King's Road. Art people headed for Mayfair, Piccadilly, or South Kensington.

Through Mick Jagger and singer Marianne Faithfull, one of the least durable partnerships of the Swinging Scene, Lennon was introduced to John Dunbar, Marianne's former husband and owner of a small art gallery, the Indica, in Mason's Yard, off St James's, Piccadilly. One of its investors was Peter Asher, whose sister Jane was Paul McCartney's girlfriend at the time. Peter had also, as half of the vocal duo Peter and Gordon, recorded a McCartney song, 'A World Without Love', whose lyrical corniness sent Lennon into fits of derisive laughter. 'Please lock me away' was, to John, hilarious.

Dunbar told John that an interesting and unusual exhibition would be opening on 10 November 1966 and that, to ensure that he wasn't harassed as part of a crowd, John might consider popping in to a private preview.

John and Cynthia often did different things in the evenings; she would draw or paint, or do needlework, happy to play the role of contented mother and wife in Weybridge. Besides, drugs had started to rock their partnership. John often went out alone.

On 9 November John's chauffeur-driven Mini Cooper with its tinted windows drew up outside the Indica and he stepped inside for what Dunbar had told him by telephone would be 'a happening'. John was intrigued. Anything that was off-beat, that fed his druggy inspirations, was going to attract him. This sounded an extraordinary exhibition. He thought 'a happening' might mean an orgy, he said. He was mentally geared up for an *event*.

The exhibition was called *Unfinished Paintings and Objects*. As he leafed through the catalogue John thought it was very freaky but fascinating, off-beat and weird enough for him to take his time walking round. The catalogue featured pictures of objects like wall cabinets, glassware, a big black bag captioned 'with a member of the audience inside', an apple, apparently meaningless to John: 'a mirror to see your behind', a 'sky T.V.' described more fully as closed-circuit T.V. set up in the gallery for looking at the sky; an 'eternal time clock'. Accompanying the pictures were words describing the exhibits: 'I would like to see the sky machine on every corner of the street instead of the Coke machine. We need more skies than Coke.' And: 'The mind is omnipresent. Events in life never happen alone and the history is forever increasing its volume. The natural state of life and mind is complexity. At this point, what art can offer is an absence of complexity, a vacuum through which you are led to a state of complete relaxation of mind. After that, you may return to the complexity of life again. It may not be the same, or it may be, or you may never return, but that is your problem.' And: 'Man is born, educates himself, builds a house and a life and then all that vanishes when he dies. What is real? Is anything real? A thing becomes real to us when it is functional and necessary to us. As long as we strive for truth we live in self-induced misery, expecting in life something that is not an illusion. If we recognize that nothing is true nor illusory. . .then we can proceed from there on to be optimistic and swallow life as it comes.'

The catalogue offered John the most bizarre introduction to 'the happening'. There was a 'Painting To Shake Hands – a painting for cowards: drill a hole in a canvas and put your hand out from behind. Receive your guests in that position. Shake hands and converse with hands.'

The carefully designed, handsomely printed catalogue had pictures on stickers for tearing out and placing over captions to feed the imagination: 'Painting to hammer a nail': 'Painting to let the evening light go through'; 'bag wear'.

A commercial sales list in the catalogue increased the smile on John's face. On offer, through mail order, were items like this: 'Soundtape of the snow falling at dawn, twenty-five cents per inch

Yoko as John saw her
for the first time. This
picture is taken from
the inside cover of the
catalogue which was
handed to John when
he walked into the
Indica Gallery in
London on
9 November 1966

(types: snow of India, snow of Kyo, snow of Aos).

'Crying machine: machine drops tears and cries for you when coin is deposited. 3,000 dollars.

'Word machine: machine produces a word when coin is deposited: 1,500 dollars.

'Disappearing machine: machine that allows an object to disappear when button is pressed: 1,600 dollars.

'Danger box: machine that you will never come back the same from (we cannot guarantee your safety in its use), 1,100 dollars.

'Sky machine: machine produces nothing when coin is deposited, 1,500 dollars.'

The list went on: a transparent house, intended so that the people inside cannot see out and the people outside can see in; special defects underwear for men; underwear to make you high, for women, description upon request; imaginary music; books called *Grapefruit*.

'What's all this *about?*' an incredulous Lennon asked John Dunbar.

'Bringing you here,' replied Dunbar, 'is my conceptual work of art.'

As John finished reading and moved round the gallery to look at the startling exhibits the artist herself, a slight woman, under five feet tall, dressed all in black, her head framed by thick, long black hair, handed him a card on which was printed one word: BREATHE.

Her name was Yoko Ono.

CHRONOLOGY
1940–1966

1933
18 Feb.   Yoko Ono born in Tokyo

1938
3 Dec.   John's future mother, Julia Stanley, a cinema attendant, weds seaman Alfred (Fred) Lennon at Mount Pleasant Register Office, Liverpool.

1939
10 Sept.   Cynthia Powell born in Blackpool.

1940
9 Oct.   John Winston Lennon born at 6.30 p.m. at Oxford Street Maternity Hospital, Liverpool.

1941
Spring John left in the care of his aunt, Mary Smith (Aunt Mimi) and Uncle George at 251 Menlove Avenue, Woolton.

1942
April   Fred Lennon, having been away at sea for long periods since his son's birth, leaves home for good while Julia Lennon moves in with her new man, John Dykins.

1945
Sept.   John starts at Dovedale Primary School, Liverpool.

1946

July   Fred Lennon suddenly returns and takes John to Blackpool, intending never to return. John's mother, Julia, tracks them down and gives her five-year-old son the choice of staying with his father or mother. He eventually chooses Julia, who returns him to Liverpool to stay with Aunt Mimi.

1952

July   John leaves Dovedale Primary School.

Sept.   John starts at Quarry Bank High School.

1955

July   George Smith, John's uncle, dies.

1957

May   John forms the Quarry Men skiffle group with some school friends.

24 May   First ever Quarry Men public performance at a street carnival in Rosebery Street, Liverpool.

6 July   Paul McCartney attends a Quarry Men performance at Woolton Parish Church Fete and meets John Lennon for the first time. He later joins the group.

July   John leaves Quarry Bank High School.

Sept.   John starts at Liverpool College of Art where he soon meets Cynthia Powell, his future wife, and Stuart Sutcliffe, to become his closest friend and a future Beatle.

1958

6 Feb.   After seeing them perform at Wilson Hall, Garston, Liverpool, George Harrison joins the Quarry Men.

15 July   Julia Lennon dies after a road accident outside Mimi's Menlove Avenue house.

1959

29 Aug.   The Quarry Men (John, Paul, George, and Ken Brown) play at the opening night of the Casbah coffee club, run by Mona Best, mother of the Beatles' future drummer, Peter.

15 Nov.   The group, now renamed Johnny and the Moondogs, fail an audition for 'star-maker' Carroll Levis at Manchester Hippodrome.

1960

5 May   The group, now renamed the Silver Beetles, fail an audition to back Billy Fury but are chosen to back another young singer, Johnny Gentle, on a Scottish tour.

20 May   That tour – the group's first – begins.

2 June   The group change their name to the Beatles for their first local 'professional' engagement at Neston Institute.

July   John leaves Liverpool College of Art.

16 Aug.   The Beatles travel to Hamburg and open at the Indra night club two days later.

5 Dec.   John arrives back in Liverpool penniless, after four months in Hamburg and a dispute with their employer there. George had been deported for being under age; Paul and Pete Best had been ordered to leave after allegedly causing a fire in their digs.

1961

21 Mar.   The Beatles make their début at the Cavern club, a jazz/beat cellar in Liverpool city centre.

June   A single, 'My Bonnie', by Tony Sheridan, with backing by the Beatles, is released in Germany.

6 July   The first edition of *Mersey Beat*, the Liverpool music paper, appears. John contributes a front-page article entitled 'Being a Short Diversion on the Dubious Origins of the Beatles' and, over the next two years, contributes many other poems and articles to the paper.

1 Oct.   John and Paul take a fourteen-day holiday in Paris.

28 Oct.   Brian Epstein, a local record shop owner, learns of the Beatles' existence.

9 Nov.   Epstein attends a lunchtime performance of the Beatles at the Cavern.

3 Dec.   Epstein invites the Beatles to his shop and offers to manage them.

1962

1 Jan.   The Beatles travel to London for an audition at Decca. They do not learn of their failure until March and are subsequently rejected by several other top record companies.

24 Jan.   Brian and the Beatles enter into an official management contract.

1 Feb.	The first Epstein-organized engagement, at a small café in West Kirby, Cheshire for £18.
2 Feb.	The Beatles' first official out-of-town date, in Manchester.
8 Mar.	The group appear on B.B.C. radio for the first time, on the Light Programme's *Teenager's Turn*.
10 April	Stuart Sutcliffe dies of a brain haemorrhage in Hamburg, aged twenty-one.
9 May	Brian Epstein secures a recording contract for the Beatles with Parlophone, a small label within E.M.I.
4 June	Epstein and the Beatles sign with E.M.I.
6 June	The Beatles' first recording session, at the Abbey Road studios, London N.W.8.
16 Aug.	Pete Best, the Beatles' drummer, is sacked.
18 Aug.	Ringo Starr leaves Rory Storm and the Hurricanes and fills the vacant drummer's seat with the Beatles.
22 Aug.	A Granada television film crew capture a few minutes of a lunchtime Beatles performance at the Cavern.
23 Aug.	John Lennon marries Cynthia Powell at Mount Pleasant Register Office, Liverpool. That same evening the Beatles, with John, fulfil an engagement in Chester.
4 Sept.	'Love Me Do', the group's first single, is recorded.
1 Oct.	Epstein and the Beatles sign a five-year management contract.
5 Oct.	'Love Me Do' is released.
17 Oct.	The Beatles make their television début on Granada's north-west regional programme *People and Places*, singing 'Love Me Do'.
27 Oct.	'Love Me Do' enters the *Melody Maker* singles chart at number 48.
17 Dec.	The Beatles make their fifth and final club trip to Hamburg.

1963

19 Jan.	The Beatles make their nationwide television début, on *Thank Your Lucky Stars*.
2 Feb.	First U.K. tour, with Helen Shapiro, begins.
11 Feb.	In one eleven-hour session, the Beatles record their first L.P.
22 Feb.	Northern Songs, publishers of all future Lennon–McCartney compositions, is formed.
2 Mar.	'Please Please Me', the group's second single, hits number one on the *Melody Maker* chart.

8 April   A son, John Charles Julian, is born to Cynthia and John Lennon at 6.50 a.m. at Sefton General Hospital, Liverpool; he weighs 6 lb 11 oz.

28 April   John and Brian Epstein fly to Spain for a twelve-day holiday.

4 May   The Beatles' first L.P., *Please Please Me*, tops the *Melody Maker* chart.

18 June   John physically assaults Cavern compère Bob Wooler at Paul's twenty-first birthday party in Huyton, Liverpool.

21 June   The John/Bob Wooler incident is big news in the *Daily Mirror*.

29 June   John's first solo appearance on television, on B.B.C.'s *Juke Box Jury*. (The programme was recorded on 22 June.)

3 Aug.   The Beatles' 292nd, and last, appearance at the Cavern.

8 Aug.   A daughter, Kyoko, is born to Yoko Ono and her husband, Anthony Cox.

13 Oct.   First signs of Beatlemania as the Beatles appear on *Sunday Night at the London Palladium*.

31 Oct.   Hysteria at Heathrow Airport as the Beatles return from Sweden after a series of concerts.

4 Nov.   The Beatles appear in the Royal Variety Performance at the Prince of Wales Theatre, London. John utters his famous witticism.

27 Dec.   In *The Times*, John and Paul are described as 'the outstanding English composers of 1963'.

1964

1 Feb.   'I Want To Hold Your Hand' tops the singles chart in *Billboard*, the U.S.A.'s premier music trade magazine.

7 Feb.   Mass hysteria greets the Beatles' arrival at Kennedy Airport at the start of their American tour.

9 Feb.   An estimated 73 million people watch the Beatles perform on television on the *Ed Sullivan Show*.

11 Feb.   The Beatles' first American concert, at the Coliseum, Washington, D.C.

2 Mar.   Back in England, the Beatles begin shooting their first feature film, *A Hard Day's Night*.

23 Mar.   Jonathan Cape publish Lennon's first book, *In His Own Write*. It is an instant critical and commercial success.

4 April   The Beatles occupy the top five places on the *Billboard* American singles chart.

23 April   Foyle's holds a literary luncheon in John's honour at the Dorchester Hotel, London. John's speech, supposed to be the highlight of the occasion, lasts just five seconds.

19 June   Charles Curran, a Conservative M.P. states in Parliament that John's book highlights the poor education in Liverpool and that Lennon himself is illiterate.

6 July   The film *A Hard Day's Night* receives its world première in London.

10 July   Liverpool honours its four famous sons with a civic reception. Estimated crowds of 100,000 line the route of their procession from Speke Airport to the city centre.

15 July   John and Cynthia buy their first mansion, Kenwood, in the 'stockbroker belt' at Weybridge, Surrey.

19 Sept.   Oxfam print 500,000 Christmas cards using a specially donated Lennon drawing.

1965

9 Jan.   John appears on Peter Cook and Dudley Moore's *Not Only. . .But Also* B.B.C. television programme reading his poetry, accompanied by Moore and Norman Rossington.

15 Feb.   John passes his driving test.

18 Feb.   Northern Songs becomes a public company, quoted on the London Stock Exchange.

22 Feb.   Shooting of the Beatles' second feature film, *Help!* begins in the Bahamas (for tax reasons).

18 Mar.   John gives his former schoolfriend and one-time Quarry Man Pete Shotton £20,000, and together they form Hayling Supermarkets Ltd and open up for business on Hayling Island, off the Hampshire coast.

12 June   Buckingham Palace announces that the four Beatles are to be made Members of the Order of the British Empire (M.B.E.).

13 June   Several M.B.E. holders return their medals, furious over the Beatles' award.

24 June   *A Spaniard In The Works*, John's second book of poetry and nonsense prose, is published by Jonathan Cape.

29 July   *Help!* receives its world première in London.

3 Aug.	John buys Aunt Mimi a bungalow in Poole, Dorset, and she moves down from Liverpool in October.
15 Aug.	56,000 fans attend a Beatles concert at Shea Stadium in New York. The proceedings are filmed for a future television special.
26 Oct.	Hysteria at Buckingham Palace as the Beatles attend their M.B.E. investiture ceremony.
31 Dec.	Fred Lennon, John's father, releases his first and only single on Pye Records entitled 'That's My Life (My Love And My Home)': it is an artistic and commercial disaster.

1966

1 Mar.	*The Beatles at Shea Stadium* receives its world première on B.B.C. television.
4 Mar.	London's *Evening Standard* publishes an interview with John by reporter Maureen Cleave. Tucked innocently in the middle of the article, John expresses an opinion that the Beatles are more popular than Jesus and that Christianity will vanish and shrink. There is no reaction from the British public.
1 May	The Beatles give what later turns out to be their last live performance in Britain, in the *New Musical Express* pollwinners' concert at the Empire Pool, Wembley.
26 June	The Beatles' emotional return to Hamburg to play a concert.
5 July	Riots rage in Manila, capital of the Philippines, after the Beatles supposedly snub the President's wife.
29 July	*Datebook* magazine re-publish in the U.S A. – out of context – John's interview with Maureen Cleave.
31 July	Radio stations in Birmingham, Alabama ban all Beatles music after learning of John's comments about Jesus. Other towns in the 'Bible Belt' soon follow and huge bonfires of Beatles records and memorabilia are organized.
6 Aug.	In the midst of the American uproar over John's comments, Brian Epstein hurriedly flies to New York to defend him publicly.
8 Aug.	After learning of John's Jesus comments the South African Broadcasting Corporation (S.A.B.C.) announce a ban on the playing of all records composed or played by the Beatles.
12 Aug.	At the start of the Beatles' third official American tour

in Chicago, John, under severe pressure, reluctantly apologizes to the world for his statement on Jesus.

29 Aug. Thoroughly fed-up after three years of constant touring, the Beatles give their last live performance ever, at Candlestick Park in San Francisco.

6 Sept. In a bar near Hanover, near the set of the film *How I Won The War*, John's Beatle locks are cut in preparation for his first solo acting role. He is given a pair of 'granny glasses' to wear.

19 Sept. Shooting of *How I Won The War* switches to Almeria, Spain.

9 Nov. John visits the Indica Gallery in Masons Yard, Duke Street, London S.W.1. for a preview of a nine-day exhibition by a Japanese artist, Yoko Ono, entitled *Unfinished Paintings and Objects*. He is introduced to Yoko by the gallery owner, John Dunbar.

DISCOGRAPHY
1962–1966

Every commercially released song John Lennon wrote and/or sang during the period covered in this book is included in this list. All Beatles tracks released during those years are named. It is John Lennon's recording career as *he* planned it. This list does not, therefore, include the many compilations and reissues or audition tapes and live albums recorded during this period but released later: these albums were marketing operations and have no bearing on Lennon's chronological songwriting pattern, which this list also sets out to reflect. This discography aims to show the reader, at a glance, what John and the Beatles did, and when.

To this end, the listing is based on British record releases, as the Beatles themselves intended The group always specifically recorded singles *as singles*, and album tracks likewise. In Britain these two paths crossed only rarely. But in America Capitol Records, through shrewd marketing practice and a great deal of song repetition, managed to produce considerably more singles and 'new' albums without using any additional material.

Songs either completely written or co-written by John Lennon are printed in capitals. But songs to which John contributed a few words, a line or a phrase — and there are a great many — are *not* ascribed to him.

Singles

October 1962	'Love Me Do'/'P.S. I Love You'
January 1963	'PLEASE PLEASE ME'/'ASK ME WHY'
April 1963	'FROM ME TO YOU'/'THANK YOU GIRL'

August 1963   'SHE LOVES YOU'/'I'LL GET YOU'
November 1963   'I WANT TO HOLD YOUR HAND'/'THIS
                         BOY'
March 1964   'Can't Buy Me Love'/'YOU CAN'T DO THAT'
July 1964   'A HARD DAY'S NIGHT'/'Things We Said
                         Today'
*November 1964 'I FEEL FINE'/'She's A Woman'
 April 1965   'TICKET TO RIDE'/'YES IT IS'
 July 1965   'HELP!'/'I'm Down'
*December 1965 'DAY TRIPPER'/'WE CAN WORK IT OUT'
 June 1966   'Paperback Writer'/'RAIN'
*August 1966   'Yellow Submarine'/'ELEANOR RIGBY'

* Denotes a double A-sided record

Albums

March 1963   **Please Please Me**
'I Saw Her Standing There'; 'MISERY'; 'Anna (Go To Him)';
'Chains'; 'Boys'; 'ASK ME WHY'; 'PLEASE PLEASE ME'.
'Love Me Do'; 'P.S. I Love You'; 'Baby It's You'; 'DO YOU
WANT TO KNOW A SECRET'; 'A Taste Of Honey'; 'THERE'S
A PLACE'; 'Twist And Shout'.

November 1963   **With the Beatles**
'IT WON'T BE LONG'; 'ALL I'VE GOT TO DO'; 'All My
Loving'; 'Don't Bother Me'; 'LITTLE CHILD'; 'Till There Was
You'; 'Please Mister Postman'.
'Roll Over Beethoven'; 'Hold Me Tight'; 'You Really Got A Hold
On Me'; 'I WANNA BE YOUR MAN'; 'Devil In Her Heart';
'NOT A SECOND TIME'; 'Money (That's What I Want)'.

July 1964   **A Hard Day's Night**
'A HARD DAY'S NIGHT'; 'I SHOULD HAVE KNOWN BET-
TER'; 'IF I FELL'; 'I'M HAPPY JUST TO DANCE WITH YOU';
'And I Love Her'; 'TELL ME WHY'; 'Can't Buy Me Love'.
'ANY TIME AT ALL'; 'I'LL CRY INSTEAD'; 'Things We Said
Today'; 'WHEN I GET HOME'; 'YOU CAN'T DO THAT'; 'I'LL
BE BACK'.

December 1964   **Beatles For Sale**
'NO REPLY'; 'I'M A LOSER'; 'BABY'S IN BLACK'; 'ROCK and
Roll Music'; 'I'll Follow The Sun'; 'Mr Moonlight'; 'Kansas
City/Hey-Hey-Hey-Hey!'

'EIGHT DAYS A WEEK'; 'Words Of Love'; 'Honey Don't'; 'EVERY LITTLE THING'; 'I DON'T WANT TO SPOIL THE PARTY'; 'WHAT YOU'RE DOING'; 'Everybody's Trying To Be My Baby'.

August 1965   **Help!**
'HELP!'; 'The Night Before'; 'YOU'VE GOT TO HIDE YOUR LOVE AWAY'; 'I Need You'; 'Another Girl'; 'YOU'RE GOING TO LOSE THAT GIRL'; 'TICKET TO RIDE'.
'Act Naturally'; 'IT'S ONLY LOVE'; 'You Like Me Too Much'; 'Tell Me What You See'; 'I've Just Seen A Face'; 'Yesterday'; 'Dizzy Miss Lizzy'.

December 1965   **Rubber Soul**
'DRIVE MY CAR'; 'NORWEGIAN WOOD (THIS BIRD HAS FLOWN)'; 'You Won't See Me'; 'NOWHERE MAN'; 'Think For Yourself'; 'THE WORD'.
'WHAT GOES ON'; 'GIRL'; 'I'm Looking Through You'; 'IN MY LIFE'; 'Wait'; 'If I Needed Someone'; 'RUN FOR YOUR LIFE'.

August 1966   **Revolver**
'Taxman'; 'ELEANOR RIGBY'; 'I'M ONLY SLEEPING'; 'Love You Too'; 'Here, There and Everywhere'; 'Yellow Submarine'; 'SHE SAID SHE SAID'.
'Good Day Sunshine'; 'AND YOUR BIRD CAN SING'; 'For No One'; 'DOCTOR ROBERT'; 'I Want To Tell You'; 'Got To Get You Into My Life'; 'TOMORROW NEVER KNOWS'.

MISCELLANEOUS
June 1964   **Long Tall Sally** (E.P.)
'Long Tall Sally'; 'I CALL YOUR NAME'.
'Slow Down'; 'Matchbox'.

December 1966 **A Collection Of Beatles Oldies** (L.P.)
Contains one track previously unavailable: 'Bad Boy'.

True collectors would also require two tracks from the 1961 Hamburg recording session when the Beatles were recruited mainly for backing Tony Sheridan. One is the first recorded and published John Lennon composition, co-written with George

Harrison, the instrumental, 'CRY FOR A SHADOW'. The other is the Lennon lead vocal on 'Ain't She Sweet'.

Songs written or co-written by John Lennon, not commercially recorded by him but instead 'given' to other artists.

'BAD TO ME': Billy J. Kramer and the Dakotas, 1963.
'HELLO LITTLE GIRL': The Fourmost, 1963.
'I'M IN LOVE': The Fourmost, 1963.

JOHN LENNON'S
CLASSIC SONG LYRICS
1962–1966

Help!

Help! I need somebody
Help! Not just anybody
Help! You know I need someone
Help!
When I was younger, so much younger than today
I never needed anybody's help in any way
But now these days are gone I'm not so self assured
Now I find I've changed my mind
I've opened up the doors.
Help me if you can, I'm feeling down
And I do appreciate you being 'round
Help me get my feet back on the ground
Won't you please please help me?
And now my life has changed in oh so many ways
My independence seems to vanish in the haze
But every now and then I feel so insecure
I know that I just need you like I've never done before.
Help me if you can, I'm feeling down
And I do appreciate you being 'round
Help me get my feet back on the ground
Won't you please please help me?
When I was younger, so much younger than today
I never needed anybody's help in any way
But now these days are gone I'm not so self assured
Now I find I've changed my mind

I've opened up the doors.
Help me if you can, I'm feeling down
And I do appreciate you being 'round
Help me get my feet back on the ground
Won't you please please help me?
Help me, help me.

I'm A Loser

I'm a loser, I'm a loser
And I'm not what I appear to be.
Of all the love I have won or have lost
There is one love I should never have crossed,
She was a girl in a million my friend
I should have known she would win in the end.
I'm a loser, and I lost someone who's near to me
I'm a loser, and I'm not what I appear to be.
Although I laugh and I act like a clown
Beneath this mask I am wearing a frown.
My tears are falling like rain from the sky
Is it for her or myself that I cry?
I'm a loser, and I lost someone who's near to me
I'm a loser, and I'm not what I appear to be.
What have I done to deserve such a fate?
I realize I have left it too late.
And so it's true pride comes before a fall
I'm telling you so that you won't lose all.
I'm a loser, and I lost someone who's near to me
I'm a loser, and I'm not what I appear to be.

In My Life

There are places I'll remember
All my life, though some have changed
Some forever, not for better
Some have gone, and some remain.
All these places had their moments
With lovers and friends I still can recall
Some are dead and some are living
In my life I've loved them all.
But of all these friends and lovers
There is no one compares with you
And these memories lose their meaning

When I think of love as something new.
Though I know I'll never lose affection
For people and things that went before
I know I'll often stop and think about them
In my life I'll love you more.
Though I know I'll never lose affection
For people and things that went before
I know I'll often stop and think about them
In my life I'll love you more.
In my life I'll love you more.

Norwegian Wood
(This Bird Has Flown)

I once had a girl
Or should I say
She once had me.
She showed me her room
Isn't it good, Norwegian wood.
She asked me to stay and she told me to sit anywhere
So I looked around and I noticed there wasn't a chair.
I sat on a rug, biding my time, drinking her wine.
We talked until two, and then she said
'It's time for bed.'
She told me she worked in the morning and started to laugh
I told her I didn't, and crawled off to sleep in the bath.
And when I awoke
I was alone, this bird had flown.
So I lit a fire
Isn't it good, Norwegian wood.

Please Please Me

Last night I said these words to my girl
I know you never even try girl
Come on, come on, come on, come on
Please please me woh yeh like I please you.
You don't need me to show the way love
Why do I always have to say love
Come on, come on, come on, come on
Please please me woh yeh like I please you.
I don't want to sound complaining

But you know there's always rain in my heart
I do all the pleasing with you
It's so hard to reason with you
Woh yeh, why do you make me blue?
Last night I said these words to my girl
I know you never even try girl
Come on, come on, come on, come on
Please please me woh yeh like I please you
Woh yeh like I please you
Woh yeh like I please you.

You've Got To Hide Your Love Away

Here I stand, head in hand
Turn my face to the wall
If she's gone I can't go on
Feeling two foot small.
Everywhere people stare
Each and every day
I can see them laugh at me
And I hear them say
Hey, you've got to hide your love away
Hey, you've got to hide your love away.
How can I even try?
I can never win
Hearing them, seeing them
In the state I'm in.
How could she say to me
Love will find a way?
Gather round all you clowns
Let me hear you say
Hey, you've got to hide your love away
Hey, you've got to hide your love away.

JOHN ONO LENNON
Volume 2 1966–1980

When John Lennon met Yoko Ono, his life changed. Volume Two of this biography mirrors the dramatic events that shaped his life in the fourteen years between meeting Yoko and his murder outside their New York home on 8 December 1980.

Cynthia Lennon vividly describes the break-up of their marriage and eventual divorce. The book traces the formation of the Apple organization and disintegration of the Beatles; and the passionate involvement of John in a campaign for peace. John Lennon gave many interviews to the author during that period. The story continues with his move to America in 1970 and the harassment he faced in staying there as a resident during a campaign by President Nixon to oust him; his embrace of the city of New York which adopted him as one of its favourite personalities; his successful battle against drugs; his five-year retirement from recording into family life, and the birth of his second son, Sean; his journeys, alone, to Japan, Hong Kong, and Singapore in his quest for a 'normal' life; his eighteen-month 'lost weekend' in California away from Yoko; his return to recording at the age of forty, and his artistic renaissance; his death and the reverberations that stunned millions, from presidents and statesmen to pop fans throughout the world.

Volume Two features more previously unpublished photographs, the continued chronology of John Lennon's life during the years 1966–80, and the words of his classic songs of that period.

343

INDEX

Page numbers in *italic* refer to illustrations.
John Lennon is abbreviated to JL in entries other than his own.